Home Recording for Musicians.

by Craig Anderton.

Amsco Publications
New York/London/Sydney

Credits

Thanks to David Karr, Barret Bassick, Bill Godbout, Jerry Martin, Merion Hair, and Ralph Benkus for their contributions to this book. Craig Anderton

All songs on the soundsheet are copyright 1977 by CAVE Music Publishing and are used with permission. All rights reserved.

Editing/John Lescroart

Book Design/Sandy Haight

Layout/Marilyn Smith-Donovan

Schematic Drafting/Craig Anderton

Illustrations/Vesta Copestakes

Soundsheet Production/Craig Anderton

Photocomposition/Frank Fletcher & Linda Turner

Administrative Assistant/Rebecca Crockett

Executive Editor/Jerry Martin

Copyright © 1978 by Amsco Publications,
A Division of Music Sales Corporation, New York, NY.

International Standard Book Number: 0.8256.0501.5
Library of Congress Catalog Card Number: 77-87208

Exclusive Distributors:
Music Sales Corporation
257 Park Avenue South, New York, NY 10010, USA
Music Sales Limited
8/9 Frith Street, London W1V 5TZ, England
Music Sales Pty. Limited
120 Rothschild Street, Rosebery, Sydney, NSW 2018, Australia

Printed in the United States of America by
Vicks Lithograph and Printing Corporation

So if, as you read this book, you find yourself confused, don't get discouraged. You don't have to understand everything instantly. If you read over the first few sections and everything makes sense except the part on, say, decibels, don't worry about it. Just put it out of your mind temporarily and forge ahead. As you gain more practical experience, as you read further in the book and start doing your own sessions, concepts that were abstract and foreign will become real and necessary, and will make more sense. It's like trying to learn to do anything from reading a book—the knowledge only becomes cemented with practical experience. Here is one hint: if something doesn't make sense, read it over out loud. Involving both the eyes and ears seems to help retention.

I must admit I never liked school and being forced to learn things I didn't really care about, but here the situation is different. We're looking to use tape machines and studios to increase our pleasure, get us high, and maybe even make us better people. This is the kind of learning that should be fun, because the results of the knowledge will be sweeter sounds, more professional tapes, and a happier musician. Also, if you know the language, you can talk to other people who know more than you do, and you can learn a lot.

Please remember that this is a handbook: hold it in one hand and operate your tape recorder with the other. Use them as a pair. If there's something you don't understand, just bull your way through and it will make sense somewhere down the road. Also remember that I generally like to put the hardest stuff first (not only is it harder for a lot of you to understand, it's the hardest part for me to write!) so that it's out of the way and we can then proceed to getting great sounds. So, let's explore the world of sound, and the language that technical people use to define the characteristics of sound.

CRAIG ANDERTON

Contents

Chapter 1:
Basics

THE NATURE OF SOUND

Sound is something most people take for granted—we hear it, so why think about it? But in recording, we have to think about sound from a somewhat more technical standpoint in order to record it, work with it, and listen to it. Towards this end, let's discuss some of the basic characteristics associated with sound.

You've probably heard the term 'sound waves.' Well, that's just what they are. Like ocean waves, sound waves, as they move through the air, have crests and troughs (see Figure 1-1). It is precisely these crests and troughs that create differences in air pressure, which we perceive as sound.

These pressure changes can occur at different rates, which gets us into the concept of *frequency.* Frequency is the number of crests that occur in a second. We can consider each crest-trough combination as a *cycle* that repeats itself along the wave. Thus, we measure the frequency by noting how many cycles pass by us in a second. This gives us a figure, in *cycles per second.* Recently, because that term was considered cumbersome, the unit of frequency became the Hertz (Hz), commemorating the person who did extensive work with wavelength and frequency. So, a wave with three cycles passing by in a single second would be called a 3 cycles per second wave, or simply a 3 Hertz or 3Hz wave. You will often see the term kHz; it is short for 'kiloHertz' and represents 1000Hz. Thus, 3000Hz=3kHz.

Audio frequencies are those from 20 to about 20,000 cycles per second, or 20Hz to 20kHz. These differences in frequency give different pitches to the sounds we hear.

With electronic circuits, we can't have air waves moving around inside wires, so electrical waves are a little different: they are waves of increasing and decreasing voltage, with respect to time (see Figure 1-2). As an

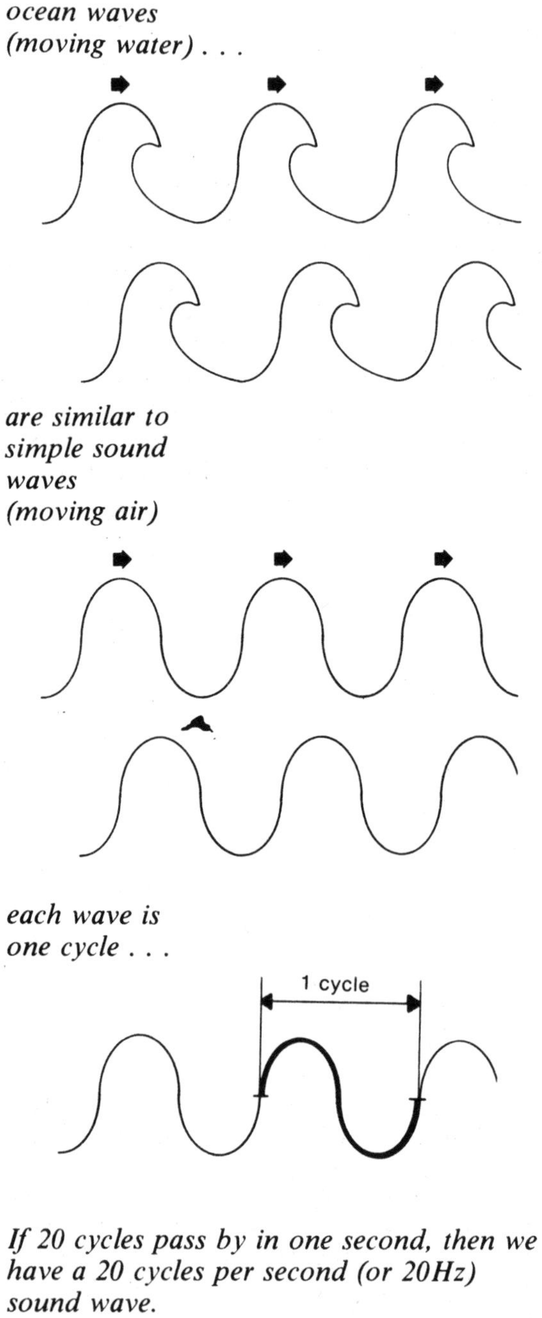

ocean waves (moving water) . . .

are similar to simple sound waves (moving air)

each wave is one cycle . . .

If 20 cycles pass by in one second, then we have a 20 cycles per second (or 20Hz) sound wave.

Figure 1-1.

ocean wave has a greater volume of water at the peak than at the trough, and as a sound wave or air wave has greater air pressure at the peak and less air pressure at the trough, an electrical wave has greater *voltage,* or 'strength,' at the crest, and lower voltage at the trough.

Now let's talk about measuring these waves. We've already figured out how to measure the frequency: count the number of cycles that occur in one second. But determining the *strength* of a varying electrical signal is quite different, and more difficult. With something like a battery, which puts out an electrical signal with a constant voltage, it's no problem to measure the voltage, but our varying signal is another story. At one point, you see the crest, and the signal strength (*amplitude*) is high, but at a different point, you see the trough, and the signal strength is very low. So, the measured strength of a varying signal will depend on when you decide to measure that signal. In order to cope with this problem, there are several different ways to measure a signal. We'll go into the two most common ways.

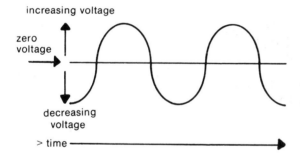

Figure 1-2. *A simple electrical wave.*

In case you are not familiar with the term 'Volt,' let's talk about it for a second. A Volt measures electrical activity—the more activity, the more Volts. This is sort of like with your car, where the speedometer reads higher as you go faster. Thus, according to Figure 1–3, we can compare the strength of one signal to another by measuring their voltages. One way to do this is to measure both signals from the

top of their peaks to the bottom of their troughs, and call this a peak-to-peak voltage. We can then see that signal X has twice the peak-to-peak voltage of signal Y. However, another way of measuring the strength of a signal is to take a mathematically correct *average* reading during one cycle, and express the average signal strength. This is known as an RMS Volt. Actually, the RMS average is *not* the same as a straight mathematical average, but we know enough for our purposes.

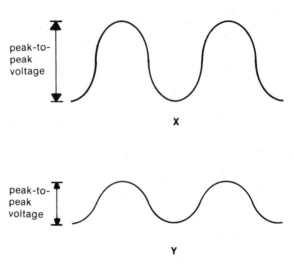

Figure 1-3. *X has twice the peak-to-peak voltage of signal Y.*

I'm sure some people are getting confused at this point. But remember—all we're really talking about is how to get a handle on these sound waves, so we don't have to simply say "this one is louder." Then we can be more precise in defining the relative levels of signals.

Since we do want to compare signals a lot, we need to look at another unit of measurement—the decibel (dB). Even engineers can have a hard time with this one, because it's a unit of measurement that can be applied in many different ways. We're only interested in applying it to signal *ratios,* though, so let's check out how it applies to them.

Simply stated, the decibel expresses the ratio between the strengths of two signals. However, before we can go any further we need to understand a little about how the ear hears (Stay with me. I told you the first part is the hardest).

If you hear a sound and then hear another sound that is twice as powerful as the first, you will not necessarily perceive the second sound as being twice as loud. Because for your ear to *hear* this:

the strength of the sound has to increase in this fashion:

As a result, the decibel increases logarithmically to correlate more closely with the ear's characteristics and to avoid using unwieldy numbers. Figure 1-4 shows a table of how the ratio of peak-to-peak signal voltage relates to the ratio expressed in decibels.

dB	Approximate peak-to-peak voltage ratio
0	1.00
1	1.12
2	1.26
3	1.41
5	1.78
6	2.00
8	2.51
10	3.16
15	5.62
20	10.00
30	31.62
40	100.00
60	1,000.00
80	10,000.00
100	100,000.00

Figure 1-4.

The decibel may seem more difficult to use, but once you get the knack of it, the decibel makes it much easier to compare the strengths of signals. For example, Figure 1-5 shows a signal that has twice as much peak-to-peak voltage as another signal. Looking on our voltage ratio vs. dB table, we see that this works out to 6dB (for you mathematical types, the formula for converting voltage ratios into dB is given in Appendix B).

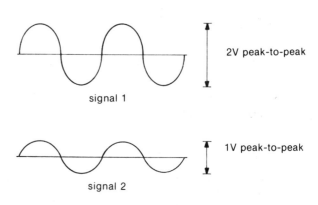

Figure 1-5. *Ratio of signal 1 to signal 2 = 2:1. 2:1 Ratio = 6 dB, according to table.*

Now we see why the dB is so useful. Referring to Figure 1-6, each pair of signals maintains a 6dB ratio, even though the actual voltage values of the signals differ. If a signal is 6dB softer than another signal, we know it is half the peak-to-peak voltage, regardless of the absolute voltage levels involved; only the ratio counts.

Sometimes you don't have a ready reference, such as a signal you want to compare other signals to. In this case, an arbitrary reference is set up and then ratios are expressed according to this reference. For example, microphones produce signals that are rated at so many dB *below* a standardized reference. This means that if you take a couple of microphones and put them in a uniform sound field, each will put out a signal whose strength can be compared to a standard signal (or reference). Thus, if one microphone puts out a signal that is 50dB below the standard, its output would be rated as –50dB, or about

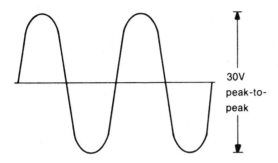

30V
peak-to-
peak

15V
peak-to-
peak

Pair 1 $\quad \dfrac{30V}{15V} = \dfrac{2}{1} = 6 \text{ dB}$

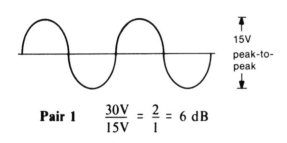

8V peak-to-peak   4V-peak-to-peak

Pair 2 $\quad \dfrac{8V}{4V} = \dfrac{2}{1} = 6 \text{ dB}$

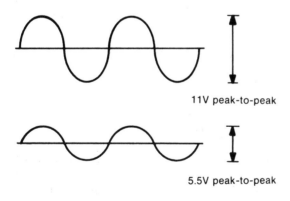

11V peak-to-peak

5.5V peak-to-peak

Pair 3 $\quad \dfrac{11}{5.5} = \dfrac{2}{1} = 6 \text{ dB}$

Figure 1-6.

1/300th of the strength of the standard signal. If a second microphone puts out a signal that is 35dB weaker than the standard signal, then the signal strength of the second microphone is about 1/60th of the strength of the standard signal. We can then directly see that the second microphone delivers more output. If an electronic device puts out *more* juice than the standard, the figure would be expressed as '+' so many dB, like +10dB, or whatever. Amplifier signals fall into the '+' dB range.

But there's no need to pursue this subject any further for right now. Let's just recap what we've got so far:

1) Sound waves are similar to ocean waves, and can be represented electronically as varying voltages.

2) Sound waves or electrical waves have specific frequencies, which are expressed in cycles per second, or Hertz.

3) We can measure the amplitude of a sound wave in several ways, two of which are the peak-to-peak method, and the RMS averaging method.

4) We can compare the amplitude of one wave to another in terms of a voltage ratio, or we can translate that voltage ratio into decibels, which reflect our hearing response more accurately than the concept of a voltage ratio. In theory, a one decibel change is the smallest change detectable by a human ear at any volume level.

There! That wasn't so bad, although there have been many simplifications along the way. We'll cover other concepts throughout the book as the need arises. Let's look at the audio spectrum next and find out about music's turf.

WHAT IS AN AUDIO SPECTRUM, ANYWAY?

We now need to understand two very basic audio concepts: the idea of an *audio-frequency spectrum,* and the idea of *flat frequency response.* Both of these concepts are vital to our understanding of sound and how we record it.

11

As any mystic or physicist will tell you, the universe is composed of vibrations—literally. Everything has its own particular resonant frequency and energy level. Some of the vibrations are very slow, others are exceedingly fast. Our ears are designed to pick up very low-frequency vibrations, known as sound waves. In fact, ears can pick up these waves from about 10Hz on up to about 15kHz, after which they have a harder and harder time responding to the vibrations. Even people with exceptionally acute hearing can't hear much sound above 22kHz. The range from 20Hz to 22kHz, which is where our various musical instruments hang out, is almost exactly ten octaves. Only electronic instruments can give a full ten-octave response, so we normally encounter instruments whose highest notes seldom get much over 3 to 5kHz. Above that we're dealing mostly with overtones and harmonics, finger noise, mechanical sounds, and so on.

One point worth considering is that this audio spectrum of sound is a tiny, tiny part of the overall spectrum of all possible forms of vibration, known as the electromagnetic spectrum. Radio waves are part of this spectrum, but are much higher in frequency than sound waves; higher still are light waves. It's kind of interesting to note that although our ears can hear ten octaves of sound, our eyes can only see one octave of light. But as far as the overall spectrum is concerned, the audio part is sort of the basement of the whole thing, a land of slow and dense vibrations that we perceive as sound, and which we arrange to form music.

To get into flat frequency response, let's invent the concept of an instrument/amplifier combination that can produce notes of exactly the same volume level, or *amplitude,* from 20Hz to 20kHz. If your ear had a flat frequency response, then whether you struck a low note or a high note you would perceive these notes as being *exactly* the same volume. In this case, the instrument is said to have a flat frequency response in terms of our ears, and this is a flat system. But our magic system doesn't exist, and our ears are not perfect, either. The biggest problem is that ears do not respond to bass as well as to treble, and, depending on the volume, they respond less to treble as well. So even before

we've built our first piece of equipment, we've already thrown in a tremendous monkey wrench. Not only does the ear react imperfectly to imperfect instruments, but every person is different: no two sets of ears respond the same way to volume changes! For a further complication, this bass response anomaly of the ears is most pronounced at low listening levels; at very high listening levels, the ears do manage an almost flat response. But as the dynamics of a song change, your ear's response changes along with it.

A partial solution to this problem has been developed over the years. Since no one doing a recording knows who will listen to the final product, or at what volume level it will be played back, the recording studio tries for a flat response—from the tape recorder on up to the amplifier and finally through the speakers—without trying to compensate for problems encountered at the listener's end. Then, a listener can change the frequency response to his or her particular requirements through the use of tone controls. Thus, if you're listening at a soft volume level, you have the option of slightly boosting the bass to compensate for your ears' deficiencies. At higher volume levels, you can leave your system flat. As you get older and the treble response of your ears starts to go away, you can add more treble.

So, the burden of maintaining the integrity of sound lies with the recording engineer, the producer, and the studio itself. If they put out an album that's bass heavy, although it may sound good at low volume, it will sound boomy and muddy at loud listening levels. By aiming for a pleasing distribution of sound throughout the audio spectrum, a standard is created. In theory, if you play back a flat recording over a perfectly flat listening system, it should sound exactly the same as the original—and it can come very close.

Before we leave the audio spectrum, let's look at how it's broken up. The audio range is traditionally divided into three broad classifications: bass, midrange, and treble. One possible definition, although there is no general consensus, is that bass extends from about 10Hz up to 200Hz or so; midrange covers 200Hz to about 5kHz; and 5kHz on up is the treble region. It's possible to divide these major categories into minor categories, and to associate particular feelings with each category:

1) *Lower bass* (about 10Hz to 80Hz) is the range where you find the lowest musical notes; this is also the area where room resonance, AC hum, and other low, rumbly entities reside. If you have some music and somehow filter out this range, you sense an immediate loss of depth, richness, and power.

2) *Upper bass* (about 80Hz to 200Hz) covers the higher end of bass instruments, and the lower range of instruments like guitar. If you were to surgically remove this range from a piece of music, almost all of your feeling of power would be lost. You probably wouldn't want to get up and dance, either, since the majority of the rhythm section's energy is located in this region.

3) *Lower midrange* (about 200Hz to 500Hz) is where a lot of rhythm and accompaniment happens; guitar falls mostly into this range.

4) *Middle midrange* (about 500Hz to 2,500Hz) is where you find violin solos, the upper parts of guitar and piano solos, and a lot of vocals. Listening to a system with poor response in the lower and middle midrange gives 'shallow' music with almost no punch.

5) *Upper midrange* (about 2,500Hz to 5kHz). Although there are few actual notes in this area, except the very topmost notes of pianos and a few other instruments, there are many harmonics and overtones within this range. Boosting this part of the spectrum results in a sheeny, bright sound, full of presence. However, if there is excessive energy in this band, the ear finds it grating after long periods of time. This is called 'listener fatigue' and is a problem with inexpensive speaker systems that artificially enhance this portion of the audio spectrum to sound 'bright.'

6) *Lower treble* (about 5kHz to 10kHz) is where the most obvious treble response occurs, and is also where tape hiss becomes most noticeable, as there are very few other sounds to block it out or mask its effects. Even though, technically, people can hear higher pitches, many times this is considered the limit of response,) because there is little of value in much modern music above this range. Sometimes a studio will cut off everything over 10kHz to minimize tape hiss problems.

7) *Upper treble* (about 10kHz to 20kHz) is our final octave, and is the home of very subtle and delicate high frequencies. Hearing good acoustic music over a system with truly fine high-frequency response is an experience, but a rare one owing to limitations in the various processes used to capture and play back sound. With this section removed, many people couldn't really hear any appreciable difference; with this part intact, and if you've got the ears to hear it, there's a feeling of 'liveness' added to the sound.

DISTORTION

Probably everyone reading this book can recognize a distorted sound—it has a grittiness and harshness not encountered with an undistorted signal. But since distortion (or rather, the avoidance of it) plays such a large part in music and recording, we should know something about what causes it. Simply stated, distortion occurs when a system operates beyond its limits. For example, let's look at why a speaker distorts. The movement of a speaker cone produces air waves that we perceive as sound; our problem is that the speaker cone can only travel a certain distance (see Figure 1-7). As long as the speaker reproduces signals within its capabilities, distortion will be at a minimum. But let's suppose we put a signal through the speaker that is loud enough to take the cone to its limit of travel; then we *double* the signal to try and get more output. Well, the speaker just won't take it—it cannot go any further. As a result, it simply can't reproduce the signal cleanly; we have gone

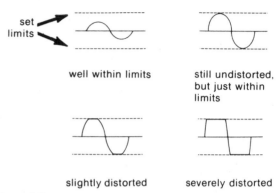

well within limits   still undistorted,
                            but just within
                            limits

slightly distorted   severely distorted

Figure 1-8.

When you encounter unintended distortion in a system, trace back through the various stages for a control that may be set wrongly, or delivering more output than the next stage can handle; then back it off until the grittiness goes away.

AN OVERVIEW OF THE RECORDING PROCESS

Let's look at the recording studio on a general level, which will make the specific aspects easier to understand.

A recording setup is composed of various parts. The first part is you! Someone has to clean the recorders, turn the knobs, push the buttons, connect the wires, and play the music. You, in turn, will need some tools to do all this.

Tool number one is a tape recorder. This can be whatever your budget can handle—even a little cassette player is better than nothing, and will give you a good idea of what you sound like. Conventional cassette and reel-to-reel consumer recorders can also be pressed into service, sometimes with amazingly good results. But to really qualify for at least semi-pro status, you need a *multitrack* tape recorder. These machines, instead of recording over the full width of a piece of tape, partition the tape electrically into four or more *tracks*. Each track is separate and independent from the others, so you can make changes to one track only, without disturbing the other ones. With this flexibility you can play and record an instrument on one track of the tape, then go back to the beginning of the tape and lay down another part on another separate track—without changing the first track in any way. The most popular and least expensive multitrack recorder for musicians is the 4-track

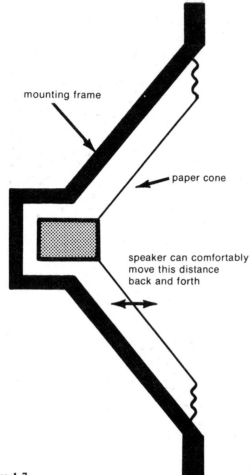

mounting frame

paper cone

speaker can comfortably move this distance back and forth

Figure 1-7.

beyond the limits of our linear, acceptable operation, and we get distortion.

Tape has limits too, which are the limits of *saturation*. As you try to push more and more signal onto the tape, there is greater and greater magnetization of the tape's magnetic particles. But if you go past a certain point, there will be no more particles left on the tape to magnetize, and therefore the sound will not be cleanly recorded on the tape. Figure 1-8 shows graphically what this kind of saturation effect 'looks' like.

It is important to recognize distortion, because its presence means that something is being pushed with excessive intensity. With a mechanical device like a speaker, you could end up damaging the unit; with a piece of tape (or many electronic devices), overloading will not cause physical destruction, but can lead to other, more subtle problems, such as leakage and, where tape is concerned, spillover to other tracks.

14

variety, which packs four different tracks side by side on a piece of ¼" wide tape. Professional studios use wider tape (up to 2" wide) to accommodate even more tracks. In only about ten years, studios changed from a 4-track standard, to 8-tracks, then to 16-tracks. Now major studios are using 24-track and even 32-track recorders. These state-of-the-art machines are marvelous, for sure, but you can do a lot with four tracks, *if* you know what you're doing.

Tool number two is a playback system. What good is recording a tape if you can't listen to it? So you must at least have headphones, but preferably a good amplifier and hi-fi speaker combination, in your studio.

Tool number three is a mixing console, which acts as a clearinghouse for all those audio signals and inputs and outputs we encounter in the course of recording. Remember how we said you can record signals on up to four separate tracks? Well, at some point we're going to want to *mix* all those signals into a composite mono or stereo signal that we can listen to, presenting the music in a finished form. This gives rise to the process of *mixing,* where all four tracks are varied in level, balance, tonal quality, or whatever is necessary to make a pleasing musical product for you to hear on your playback system.

Tool number four is another tape recorder to record the final version of your mixes. This recorder produces what's known as a *master* tape, which contains the mixed and edited versions of musical pieces. A professional studio will have a separate, high-quality machine (usually a 2-track model for stereo and a 4-track for quad) for making master tapes; but with our relaxed home requirements, you can use any good reel-to-reel or cassette deck. As long as you have your original tracks preserved on the 4-track tape, you can remix at a later date when you become an accomplished mixer, or you can remix into a better machine if you upgrade your studio.

Tool number five covers lots of separate accessories, which depend upon your circumstances. A microphone, for example, is a necessity for almost all studios, as are any tools required for routine maintenance. You also need tape, a razor blade and splicing block to splice tapes, microphone stands, extension cords, and so forth.

When you combine all these tools together into an acoustically acceptable environment, you have all the basics of a studio. But, just as buying a superb instrument doesn't make you a superb player, all the equipment in the world won't do you any good unless you have the knowledge, patience, experience, and *practice,* to back it up. You don't gain these overnight—in fact, any good sound engineer will tell you that you never stop learning, and, literally, you never do. There are always new techniques to be tried, new devices to experiment with, new music to record. In any event, strive to run your studio as efficiently, professionally, and pleasantly as possible. When you know what you're doing, it's fun; when you have to fight the equipment, it's work. So let's begin by looking inside the tape recorder and talking a bit about the physical process that actually puts sound onto a piece of tape.

GROUND RULES—AND THE CASE FOR MONO

Throughout the book, we will generally assume that your studio will be monaurally oriented, and that your final tapes will also be mono. Now I know that this is going to disappoint some people, but there are some very solid reasons for it.

First of all, many people are into home recording because they plan on making demo tapes to send to record companies. This is fine, but you should be aware that some lower-echelon company listeners don't necessarily have wonderful stereo rigs in their offices; and even if they do, you have no guarantee that the balance is going to be correct: in short, life is most goofproof with a mono tape. It's always good to take Murphy's Law into account ("anything that can go wrong, will"), and that's one reason to go with mono demo tapes.

You'll also find it a lot easier to put the studio together. Your mixing board doesn't have to be as complicated, and, instead of needing two expensive monitor speakers, you need only one. You don't have to be as critical about level setting, or do dreary things like match resistors for balanced response (if you build your own stuff).

15

Finally, you'll find that it is difficult to create very satisfying stereo mixes with a 4-track recorder (for reasons that will become clear when we get into mixing); this is especially true for solo artists playing all the instruments themselves. If you have an 8-track recorder, then stereo becomes much more accessible and is decidedly the way to go.

BASICS OF RECORDERS

The whole point of recording, really, is to 'freeze' sound so that later we can listen back to it. As a photograph holds an image, a tape must hold sounds in a form that can be played over and over again if need be. When you consider that sounds are caused by moving air, you see the problem we are up against: how do you store a bunch of airwaves, anyway?

Over the years, people have been working on how to translate air waves into electrical impulses. This has led to the invention of the microphone, which does a fairly good job of reacting to air waves, and generating electrical impulses in response. A microphone is similar to a loudspeaker, but designed to work exactly in reverse: instead of making sounds, it picks them up. Both microphones and speakers are *transducers,* or devices that translate one kind of impulse or energy into another kind of impulse—in this case, air pressure translates into electricity. Let's get into this a little further, since many of the principles we will discuss relate to tape recorders as well.

Figure 1–9 shows how a speaker works. Note the three important parts: the permanent magnet, the electromagnet, and the paper cone. Permanent magnets are like the bar magnets you have probably played with at some point in your life. Magnets have the interesting ability to repel or attract each other, depending on their relative positioning (see Figure 1–10). This ability of one magnet to cause another one to physically move forms the basis of the speaker's operation, as we will see.

An electromagnet is a coil made of many turns of very fine wire, and is similar to a permanent magnet in its effect; but it requires an electrical current passing through it to create a magnetic field. A varying electrical current creates a varying magnetic field.

Now, getting back to the speaker, note that the electromagnet is attached to the paper

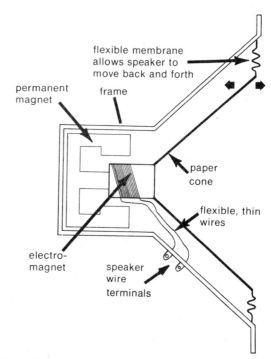

Figure 1-9.

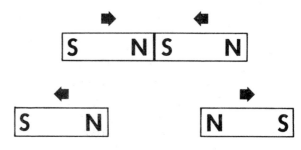

opposing poles of bar magnets attract

like poles of bar magnets repel

Figure 1-10.

cone, and placed within the field of a permanent magnet. Passing a varying electrical current—like the audio signal of a power amp—through the electromagnet, generates a magnetic field around it that interacts with the

16

field created by the permanent magnet. Because of the attraction-repulsion effect of the magnets, this magnetic interaction translates into movement of the speaker cone. Since the speaker cone is now moving back and forth at a rate determined by the magnetic field created by an audio signal, that audio signal is controlling the speaker cone. As the speaker cone moves back and forth, it sets up air waves that we perceive as sound. So let's recap: we have managed to convert electrical current into air waves by using a combination of electrical signals and magnetism.

Interestingly, a speaker can also work like a microphone (see Figure 1-11): Air waves striking the speaker cone cause the electromagnet to move within the magnetic field of the permanent magnet. As the electromagnet coil cuts across the permanent magnet's magnetic field, the interaction causes a tiny, fluctuating signal—the electrical equivalent of the air waves striking the cone—to be induced into the coil. This is very much like the case with a guitar pickup, where a vibrating string induces a voltage into an electromagnetic coil. However, when a speaker is used as a microphone, the paper cone is usually too stiff to give very good frequency response; so we have microphones that work on this principle, but are specifically constructed to receive air waves rather than create them. The minute voltage present at the windings of the microphone's electromagnet duplicates the motion of the air waves striking the microphone's diaphragm; we have managed in this case to turn airwaves into a feeble, but measurable and usable, electrical signal. Not just any electrical signal can drive a speaker; try plugging your guitar directly into a speaker for a graphic illustration! Any signal intended to drive a speaker has to be properly conditioned, usually by giving it enough power to make that cone really move, and push the air around. A tiny electrical signal won't drive the speaker at all. The output of your microphone also needs some conditioning; the signal is so low that we need to amplify it in order to make it usable.

The reason we want to generate an electrical signal is that electrical signals are much easier to store than air waves. It's time to examine how we store these signals with tape.

A reel of tape is nothing more than a base material, usually some kind of very thin,

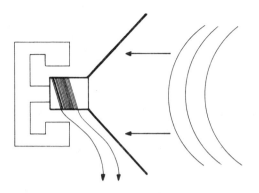

Sound waves strike the speaker cone, making it move back and forth . . . this induces a small voltage in the coil, which means we have translated air waves into an electrical signal.

Figure 1-11.

space-age plastic, uniformly coated with zillions of tiny magnetic particles (see Figure 1-12). These particles are like miniature bar magnets, and are only about one micron long; so, you can fit a whole lot of these particles on a piece of tape. Normally, these particles are just kind of floating around in their little molecular world, randomly orienting themselves in a variety of positions and directions, sort of like a crowd of people at a party. What we can do, however, is to make these particles line up in a meaningful way. This would be the difference between having a bunch of people just standing around, and a bunch of people all walking together in a straight line. When they're walking in a straight line, there is a defined and obvious pattern. Otherwise, it's just a mob scene.

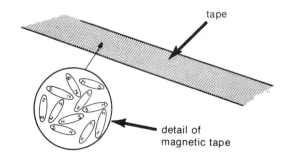

tape

detail of magnetic tape

Figure 1-12.

Taming these particles requires the introduction of a new transducer, the *record head*. Like a speaker, this device takes electrical signals and uses them to create a magnetic field by going through the windings of an electromagnet. The windings are wrapped around a permanent magnet; but the magnet is *not* free to move. However, this particular magnet is interestingly constructed: there is a small gap at one end. Because the magnetic 'circuit' is not complete, a fairly intense magnetic field is generated at the gap; this field fluctuates in accordance with the strength of the electrical impulses, or signal, applied to the record head (see Figure 1–13).

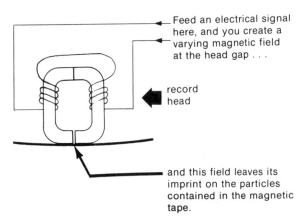

Feed an electrical signal here, and you create a varying magnetic field at the head gap . . .

record head

and this field leaves its imprint on the particles contained in the magnetic tape.

Figure 1-13.

But we still need to listen back to what we've recorded. Again, we apply the same principles, but in reverse. We now introduce a *playback head,* similar to a record head but optimized for playback. As the tape goes past this head, the magnetic field pattern imprinted on the tape causes very small voltage changes in the windings of the playback head's electromagnet; once amplified in a suitable way, we have an electrical signal. Generally we'll drive an amplifier/speaker combination, or use headphones to hear what's happening on the tape. But we've accomplished what we set out to do: created a permanent record, coded in a magnetic language, of what we wanted to record; and we can take that magnetic language and translate it back into something we can listen to and understand.

A tape recorder has one more head in addition to the record and playback heads; this third head, called the *erase head,* simply erases signals previously put on the tape. As tape travels through the machine (see Figure 1-14), it goes past this head first, any signals are erased, and the tape is fresh and clean for recording. Well, not perfectly fresh and clean. A virgin, unrecorded tape has less noise. However, there are devices called bulk erasers which can erase an entire tape in a few seconds to better than new condition.

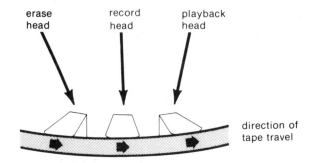

erase head   record head   playback head

direction of tape travel

Tape first travels past the erase head, where previously recorded signals may be erased if desired. Then signals are recorded at the record head, and finally pass by the playback head where they can be monitored. In practice, the head extends slightly above and below the tape.
Figure 1-14.

This is a very simple explanation of the workings of a tape machine, and in order to get the point across, we've simplified, and also ignored, some of the complications and limitations. But it's important to basically understand these workings if we're going to get the most out of our equipment. So now let's turn to some of the components and eccentricities of the tape recording process.

THE TAPE TRANSPORT

There is more to tape recording than electronics; much of the tape recorder is a mechanical system. Whether we're talking about a cassette or a fancy studio recorder, the mechanics of a tape transport are similar, and designed to accomplish the same goal: pulling the tape past the machine's various heads in the most uniform, constant way possible. Tape speed is given in inches per second (ips), i.e. how much tape goes past a given point in one second. Typical studio tape speeds are 7½, 15, and 30 inches per second.

Variations in tape speed show up as *wow* and *flutter.* Wow is a cyclic speed change which is fairly slow; flutter is like a vibrato effect applied to the tape. Neither is desirable, and a lot of engineering effort has gone into making tape transports that move the tape efficiently and reliably, reducing wow and flutter.

The most common system is shown in Figure 1-15. In this, a precision motor turns a cylinder called a *capstan,* which revolves at a constant speed. The capstan works in conjunction with a device called a *pinch roller.* When the pinch roller is disengaged from the capstan, the tape is motionless. However, pushing the play button will swing the pinch roller against the capstan, with the tape pinched in between. As the capstan and pinch roller rotate, they feed the tape through. Because the capstan is a constant-speed device, the tape is pulled through at a very uniform rate. Speed accuracy within .1% is considered good for consumer-type equipment, with .05% accuracy considered outstanding. Very few people can detect this amount of variation, except perhaps on long, sustained notes, like the bass notes of a piano or organ.

Part of the transport holds the *supply reel* of tape, and part holds the *take-up reel.* Tape is 'supplied' from the reel on the left and is 'taken up' by the reel on the right. A slight, counterclockwise 'pull' is applied to the takeup reel in order to eliminate any slack as the tape passes through the capstan and pinch roller. Similarly, the supply reel has a slight amount of clockwise pull to insure the smooth flow of tape. This pull, or 'back torque,' must be slight and precise. Otherwise, the capstan/pinch roller would have to work harder to pull the tape from the supply reel. Without these compensating tensions on the supply and takeup reels, the tape would not run smoothly; this would give rise to tape handling problems and speed inaccuracies. The capstan-pinch roller has to control tape speed, but the takeup and supply reels are an important part of the process.

To rapidly advance the tape 'fast forward' —say to find a later selection on the tape—the pinch roller and capstan are disengaged, and the takeup reel rotates rapidly in a counterclockwise fashion, pulling the tape at a fast speed. Rewind works in reverse: the supply reel rotates rapidly clockwise to return the tape to itself (see Figure 1-16). Complex braking systems are also a part of the transport. These prevent tape spillage as tape is shuttled rapidly back and forth between fast forward, play, and rewind. The higher-class

In rewind, reels go clockwise at high speed. In fast forward, reels go counterclockwise at high speed.

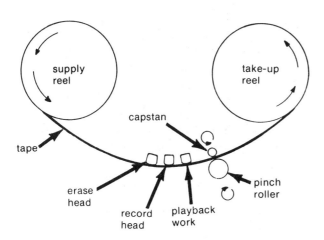

Simplified top view of tape transport in play or record mode.

Figure 1-15.

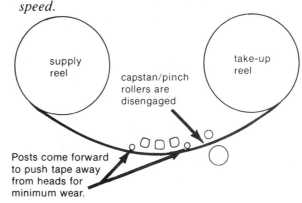

Top view of transport in fast forward or rewind mode.

Figure 1-16.

tape machines have special electronic logic circuitry that controls all these various motions, making sure that braking is applied at the right time, that the speed is maintained at a constant rate, and so on.

Inexpensive tape recorders, through an intricate collection of pulleys, gears, and levers, use one motor to drive the capstan and the supply and takeup reels. More sophisticated decks use three separate motors: one for the capstan, one for the supply reel, and one for the takeup reel. Not only does this latter system eliminate all the pulleys and belts and gears (which need to be maintained and can be a source of trouble), but it also removes a fair amount of load from the capstan motor, contributing to better speed reliability. Also, three motors are necessary in order to use the electronic logic gadgetry that we touched on a few sentences ago.

No matter what kind of machine you have, it is important to keep a couple of rules in mind:

1) If the pinch roller gets dirty and flaked with minute pieces of tape or dirt, the effective diameter of the pinch roller increases, throwing off the speed. A dirty capstan will have the same problem (see the chapter on maintenance for cleaning instructions).

2) Since, with one-motor machines, various play, rewind, and fast forward positions bring a variety of motors and mechanical gizmos into play, it's best to switch quickly, authoritatively, and gently from one function to another. Switching like a demon from play to fast forward to rewind may be fun, but your machine will dislike you for it. If you want to go from fast forward to play, switch to stop for a second, *then* go into play. Treat your tape machine gently. More expensive machines are made foolproof so that you can go directly from, say, rewind to play; but chances are you're not going to encounter this in anything but professionally-oriented equipment. Play it safe.

Naturally, engineers haven't been sitting still when it comes to designing transports, and there have been constant improvements.

One of these is the *servo-controlled* transport, which provides extremely stable speed and has the bonus of making possible moderate tape speed changes. Conventional motors lock onto the frequency of AC house current (60Hz in the USA, 50Hz in Europe and many other parts of the world), and derive their accuracy from the fact that the AC power line frequency is also quite accurate, typically within .01%. It is very difficult to change the speed of these kinds of motors, since it isn't very likely that the power companies are going to change 60Hz over to something else just so you can fiddle with your recorder! But a servo-system does not need to lock to the AC frequency and may be fed correction information that yields a fairly wide pitch variation—typically, ±3% to ±10%. This can be very handy, but again you pay money for the privilege. Top-of-the-line cassette decks are beginning to incorporate servo-controlled motors, and no doubt the trend will be toward increased use of this type of drive system in more recorders.

THE VARIOUS JACKS

All tape recorders have at least two kinds of jacks: a set of input jacks and a set of output jacks. The signal you want to record goes into the input jacks; these may be called REC IN, TAPE IN, LINE IN, or whatever. Frequently there will be two different types of input jacks: a MIC IN jack and a LINE IN jack. The MIC IN jack goes to a booster amplifier, called a *mic preamp,* which brings the (usually weak) microphone signals up to usable levels. The LINE IN jack accepts signals which are already at a suitable level, such as the signal from another tape recorder, certain electronic instruments, and so on. It is always a good idea to go through the line inputs wherever possible, since you avoid any noise that may be added in the mic preamp. Also, you can easily run into mismatch problems that give distortion with mic inputs.

In a stereo machine, you have two duplicate sets of input and output jacks: one set for the right channel and one for the left. In a 4-channel machine, you'll find four sets of input-output jacks.

The playback head connects via some electronics to the output jacks, and these get patched into your playback, or monitoring, system. In the majority of cassette machines, there is no extra playback head. A single head is made to do double duty, and if you think this might interfere with high-quality sound, you're right. Trying to use one head for two purposes involves a necessary compromise. Nonetheless, there will also be a set of output jacks on a cassette recorder.

You might also find a headphone jack, so you can monitor the tape directly at the machine. Other jacks may include a jack for a remote control adapter, a spare output, or some other function; but the important ones are the IN and OUT jacks.

THE RECORDING ELECTRONICS

You can't stick a signal into the record head and expect it to come out on the tape. First of all, with the tape recording process, good, high-frequency response is harder to achieve than good bass response, due to the physics of tapes and heads. So there is a high-frequency boost called *pre-emphasis* built into a recorder. The amount of pre-emphasis is set to compensate exactly for the treble loss that occurs (see Figure 1–17). There is also a

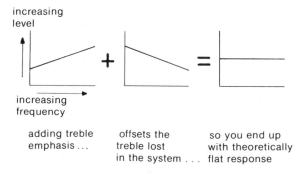

adding treble emphasis . . .   offsets the treble lost in the system . . .   so you end up with theoretically flat response

Figure 1-17.

circuit called a *bias oscillator.* This is a supersonic tone generator, which in essence provides a 'backdrop' against which to record your audio signals. Without this backdrop there are severe distortion problems due to the nature of the tape itself. Luckily, we don't need to know a lot about bias oscillators, except for one aspect: different types of tape require different levels of bias for optimum results. The bias setting influences your noise level, frequency response, distortion, and so forth. Like everything else, it can't be perfect,

so the bias setting is a compromise for the best average characteristics. Most recorders these days have switches that allow you to change the bias for different kinds of tape while recording, and also tend to include instructions for the settings to use with different brands of tape. Usually the recorder's bias oscillator is calibrated for a particular brand of tape (stated in the owner's manual), and using that type of tape will generally give optimum results.

THE PLAYBACK ELECTRONICS

There's nothing too exciting here. With more amplification and more frequency shaping, you end up hearing your sounds at the output jack.

THE VU METER

VU (volume unit) meters are wonderful to look at as their pointers swing merrily back and forth across their brightly-lit faces. Their intended function is to monitor the signal level being put on the tape, because if you exceed the tape's signal-handling capacity, you generate distortion, which ends up as a 'grunching' sound on playback. VU meters, therefore, have a calibrated scale, with a point marked 0 VU (dB). Above this, the meter has a red band to indicate that you might be overloading your tape, sort of like the red line marks on a sports car tachometer. Now, it would be nice if all we had to do was look at the meter, and whenever the signal went into the red, we'd know that we had to turn down the level of the signal going to the record head. But meters are not that simple. For one thing, the meter's pointer has a certain amount of inertia; it takes a finite amount of time to swing from one end to the other. Although it can react to slowly-changing signals adequately, the pointer lags behind sharply percussive sounds that may be over before it has had a chance to start moving, so although the meter didn't show you going into the red, you may have been there anyway. Secondly, not all tapes react the same way. One may saturate and distort easily, yet with another you may be able to keep the pointer in the red most of the time and still obtain a good recording.

Why, then, do you want to record at the highest signal level possible, since that clearly increases your chances for a distorted tape? Well, tape tends to have a residual amount of hiss, and nothing will remove it, although noise-reduction equipment can help (more on this later). This hiss is unpleasantly audible and interferes with the music, especially during quiet passages; the louder the hiss, the more the annoyance. Now, there's not much we can do to lower the hiss, but we *can* raise the amount of signal compared to it, so that any hiss *appears* small. From this, it's pretty clear that the more signal we get on the tape, short of distortion, the less noise we'll hear on playback. This concept is expressed as signal-to-noise ratio (see Figure 1-18)—the higher the ratio, the quieter the machine. A good tape recorder will have a signal-to-noise ratio of about 1000:1, which at least puts the noise in the background. It may sound like 1000:1 is a lot, but when you consider that your ear is so remarkably sensitive that it can discriminate dynamic changes of 1,000,000,000,000:1 (not a misprint!), then it doesn't look so good; but it is adequate. Signal-to-noise is typically expressed in decibels, which we talked about earlier.

So a VU meter helps us keep the noise down and the signal undistorted, and that makes it unmistakably one of the good guys. But meters are fragile; don't let them swing wildly over to the right-hand side of the scale, as an extra-strong signal can bend the pointer, necessitating an expensive repair.

GETTING THE SIGNAL ONTO THE TAPE

As we mentioned earlier, tape is composed of lots of little magnetic particles, attached to a plastic backing. The layer of particles is extremely thin and is measured in microns (1 micron=1/1,000,000th of a meter). For this reason, you can see that the backing material must be very uniform or the particles will form an uneven surface (see Figure 1-19). An uneven backing prevents the tape from making good contact with the heads, and can cause *drop-outs*, where the sound simply disappears for a few milliseconds (or longer, if the tape is a cheap variety).

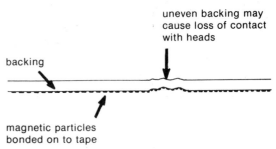

Figure 1-19. *Exaggerated and magnified top view of tape.*

An important characteristic of the tape is the distribution of the magnetic particles in terms of their density and uniformity. Since they carry the information, you want them to do the best possible job. One way to insure that they do is to pack as many particles on the tape as possible; this increases the potential fidelity as we can illustrate by an analogy.

If you tried to communicate a symbol, like the letter 'R,' by darkening a series of squares in a grid, you would get better definition (or fidelity) of that symbol as you increase the number of squares that you darken (see Figure 1-20). A similar process happens in

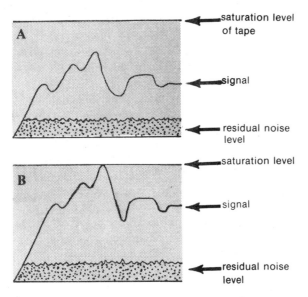

In B, we have put more level on the tape, while still avoiding saturation of the tape. Thus, this increased signal masks residual noise better than the under recorded signal in A.

Figure 1-18. *Pictorial representation of tape noise and signal.*

recording; the more particles, the better the definition of sound.

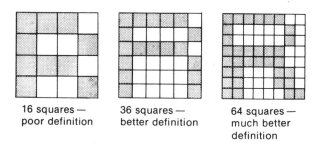

16 squares — poor definition   36 squares — better definition   64 squares — much better definition

Figure 1-20.

There is a limit to how many of these particles can be packed on a given inch of tape, but we can increase the *apparent* number of particles at the tape head by increasing the speed of the tape. For example, let's say we have a sound that lasts exactly one second, and we apply that sound to the record head. If the tape is running at 7½ ips, then 7½ inches of tape will go past that record head in one second, and present a finite amount of particles to the head for magnetization. But if we increase the speed to 15 ips, then twice as much tape will go past the head in the same amount of time, making twice the amount of particles available for magnetization. This increases the fidelity, and explains why cassette recorders, which only run at 1⅞ ips, are so picky about having the very best tape possible: you can't increase the speed to improve the performance.

When we talk about tape fidelity, the most important factors are the level of a signal we can produce on the tape, to overcome noise; and the amount of high frequencies we can put on the tape, since that is usually where tape performance falls off the most. Along with tape speed, another factor influencing fidelity is *track width*. To understand this particular concept a little better, we need to look a little at the evolution of the tape recorder.

There are many contradictory stories about just who invented the first recorder and when; however, we do know that the very first machines didn't use tape, but rather wire, and were called wire recorders. When magnetic tape was introduced in Germany, the record head would record signals over the full width

of the tape (see Figure 1-21). This is a good example of a *full-track,* monophonic tape recorder.

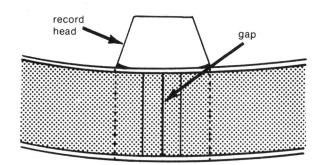

Full track — records over full width of track.

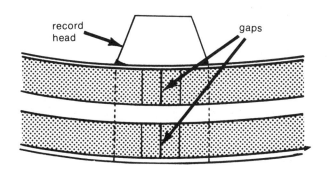

Half track — records 2 tracks of audio on a single piece of tape.

Figure 1-21.

Next, someone got the idea of splitting the head into the separate, smaller, record heads, and recording in stereo. Each track now occupied half the tape; this was called *half-track* recording. But we paid for this privilege: we had two tracks of tape hiss as well as two tracks of signal, and we decreased the amount of tape available to each of the two record heads. But none of these problems were considered serious enough to offset the extra flexibility, so we progressed to *quarter-track* recording, which became a little more complicated. There were still two record heads, but they were staggered. So, when we put on a tape, we could record two stereo tracks, with each track taking up a quarter of the tape (see Figure 1-22). Then, we could turn the tape over, and record two more stereo tracks on the remaining half of the tape. But now we added another price: we could not make splices in the tape anymore, at least not without interfering with the information going the other way on the tape (see Figure 1–23). For this reason, in professional applications, where splicing and editing is important, tapes are always recorded in one direction only.

But luckily for us, head technology didn't stop there. Soon, four record heads were put in a line, and now we had 4-channel, or quad recording, because we could record four separate tracks. This went on to eight record heads in a line for 8-channel recording, then twelve for 12-track, and so on.

Although we reduced the fidelity somewhat in theory, in practice, recording electronics, tape formulations, and other whizbang technological events have kept the

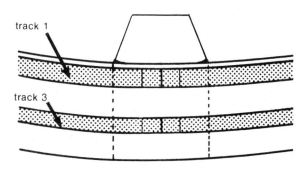

Quarter-track format splits the tape into quarters, and records on two of the quarters (tracks).

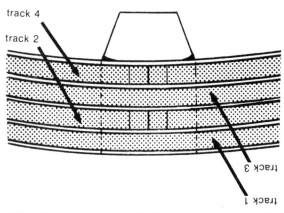

Flip the tape over, and the previously recorded tracks now go in the opposite direction, out of the way of the head gaps, and we can record on the other two quarters of the tape.
Figure 1-22.

24

quality of the tape recorder moving right along to compensate. But perhaps the most important addition to the recorder, as far as we're concerned, is the subject of our next-to-last basic concept: *synchronization.*

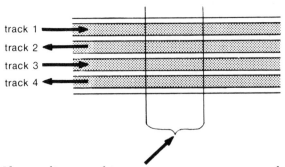

If we splice out this section to remove a sound on tracks 1 and 3, then we also remove part of tracks 2 and 4 whether we want to or not.

Figure 1-23.

You have all probably heard the term *overdub.* An overdub is when a musician can come into a studio, listen to a tape, and add a part to what he or she hears. For example, let's suppose you have a 4-track recorder, and a trio comprised of guitar, bass, and drums. You could record the guitar on track one, the bass on track two, and the drums on track three. Then, as the guitarist listened to tracks one, two, and three, he could play a lead guitar part on track four. This lead guitar part is called an overdub.

Now this doesn't sound complicated, but it is, because overdubbing must be done *in synchronization with the basic track.* There would be no point in putting a lead guitar solo on a track if it were going to be half a beat late all the way through, and that's the difficulty we face with most tape recorders. Here's why (see Figure 1–24):

As the tape travels past the playback head, we hear the sounds on the tape. But remember that the tape passes by the record head *before* it hits the playback head, so that if at the moment of hearing a sound, we put a signal into the record head, *it will not go on the tape at the same physical location as the sounds we hear,* but rather it will be stored at the place on the tape over the record head.

When we play that tape back, the overdub comes in late, and it sounds terrible because it is not synchronized with the original signal.

But luckily, some astute engineering overcame this problem. A signal can now be monitored *at the record head,* so you don't have to wait for the signal to pass the playback head in order to hear it. The most common name for this is Selective Synchronication or 'Sel-Sync,' a name originated (and owned) by Ampex. Other companies have other terms, like 'Multi-Sync' (TEAC), 'Trak-Sync' (Crown), just about everything-but-the-kitchen-sync—the net result is the same.

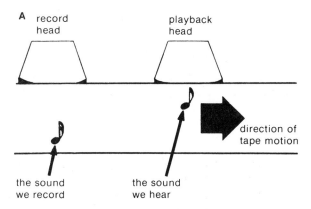

Without synchronization, when we hear a sound at the playback head, and record an overdub at the record head, the sounds are separated on the tape. Thus, on playback the first sound plays back before the overdubbed sound. But with synchronization, on playback both sounds hit the playback head at the same time.

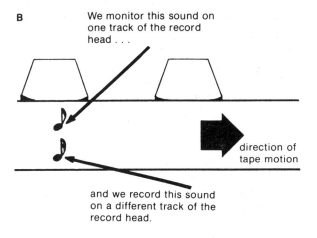

Figure 1-24.

Again, we have compromised ourselves somewhat since, as we pointed out earlier, heads don't like to do double duty. The solution is to optimize the record head for recording only, and just ignore the inferior playback qualities—they really don't matter in the long run because, after all, we are simply monitoring the tape for the purposes of synchronizing an overdub. When you want to hear all tracks in glorious full fidelity, then you listen to all the playback heads after the tracks have been recorded, and the synchronization and fidelity will both be there.

The same type of sync technique is applicable to 8-track, 16-track, and other multitrack recording equipment.

TAPE RECORDER SWITCHES

The sync switch isn't the only switch you will encounter; there will also be an output switch that selects what kind of output the tape recorder will give. In the *source* position of the output switch, you can monitor the signal going into the recorder at the same time it is being played. In the *tape* position, which becomes operative only when the tape is running, you monitor directly from the tape— either via the playback head, or from the record head in the sync mode. If you monitor the tape position while playing an instrument, the signal from the recorder will appear delayed; nonetheless, by listening directly to the tape it is easy to tell if the recording levels are too high (giving distortion), or if the tape has any imperfections.

As you can imagine, super tape formulations, multi-track recorders, and super-accurate tape transports have all contributed greatly to the increase of good recorded sound we are fortunate to be able to enjoy. These systems are by no means perfect, but continuous improvements are being made.

Going through all these basics may have been a little heavy, but this knowledge will come in handy. Tape recorders aren't used in a vacuum; for example, they need microphones to turn air waves into usable signals. They also work with a collection of electronic circuits that help route signals to correct inputs and outputs, add modifications to the basic sound, and so forth. These electronic devices are housed in a *console,* which we will explore in a little while. But for now, before we leave the subject of tape recorders, let's look at what is available in terms of recording equipment.

BUYING THE TAPE RECORDER(S) FOR YOUR STUDIO

In this section, we come to grips with a harsh reality: you are going to have to tie up a fair amount of money in your studio and tape deck. Although most professionals would put the price tag on a minimum system at around $20,000 (!), you can get by for much less. I put together a very good, basic, demo studio for under $1500, which is considerably less. But even if that looks like an impossible figure, there are alternatives.

If your budget is very limited, I would suggest a 3-head, reel-to-reel recorder. With this you can do some fairly interesting tapes, and at least layer three or four tracks into a single mono tape (see the section on recording techniques). You can expect to pay anywhere from $150, for a used model, to $500-$600 for a newer type with good transport, heads, and so forth; for deluxe types you can spend even more. Reel-to-reel machines are pretty common in the audiophile market, and popular brand names include ReVox, Hitachi, Akai, Sony, TEAC, Pioneer, Dokorder, JVC, and many more. The best place to find information on this type of equipment, as well as what's new, is in the various hi-fi magazines available at newsstands. Remember, though, that if you plan to do this primitive overdubbing, you must have a 3-head, and not 2-head, model.

The choice narrows down considerably when considering multitrack recorders. We are now dealing with a more specialized market, consisting of serious musicians and smaller studios who need studio-type features, but don't want to pay the high price of truly professional gear. The following are descriptions of some models available as of this writing (12/76). Keep in mind that new machines are constantly being introduced, while older models are discontinued; so, there is no way this type of list can be current. However, it

should give you a pretty good idea of the type of features you can expect to find on both new and used models. Since I have not had hands-on experience with all of these models, I cannot recommend any particular type.

1) *TEAC A-3340S.* Probably the best selling 4-channel deck for musical purposes, this deck can hold 10½" reels, which means that you can get a lot of tape time (consumer decks only accommodate 7" reels). Reels can move at either 15 ips or 7½ ips. To produce tapes approaching professional quality, 15 ips is mandatory, although this speed does eat up twice as much tape. If you're not all that much into turning out super-quality sound, the TEAC 2340S is available for slightly less, but it only handles 7" reels and the choice of speeds is 7½ and 3¾ ips. Otherwise, the machines are very similar.

Like other competing 4-track recorders, the TEAC transport uses three motors: one for the take-up reel, one for the supply reel, and one for the capstan. This approach is the most reliable and flexible, and moves the tape gently and without unpleasant surprises (like spillage).

The 3340S also includes three heads (erase, record, playback), four VU meters, separate record buttons for each channel, and switches to move the output of the recorder from source to tape. These are all standard features for this class of deck.

A feature added for the convenience of the user is a cueing arm, which allows you to bring the tape into contact with the head even if the machine is in the pause position. This is very useful for editing and cueing. The TEAC also has mic-line mixing at the recorder, so if you have up to four line-level instruments and four high-impedance microphones, you don't need an external mixer. This feature becomes less important if you have a good console, but it does have its uses. You also get output-level controls, and the ability to accommodate 7" reels if you want to.

None of these features is of the 'toys and games' variety; in fact, remove any one of these and you have a seriously crippled studio. Many lesser-priced consumer decks, intended to hang out in living rooms to impress friends, have more gimmicks, such as auto-reverse of the tape, slider pots, fancy lights, and so on. None of these is really necessary; for semi-pro use, companies tend to produce fairly stripped-down decks, and put the extra effort and money saved into reliability. I highly approve of this approach; what fun is a tape recorder if it doesn't work?

2) *Akai GX-630D-SS.* Another contender in the 4-channel sweepstakes, this machine lists for $1000, or slightly less than the TEAC. Akai claims to have great tape heads, but then again, most manufacturers have introduced some kind of innovative thinking towards producing a better head. This machine does not handle 15 ips; but it does have a pitch control, a feature I wish every tape recorder had. Frequently, when you're overdubbing, you need to add an instrument that may be slightly out of tune with the other tracks. Rather than retuning the whole instrument, you can simply raise or lower the pitch of the tape to match it, which is much simpler. Variable speed is also useful for special effects, and can compensate for the speed variations that occur in any lower-priced deck, no matter how well designed. As of this writing, Akai has announced the model GX-270D-SS, which sells for somewhat less.

3) *Sony TC-788-4* (no price available, but competitive with the TEAC 3340), and the *TC-388-4* (competitive with the TEAC 2340). The TC-788-4 gives wow and flutter figures that equal the TEAC's (.04% at 15 ips, .06% at 7½ ips—very good figures for consumer products); the biggest difference between it and the TEAC models is that it includes a memory rewind feature. This is another nice convenience; it means that you can be recording, and have the tape rewind to a location that you have previously specified, when you hit the rewind button. This is handy during mixdown, for example, where you run the tape through many times and frequently have to return to the beginning of a section. Set the memory rewind for the beginning, hit the rewind, and it stops at that place every time. This is one gizmo that doesn't noticeably degrade reliability and it can be quite helpful. The TC-388-4 is designed for 4-channel listening setups, and does not include track synchronization, so it's not recommended for our purposes.

4) *Dokorder:* This company has gone out of business but used Dokorder machines are often available. They have put out three models: the 7140 (approximately $670 list), 8140 ($750 list), and the 1140 ($1300). The 7140 is the lower-level entry into the 4-channel world in terms of price, but the performance is quite adequate, and many people have gotten their start with this machine. However, it is limited to 7½ and 3¾ ips with 7" reels. It does have two extra toys: an echo, and a sound-on-sound switch with an associated level switch to control these effects; nothing earth-shattering, but nice to have when you need some tape echo. The 8140 is more or less the same machine in a different and more professional-looking enclosure.

The 'top of the line' is the 1140, which looks like it's designed to compete with TEAC's 3340. To woo you away from the established standard, they throw some extra features at you: memory rewind (which goes either play-rewind-play or play-rewind-stop), peak-level-indicator LEDs (which, in conjunction with the meters, make it easier to consistently obtain distortion-free levels); an automatic sync feature that simplifies the procedure of going in and out of sync while recording; and also, a built-in test signal generator, and front-panel bias controls (something I haven't seen on other multitrack decks, incidentally), so that you can set the bias for whatever type of tape you use. This feature shows that Dokorder has more faith in the consumer than other manufacturers, who pre-set the bias adjustments and hide them in the recorder. The Dokorder manufacturers recognize that bias adjustments are often a matter of individual tastes and varying recording requirements. So with this recorder, they make it easy for you to readjust the bias to suit your needs. The recorder itself is packaged as a two-part affair, with the electronics standing vertically behind the transport. This may not sound like a big deal, but it's a lot more convenient than the self-contained-type recorders.

I should add at this point that all these features are handy, but only that. You will not necessarily make better tapes on this machine, but it is nice to see a company that has looked at what's available and attempted to add features which are meaningful to the musician.

Most early decks were outgrowths of 4-channel technology, adapted to musical use; the latecomers in the field had the chance to design from the ground up for this new market.

5) The *Pioneer RT-2044.* Priced somewhat higher than the standard TEAC 3340, it includes some interesting features and seems to be more of a professional, field-type deck that can be transported easily and without fear of damage. It is a modular system, and offers plug-in head assemblies. Pioneer also claims rugged construction. If you're mostly interested in recording at home, this probably isn't worth the extra money; but if you plan to do a lot of remote or field recording, or if you need head configurations other than the 4-track sync format (which makes the replaceable plug-in heads look attractive), look this over.

I'll bet you didn't know that there were so many other choices, but we're still not through. If you're ready to commit about $1200 more, you can buy the *Otari MX-5050-QX* compact professional recorder. This is designed more with professional applications such as broadcast and jingle studios in mind, but shows up in home studios among the more serious (and affluent) recordists. The design is very simple and very rugged, and there are some nice touches. For example, the tape counter, rather than simply reading off a series of sequential numbers, indicates minutes and seconds of elapsed time—very handy. The hinged head cover makes it easier to clean and demagnetize heads; this is an example of paying more and getting more for it. Like Teac, Otari also makes an 8-channel semipro recorder. The TEAC is approximately $3000, the Otari $4000, with differences again comparable to the differences between the 4-track versions. I'm sure that as the years go by, 8-track will usurp 4-channel's place in the home, just as it did in professional studios.

The Otari machines already start to blur the difference between amateur and professional units, but you can go still further to the 4-track recorders made by Crown. This company is well known in the hi-fi business for their clean and ultra-responsive power amps. Users state that the recorders are excellent and most lab test reports bear out the users'

claims. Be prepared for a bit of a wait if you want one, though; they only put out a limited number of recorders a week, and there are also multiple options which lengthen the decision-making process. The basic 4-track unit costs about $3000, but to syncronize tracks you'll have to add an accessory unit that costs about $280 extra. The recorder will operate at three speeds, 15, 7½, and 3¾ ips, and this is convenient for broadcast studios. Naturally, machines like the Otari and Crown are beyond the means of the majority of home recording enthusiasts, but they serve as an interesting comparison of what more money will buy you in terms of features.

Features alone should not make you decide what kind of deck to purchase. For example, how easy is it to get the machine serviced? How much of a discount can you get on it? What kind of warranty covers you? How reputable is the company? All these factors complicate the decision; then there is the traditional problem of whether to go with the old, reliable, proven decks, or with some of the ones from new companies that have fresh ideas and a desire for a greater share of the market.

All in all, keep several thoughts in mind when you go out to buy a 4-track deck:

1) You are spending *lots* of your hard-earned money on a product—let them sell you on it.

2) Get a couple of different opinions, and go to a couple of different stores. Call up other stores for quotes. You wouldn't just buy the first car you saw advertised in the paper, and a good tape deck can cost as much as a car and sometimes more.

3) Assume that you can get a discount. Let's say store A is selling a Supertaper Model X and hangs a sign over it that says "$1250" (this is the list price). However, Harry's discount hi-fi warehouse around the corner sells the same item for $1000. The only trouble is that a friend of yours bought a cassette deck from Harry's and it took six months to get a replacement part—whereas store A has some in-house technicians who get repairs

done in ten days or less. So, you go to store A and offer them $1000 for the tape recorder. Let's say the store buys the machine for $800; they'd rather sell it to you for $1000 and make $200 than give the business to Harry's; they *also* know that he is around the corner. If you don't barter and play a little hard to get, you'll probably pay what the traffic will bear (after all, no salesman is going to tell you where to get something cheaper); but know what you're talking about. Compare what's available and compare prices. An intelligent, informed buyer can often get a better deal—like they say on the record, you'd better shop around. I tend to prefer local stores; then, if there is a problem, I can yell at a person rather than at a telephone.

Since you've just committed yourself to spending at least $500 for a 4-track deck, now may not be the most pleasant time to discuss another deck: however, you will need it. Having all those little separate tracks on your multitrack recorder is just fine, but then you have to mix them every time you want to listen to them. It's better to mix them once and for all onto a good-quality tape, and listen to that. But to make that high-quality tape, you need a high-quality recorder.

If you've got the money, there are some excellent stereo (2-track), reel-to-reel tape decks on the market which will add virtually no noise to your finished product. The *Revox A-77* is considered the standard of comparison in its price class by many audiophiles. Most of the companies supplying multitrack machines also have attractive stereo units; but these machines cost almost as much as the 4-track recorder. For some applications, simply buying another multitrack recorder would allow you to mix on it, and gain extra flexibility at the same time, but there is an alternative.

In recent years, the cassette recorder has really come into its own. New tape formulations, head technology, sophisticated transports, and a never-ending series of minute technical advances have all turned the darling of the dictation set into a true hi-fi medium.

Well, not as hi-fi as good reel-to-reel, but definitely acceptable. Almost all decent cassette decks now include Dolby noise-reduction units, which make the cassette far more listenable by getting rid of that nasty tape hiss. You can buy a very good cassette deck (at a discount, of course) for around $300, and even for $200 you can wring out some pretty respectable performances. Additionally, by having a cassette deck you can make dubs for friends, tapes for car players, and so forth. And as mentioned, if you ever move up to a really good second deck, you still have the multitrack master tapes available, so you can always do a re-mix if you want higher fidelity finished tapes.

I suppose the ideal arrangement would be to have a multitrack machine for basic tracks, a good 2-track deck for mastering (and perhaps for use as an echo unit while recording), and a cassette recorder to make dubs from the master, but all this isn't absolutely necessary. Some kind of second machine is, however, so allow for that in your budget.

There are so many manufacturers of cassette decks, with so many new models and improvements (real or imagined) coming out, that your best place to look for current information is in hi-fi-oriented magazines. To pick a good cassette recorder, you have to do your homework; although multitrack recorders are mostly variations on a theme, cassette decks vary widely in their features. Some are designed to fit in with the 'decor of a modern living room'; skip over those and get to the machines designed for the typical audio fanatic. Make sure it has Dolby, bias and equalization controls that allow you to handle standard, chrome, and ferrichrome tape (nobody knows which type will dominate as the years roll by, so hedge your bets), and a fast-acting pause or edit control. Some other features, nice but not essential, are memory rewind (saves time during mixdown), front-loading, which really is more convenient than top-loading; and a two-motor transport. Very few cassette decks have a two-motor system, but I feel that this contributes to increased reliability. A pitch control (variable speed) knob is very handy, but hard to find except on top-of-the-line decks.

One final point worth mentioning: Cassette decks need to have every aspect optimized in order to give good performance. All the hints about regular cleaning (see the chapter on maintenance) apply here also; but the factor that can really make or break performance is the tape you use. Don't pay $300 for a deck and use tape from the corner drugstore. If you're expecting to get high quality, make the job easier for the deck and its associated electronics by giving it really nice tape on which to record. How do you go about choosing this tape? See the next section.

SELECTING THE RIGHT TAPE

Stated as simply as possible, buy the best tape possible, consistent with the recommendations of your machine's manufacturer. Since it is often not possible to custom adjust your machine for a specific tape, using the best tape recommended in your manual will usually give the best overall results.

Tape manufacturers often have two or more lines of tape; you want the highest-quality line. A lot of the tape market goes to speech recording, so less expensive tapes can be used in these circumstances; but none of them are really suitable for getting the most out of your machine in terms of music.

Tapes also come in different thicknesses; one 7″ reel may have 1800 feet of tape, whereas another may have 2400 feet. The difference is that the longer tape is a *thinner* tape. Although acceptable for consumer situations, where somebody wants to tape background music or something similar, thin tapes can cause problems in the studio environment. For one thing, they are more susceptible to print-through, where signals from one piece of tape alter signals on an adjoining layer of tape. They are also more fragile, and have a greater tendency to stretch or deform under repeated back and forth tape motion. So, given two reels of tape occupying the same size reel, I'll take the one with the least number of feet every time.

Before settling on any specific type, try several available brands and see if any one develops a particularly good relationship with your machine. Once you have settled on your favorite, then you can buy a quantity of it and save yourself lots of money compared to the single piece price.

The rules for buying cassette tape are similar: use a type designed for music, don't use the extra-long, 120-minute cassettes, and get a tape that's compatible with your recorder. This last point is a little more difficult to deal with than it was with reel-to-reel, since cassette machines are more finicky in their choice of tape. Again, experimentation is the key. Try several cassettes, recording identical material at identical recording levels. You may be surprised at the substantial differences between tapes; one may have better sounding highs at the expense of slightly higher noise, one may sound distinctly better than all the rest, whatever. But, in most of the cases, you are not really listening for the 'best' cassette, but for the one that is best mated to your machine and ears. Do, however, look for mechanical rigidity; if you plan to salvage your tapes in case you have an accident or jam them on a friend's machine, better get the kind with screw housings, rather than the sonic-weld variety that is destroyed upon opening.

Make sure you *avoid* house brand and unmarked tapes, and stick to reputable brands. Inferior tape can cause all kinds of problems in terms of drop-outs, oxide flake-off, and the like. It's easy to make tape; it's just hard to make it well. I tried a tape which was advertised as being just super, and although a casual hi-fi fan might not have been too displeased, I found it unusable with a good machine in a studio environment—an edge had been crunched where track four was supposed to be, giving a little series of explosion sounds for about the first 200 feet of the tape. Naturally, I did not discover this problem until I had carefully recorded on the three other tracks. Good tape costs money, but the reduced aggravation compensates for the extra cost.

Chapter 2
Creating The Home Studio Environment

Now that we've covered some of the electrical angle of tape recording, it's time to set about creating the studio. There are many facets we need to cover: the acoustical aspects, the layout of equipment for greatest efficiency and ease of use, proper monitoring, cables, accessories, and more. As we discuss each item, we'll mention how it's treated in a professional studio where money is no object. From there, we'll figure out how to cut corners and make changes to adapt the studio to fit our specific conditions and budget.

THE ROOM(S)

A recording studio usually consists of the studio itself, where the musicians actually play, and a control room. If the recording facility is big, like Columbia studios, there can be several studios; they're usually given letter designations (studio A, studio B, etc.), and can be spread over several floors of a building. The studios are different sizes, have different characteristics, and can accommodate different numbers of musicians. While this dramatically increases scheduling flexibility, it creates horrendous soundproofing problems. You also have city noise to contend with. I remember one story of a prominent New York studio that had selected a prime location—which was later discovered to be directly over a subway! They spent a lot trying to dig out from that mistake, but it just goes to show what kind of problems you run into.

Chances are that, as a home recordist, you'll run into a different set of problems. For one thing, you have neighbors and perhaps other members of the household who might not appreciate hearing a piece of tape go by for the 23rd time en route to the ultimate mix. Also, chances are that you will have to compromise as far as construction is concerned (very few houses were built with the idea that they would become studios one day), and also in regard to size. A large, dead room is the best general-purpose recording area, but you may not be able to afford that luxury.

A lot of the choice of the size of your studio depends upon what you want to record. Probably the hardest single entity to record is a symphony orchestra, and I think the average home recordist is going to have a hard time finding a room that could hold one. But a three- or five-piece group is another thing. For that, a much smaller room will do. If you're a one-man-band making a demo, then all you really need is some place to stuff the recorder and a mixer. And if you can feed directly into the tape recorder instead of using a mic (i.e. plug an electric guitar directly into the board rather than use a microphone and acoustic guitar), the acoustics are of very little importance, and you'll get the added benefit of a generally 'cleaner' sound. Let's define, and talk about, four common situations: In situation No. 1 you have access to two separate adjoining rooms for recording; in situation No. 2, you have one room; in No. 3, you have a part of a large room (like a corner of the living room); and in No. 4, we'll talk about building your studio into a closet (no jokes, please). We will refer to these situations by number throughout the chapter.

With situation No. 1, you're right in there with the big guys, because you can have a separate control room and studio, achieving the best possible acoustic isolation between whoever is running the tape and whoever is making the music. In this type of situation, some kind of talkback or intercom system is mandatory for communications; also, you have to consider the extra cable runs required to feed mic signals into the control room, and cue signals out to the musicians. If you're doing a solo effort, and your own engineering, then using a separate control room and studio would be unworkable. A lot of times, when I would work in studios on multitrack instrumental recordings, I would let the studio itself go to waste, since I did all my recording directly into the console in the control room. In the big studios, you will generally find a thick glass pane (triple-thick with air spaces in between, in fact, for maximum sound rejection) between the control room and studio so that the engineers can see the performers. This isn't really necessary for a home environment, so you can save yourself a bundle by forgetting about visual contact. About the only time you need contact is if someone in the control room needs to cue the performer; but that may also be accomplished by hooking a little cue light up to a switch, with the engineer's hand on the switch and the performer's eye on the light.

Number 2 is probably the most common situation that the home recordist will encounter. The bigger the room you can use, the better. For one thing, large size will cut down on resonances that occur in the room; 'resonance' is the quality of having a room vibrate when certain notes are played. Probably any bass player is familiar with room resonances and how they can make a bass 'boom' on certain notes; it is best to minimize these because they will drive you up the wall when recording, and later on, maybe even make you wonder why your tapes sound good in your studio, but strange everywhere else. In this respect, the room acts almost like a random-action tone control, peaking and dipping the frequency response at several fixed points throughout the audio spectrum. A larger room will mean a lower resonant frequency.

One other consideration is that a larger room will give more reverberation; this can be either an asset or a liability, depending upon what you are recording. However, it is my opinion that a studio should be as acoustically 'dead' as possible. You can always add reverberation or echo electronically, but it's very difficult to add deadness.

I feel that, when recording, you want to obtain a sound as close to the original as possible, because that gives maximum flexibility in the mixdown process. There are exceptions to this rule, but experience has shown me that a dry, natural track is best most of the time. Also, if you have to combine the control room and studio into one room, a dead one is the best for mixing down. 'Live' rooms are a nightmare for mixing.

The ultimate non-reverberent recording area is outdoors, where the reverberation is essentially non-existent because there are no reflective surfaces. If you can set up drums outside, not only will you get no leakage from the other instruments that are located inside, but you will achieve a very crisp sound. You'll probably have to add a little reverb, in fact, to get some warmth.

To make a room as dead as possible means either tearing down the walls or putting up new ones, renovating the ceiling and floors, and adding sound-absorbent material. Good luck, especially on the part about tearing down the walls if you're a renter! Professional studios have elaborate wall structures made of interwoven fiberglass boards and air spaces filled with more absorbent material, like cloth, foam, etc. Ceilings, and sometimes even floors, are treated along the same lines, but chances are that anybody reading this book will have to settle for less.

One positive step is to line the walls and ceilings with sound-dampening material, and to carpet the floors with the thickest carpet possible. Also, make sure you use one or two pads under the carpet. This will help to absorb vibration being transmitted through the floor; it will also have the side benefit of making a drum kit seat more firmly into the floor. To sound-dampen walls, there is one trick: go to a carpet-overruns/cutoffs shop, and buy a larger piece of carpet than you need. Then, run the carpet up the walls as far as it will go.

Another excellent sound dampener is a piece of canvas suspended from the ceiling (see Figure 2–1). These are not too expensive (look under 'canvas' in the Yellow Pages), and do a pretty good job of absorbing sound. Bedspreads hung from the walls are good, and there is always the traditional egg carton. These do, in fact, work very well for studios,

32

although the new styrofoam kinds have harder surfaces and are therefore suspect (I haven't run any tests myself, though). But the old fibrous cardboard ones are just dandy; old clothing or anything 'clothy' and soft will do a good job of sound absorption. Keep lots of pillows around, too.

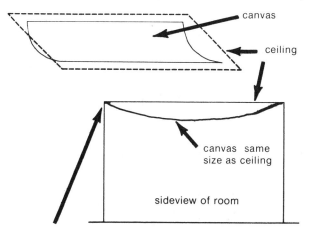

Securely attach canvas in four corners of ceiling; add additional fasteners to sides if required.

Figure 2-1.

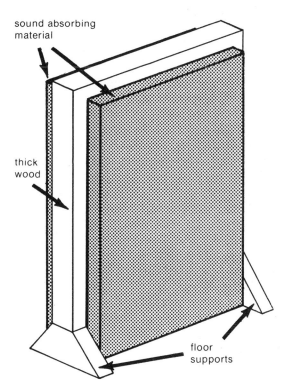

Figure 2-2.

In addition to the general soundproofing and deadening you need, you may also need localized, acoustically isolated, dead zones. In professional recording studios, there are usually two permanent or semi-permanent dead zones: a vocal booth, which is extensively padded and deadened in its own right, and some kind of drum booth. This can be anything from a corner of the room that is heavily padded, to a cage-like structure, or even a separate booth. Professional studios also have structures, called baffles, to help create localized acoustics. These are large plates (see Figure 2-2) that are usually built of some thick wood, with panels of sound-absorbent materials on either face of the baffle, which are placed between drums and amps, around pianos, or wherever they are required to minimize leakage (see Figure 2-3).

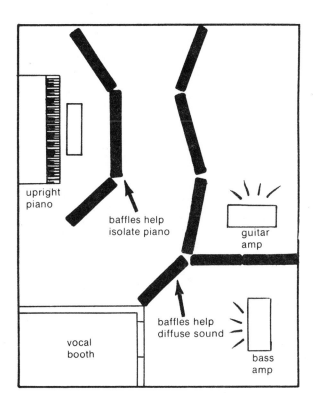

Figure 2-3. *Top view of studio room.*

33

We have talked a lot about eliminating leakage, but what makes leakage such a bad thing?

A lot of times during mixdown, you'll edit out some parts of a track. Let's say you want to fade the drums way back on some part, but there's a substantial amount of leakage on the bass track. The leaked sound won't have the quality of the original sound recorded from the drums; but as you fade back the drum track, this leakage becomes the dominant drum sound. No good! Also, let's suppose the bass sounds a little thin so you boost its track. You simultaneously boost the bass on the leaked drum, perhaps forcing the bass drum into a prominent position not originally intended. Too much leakage defeats the purpose of having instruments on separate tracks in the first place.

If you don't feel like building baffles for your home studio, there's an easier (though not as effective) substitute: suspend bedspreads or heavy cloth from the ceiling as required (see Figure 2-4). If you elect to use some kind of drapery pull for a semi-permanent installation, make sure that the draw mechanism doesn't have any little rings or metal buckles that could rattle when subjected to high noise levels.

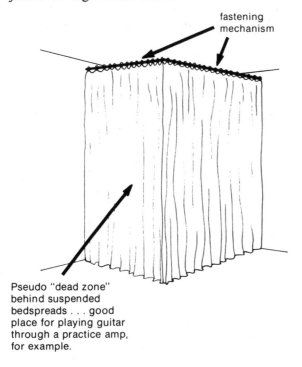

fastening mechanism

Pseudo "dead zone" behind suspended bedspreads . . . good place for playing guitar through a practice amp, for example.

Figure 2-4.

34

In addition to room considerations concerning sound, you probably have to contend with keeping sound away from other people, like neighbors. This is seldom easy with loud music. A solution that relies on changing the fundamental acoustics of a room is bound to be very expensive. Your best bet is to do as much direct-into-the-console recording as possible, record only during legal noisemaking hours (most towns have ordinances which specify no 'excessive' noise after a certain hour), and keep all windows and doors closed. You can also do your monitoring on headphones. Other than that, there's not much you can do.

Well, now we've covered ideas on how to optimize situations No. 1 and No. 2 for home recording. But if there isn't an entire room available, we're back to situations No. 3 and No. 4, which we talked about earlier.

If you're just set up on a table, with your tape recorder as part of the room, there probably isn't much you can do about the acoustics. For example, if you're set up in a living room, you obviously aren't going to run carpets up over the windows and hang old clothes from the walls unless you have very tolerant friends. One of the tricks mentioned before is applicable, and that's hanging canvas from the ceiling. The canvas also helps keep your room warmer in winter since it adds insulation between you and your roof, so that it not only improves the sound, it's ecological. The aesthetics are nice, too—sort of like hanging clouds. Although this may not appear to make too much of a difference while recording, for monitoring and mixing the difference is very clear. Also, putting a drape or two, pillows, padded furniture, etc. in the room, helps to absorb sound, so that you may end up with a decent acoustical environment in your living room after all.

Situation No. 4 is when you just don't have any room at all. If you have a closet, you have a studio. Here, though, you really have to pretty much relegate yourself to solo-type recordings. However, since closets usually do lead out to a room or at least a corridor, you do have a spot where you can sing, play, or whatever. As far as shaping your acoustics, there's not very much you can do. Your best bet is to buy a set of headphones and develop a good relationship with them.

This gives you some idea of what to do with the room you've got. Now we've got to fill out that room, and it's time to consider layout.

LAYOUT FOR STUDIOS

Many people fail to recognize the absolute necessity of an efficient studio layout. You can't trip over cords or adjust monitor speakers every day; you don't want people banging into tape recorders, so they have to be out of the flow of traffic, and so on. An efficiently-laid-out studio can make all the difference between effortless sessions and hard work.

How you lay out your studio will depend in part on what kind of machine you use. There are three basic styles of tape recorder (see Figure 2–5): horizontal self-contained, vertical self-contained, and right-angle (with the transport oriented horizontally and the electronics vertically). The right-angle type is the most popular in professional studios, but the majority of consumer recorders are self-contained.

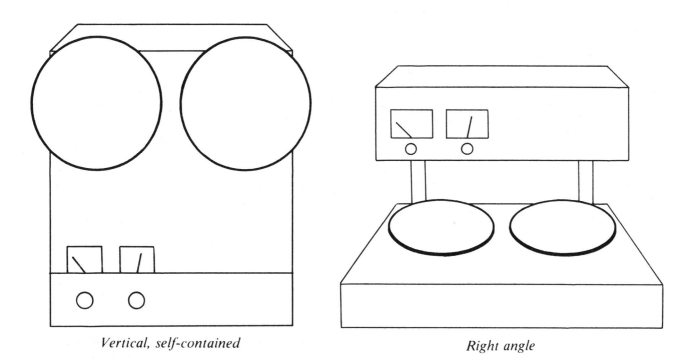

Vertical, self-contained   Right angle

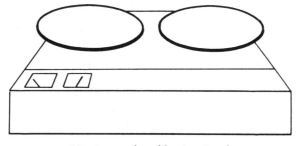

Horizontal, self-contained

Figure 2-5.

Figures 2-6 through 2-9 show various possible layouts for the situations that we've been talking about. In each case we've assumed a medium-size console, some bookshelf-size monitor speakers, and a single person operating the machine and mixer.

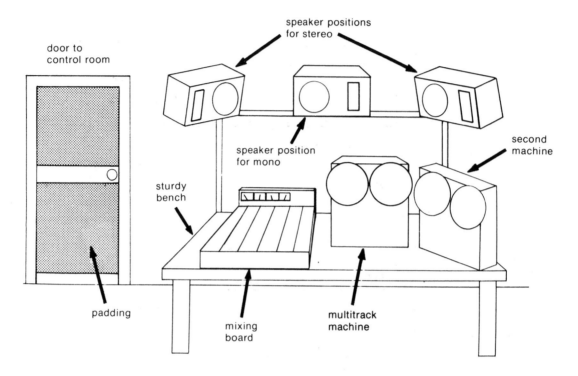

Figure 2-6.

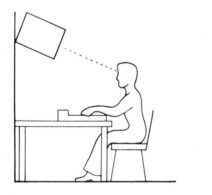

Mount speaker against wall at angle so that it aims towards ears while mixing.

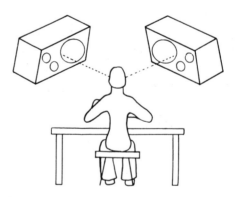

With stereo, I've had best results by placing speakers horizontally at ear level with tweeters at the extreme right and left corners.

Figure 2-7.

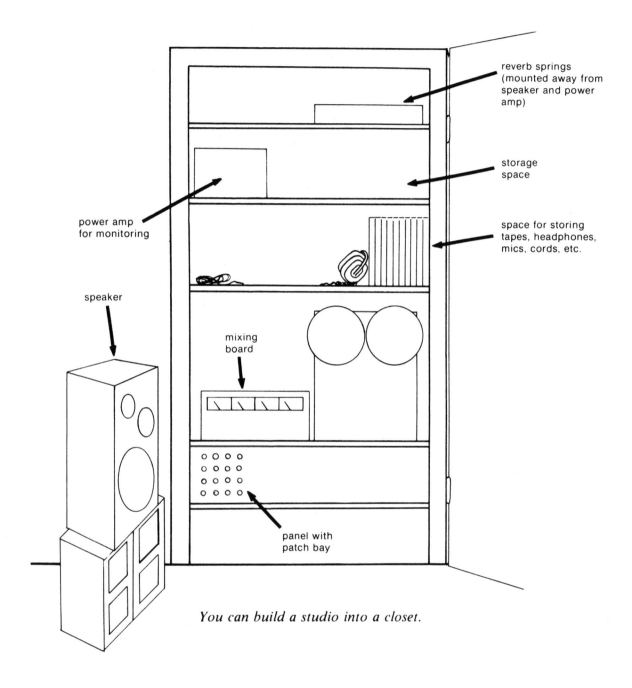

reverb springs
(mounted away from
speaker and power
amp)

storage
space

space for storing
tapes, headphones,
mics, cords, etc.

power amp
for monitoring

speaker

mixing
board

panel with
patch bay

You can build a studio into a closet.

Figure 2-8.

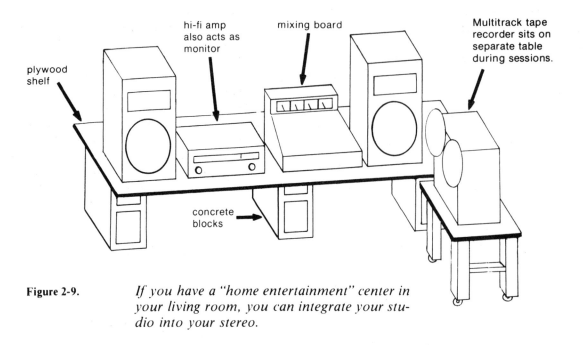

plywood
shelf

hi-fi amp
also acts as
monitor

mixing board

Multitrack tape
recorder sits on
separate table
during sessions.

concrete
blocks

Figure 2-9. *If you have a "home entertainment" center in your living room, you can integrate your studio into your stereo.*

THE MONITORING SYSTEM

There are many times when you want to do some careful monitoring as the session goes along. You want to hear exactly what is going on the tape, for one thing; and when mixing the various tracks together, you also want to have as accurate a representation as possible of what's on the tape. If you're listening to the tape and mixing on speakers that have poor high-frequency response, then you're going to mix the tapes with more treble in order to compensate. This is fine until you play the tape on a system with normal high-frequency response, at which point the highs sound super-boosted. For this reason, you want a monitor system with as flat a frequency response as possible. This means that your sound will be butchered the least amount possible by other systems, all of which are bound to deviate from the flat position.

Achieving this flat response is no easy task. First of all, the monitor amplifier must be flat, but this is the simplest part. Almost all high-fidelity amplifiers these days have flat response (or very close to it) from at least 50Hz to 50kHz. One of the best monitor amps

you can use is a good, clean, 25- or 35-watt, hi-fi unit. You don't really need more power unless you're driving a very inefficient speaker. Just connect the inputs of the monitor amp to the output of the mixer or appropriate audio output of the tape recorder and you are ready to monitor.

Now we're faced with the prospect of finding a flat monitor speaker. Prepare to separate yourself from your money, as this means a quality bookshelf speaker costing at least $100. If you have a hi-fi system, you're off to a good start, as you can possibly work out some kind of time-sharing arrangement— when you're recording, you take a speaker into the studio. If you're in situation No. 3, where your studio could be your living room, then it might be possible to integrate your hi-fi system into the studio; probably both will benefit as a result. But we still have the real problem of creating a flat listening room. Luckily there are some electronic gizmos called *room equalizers* which can help tune the monitor system to compensate for improper room acoustics; unfortunately they're not cheap. We briefly cover these in the console section.

A lot of people ask about using headphones for monitoring. I think they work fine for cueing and possibly for recording tracks and overdubs, but for mixdown, where all sounds are super-critically evaluated, speakers are a must. More people listen to music over speakers than through headphones, and a piece of music mixed on headphones will only sound right played back through headphones. In addition, headphones have inferior bass response on the whole and are much more sensitive to subtleties. What sounds like a bit too much reverb on headphones, for example, can literally appear non-existent on speakers —another reason for choosing speakers for monitor and mixdown work.

LAYING WIRES

Here's where a lot of potentially good studios turn into noisy, nasty studios. But before we talk about cables, let's discuss the electrical environment in general.

The AC line can carry a lot of garbage and noise on it; these spurious signals ride along with the electricity and get into your equipment. You've probably noticed how light dimmers can create interference with radios and guitar amps; fluorescent lights are also a problem. For this reason, if you're starting a studio, do not use fluorescent lights and *do not use dimmers*. Incandescent lights may be too bright for the relaxed atmosphere of a studio environment, but you can always use bulbs of low wattage and provide indirect lighting.

You'll also be drawing a fair amount of current—maybe 150 watts for the tape recorder, another 50 watts for the monitor amp, more for instrument amps, lighting, and the console. All that adds up. *Proper electrical outlets are of the essence.*

Much of your equipment will have a three-wire plug which requires a good ground. You *must* provide that ground connection. During one session I remember, a flute player's modification boxes started giving a low, but audible, output of 'hash' from the AC line; it was because the third wire was not connected. Once it was, the problem went away. Many people don't pay very close attention to ground wires because they don't hear any sound at the time they set up their equipment; but insidious noises can come along the AC line when you

least expect them, not necessarily while you're listening for them. Also, the more equipment you use, the greater your chances of experiencing problems.

I recommend purchasing one of those multi-outlet barrier strips (see Figure 2-10); you may need two if you have a fair amount of equipment. Brace yourself: they aren't cheap, but they're worth it. While you're at it, get one with a fuse or circuit breaker built in, and make sure that the strip accepts three-wire cords. The cord coming out of the strip will be a three-prong plug. If you have a three-wire receptacle feeding the stuidio, fine. If not, you'll have to hook up an adapter and connect a ground to the AC receptacle (see Figure 2-11).

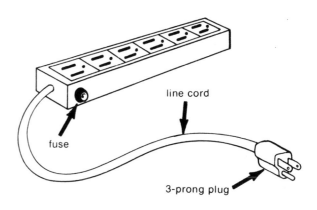

Figure 2-10.

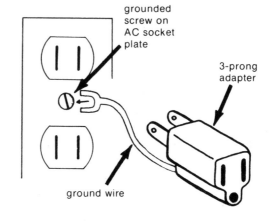

Figure 2-11.

The outlet should be able to handle any power required with a very large safety factor. This is not just for safety—although that is the primary reason—but to keep the line voltage from pooping out. I remember one home studio where the line voltage was about 100 volts. The outlet for the studio was not being fed with large enough wire to carry the electrical demands of the studio. As a result, the electronic instruments played out of tune and had general stability problems, and the tape deck's motor was working under a strain, not to mention the fire hazard. If you have a voltmeter and know how to use it, check your power-line voltages with the studio on full blast. If there is a voltage drop compared to the normal reading, you had best contemplate rewiring, and soon.

In situation No. 1, each room will probably have a couple of different outlets, possibly on different electrical circuits. This is good, as you can run the control room electronics from one circuit and the studio amps from another. But make sure that whatever circuit you plug into is fused at a master fusebox. I can't emphasize enough the importance of safety in terms of electrical wiring. This isn't meant to make you paranoid, but to make you aware that electricity coming from the wall is not something you can take for granted: it has limits, it has tremendous power, and it can be lethal.

You also want to keep any extension cords as short as possible; this may force you to locate equipment near the part of the studio that happens to have power. So be it; those are the breaks.

In situation No. 2, you have to be even more careful, as putting everything in one room generally means that one circuit has to take the load. Again, find out what the ratings are for the line, add up the wattages of your various devices, and make sure you come out with a comfortable safety margin. Rewiring is not particularly difficult, but the chances are that you will not be able to do it yourself. Local zoning laws establish certain mandatory building codes, and you must conform to those codes or risk possible lawsuits. Let's say some neighbors don't like the noise, and want to stop you from doing sessions—maybe they even have a legitimate gripe. If someone comes to investigate the situation and you have strange, non-code wiring draped all over the place, you aren't making things any easier, and you could get into trouble. I hate to bring up stuff like this in a book that's supposed to get you closer to the joys of music, but I would be overly optimistic if I didn't mention potential problems as well as potential delights. This is a complex world, and as our toys get more complex, it is our responsibility to use them correctly and wisely.

After plugging your three-prong cords into the barrier strip, you will probably have some equipment left over that has only two-prong plugs. How do you handle the ground situation on these? If you're lucky, the piece of equipment in question will have a little binding post labeled 'ground' (or, on British equipment, 'earth'), suitable for holding a piece of wire (see Figure 2-12). This is called a *ground wire,* and you run it to the central ground point of the terminal block. If there is no ground point on the block, the odds are excellent that the case itself is grounded. In this instance, you can attach some kind of binding post to the metal, or screw it into something metal with a solder lug attached; the point is to make good contact between the ground wire and the terminal block case.

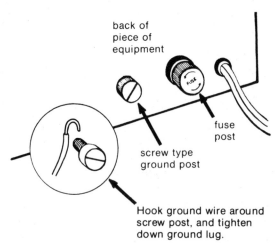

back of piece of equipment

fuse post

screw type ground post

Hook ground wire around screw post, and tighten down ground lug.

Figure 2-12.

Grounding all the metal enclosures of electrical equipment is a universally recommended procedure for reducing hum and shock hazard. What is not often mentioned is that grounding everything may actually set up a *more* hazardous circumstance in some situations. When you have a defective or poor-quality piece of equipment with a 'live' chassis, and you just touch it with one hand, you're not going to get bit too badly. But if your other hand is touching a good ground connection at the same time—zap! Electrical current will flow from arm to arm, frequently through the heart (which doesn't like it). Grounding the 'live' chassis prevents this by diverting any leakage currents to ground; so, if you're going to ground one enclosure, ground them all. If grounding a piece of equipment blows a fuse, replace the piece of equipment—it's unsafe. Even with all this grounding, you may still experience some hum problems. If you do, try reversing the plug going into the wall (just pull it out, turn it around 180 degrees, and re-insert), or try running the ground wires to a different ground point. The subject of grounding is quite complex, but luckily, in our home recording studio, there probably won't be enough equipment for really serious ground problems.

About the only additional point worth making about AC lines is that they should be kept away from sensitive electronic circuits like preamplifiers, reverb units, audio inputs, etc.; the current flowing through the line can induce hum into the equipment. Also, AC lines will frequently terminate in a transformer inside the equipment they are powering. These transformers create stray AC fields, so it's essential that you *never* set your tape on top of a transformer; in fact, you should keep your tape as far from the transformer as possible. Also, keep transformers away from sensitive audio inputs or you'll get some pretty severe induced hum. Two pieces of equipment that are likely to pick up hum are guitar pickups (by changing the position of the guitar, you can frequently minimize it) and reverb units. Get a reverb spring anywhere near a transformer and you'll get some top-notch, 60Hz, AC hum. So, positioning is important, and must be taken into account.

For situations nos. 3 and 4, we're talking about very limited and compact situations, so the problems are less acute. Nonetheless, it is just as vital to ground, to make sure that the current drain is proper, and to pay attention to the other points we covered when we were discussing larger setups.

But we need to run more than AC lines from one place to another. In situation no. 1, mic cables have to get from the studio to the control board; and cue signals have to get from the board to the studio. Most often, mic cables should use low-impedance, balanced line; this tends to reject hum and may be used for long cable runs—not with impunity, but with a fair degree of confidence (see the chapter on microphones for background on balanced-line systems). If you have a fair number of individual, shielded cables, you can surround them all by another shield; this produces one big cable. Professional sound people refer to this as a 'snake.'

Handling the cue function is another matter. In a situation where you need to drive four or five headphones, if each earcup draws half of a watt, you still need an amplifier capable of providing at least 5 watts to handle the load. Usually an audio power amp is connected to the output of the *cue bus* (any output line is called a bus), and the amp output wires run from the control room into the studio, there you'll find a number of little boxes with headphone jacks, usually connected to the main line through some isolating resistors. These are chosen for the headphones in question, and are typically 47-ohm power resistors.

When you buy headphones for cueing musicians, don't bother to get really expensive ones, since they usually have to be turned up loud to overcome the sound of whatever instrument the musician is playing. As a result, they tend to have a short life expectancy. They also get kicked around a lot and fall on the floor. Your best bet is to get one particular model of headphone and stick to it. This way, they'll present similar loads to the cue amp (and you may be able to obtain a quantity discount). Different brands may have different impedances and 'hog' more output from the cue amp than others. I would also strongly recommend that you get headphones with those little built-in volume controls. I hate them for hi-fi use because they generally don't use really high-quality pots, but they sure are a handy feature for cue systems, since no two musicians ever seem to want the same cue level.

The only other cables necessary for the studio would be those for the intercom system in situation No. 1.

ACCESSORIES

So far we've picked a room, done our best to soundproof it, tentatively laid out where we want everything to go (which will inevitably change some day, but probably later than sooner), set up a monitor so that we can hear what we're doing, and run our power and audio lines. You'd think we'd be ready to start recording. But what about the mic stands, microphones, tape, and the other recorder or two that we have for making cassette or reel-to-reel dubs or masters? In short, what about all the accessories that are necessary to make a good recording—the editing block and splicing materials, tape cleaning tools, maybe even a soldering iron for quick repairs of cords and equipment? All these accessories must be stored so that they are instantly accessible, yet out of the way. A batch of shelves is usually the best solution, with a few cardboard boxes to hold items like percussion toys, logbooks of various sessions (more about this important aspect in the section on recording techniques), patch cords, and extra cables. Don't keep microphones, or for that matter anything else of value, on the floor—whatever you keep there will surely be accidentally stepped on somewhere along the line.

When you set up the accessory shelves, keep in mind that tapes should be stored away from moisture and kept away from electrical devices.

Chapter 3:
The Console

If the tape recorder is the guts of a studio, and if the rooms that you use form the body, then the console (or mixing board) is the brains. It is responsible for combining signals, routing them to appropriate places along the signal path, providing headphone monitoring signals, generating playback outputs—in short, it's the traffic director of the various audio signals.

The console is a wonderfully imposing piece of equipment, filled with little lights, zillions of controls, meters, cryptic calibrations, and bright colors; it resembles the cockpit of a 747. A mixing board appears very intimidating, and I guess it has a right to, since it demands practice and study from anyone who wants to master it. In that sense, it's like a musical instrument. But luckily, a console is *not* a large, monolithic batch of circuitry. It is actually composed of a number of modules, many of which is identical to the others. So, once you've learned how one module works, you know how 90% of the board works. Since consoles scare a lot of musicians, we'll start simply and work our way up to a professional-type setup. In order to talk rationally about them, we can't describe in detail all the different types—they are all different. Virtually every console has its own quirks, features, and applications. Some are designed for sound reinforcement or PA work, but can also be used with multitrack facilities. Some are designed for minimum cost, some for maximum flexibility, and so on. The important point here is to understand how the various components that make up a console operate. Then, no matter what combination or variation we encounter, we'll usually be able to make some kind of sense out of it.

A SIMPLE MIXER THAT BECOMES COMPLEX

The primary function of a console is to mix signals together. We can illustrate the basic mixing principles by using a simple example: a 2-input, 1-output mixer. Let's suppose you have two keyboards on stage, one an electric piano, and one a synthesizer. By feeding these into the mixer, you can adjust the volume level of one relative to that of the other. That way, if you're playing a right-hand part on the synthesizer and a left-hand part on the piano, you can balance their volumes exactly, so that neither instrument dominates; instead, they form a unified, blended sound. Figure 3–1 shows this type of arrangement: the mixer has two *inputs,* which accept the outputs of the instruments; these go through two *faders,* which are volume controls that regulate the balance; then the combined signals feed to a common *output bus,* which then goes to your amplifier. We don't have to limit ourselves to 2 inputs; many mixers designed for PA work will have 8 to 12 inputs (Figure 3–2). These inputs to the PA system can mix together microphone and instrument signals.

In spite of its simplicity, a 4-input mixer can be a very useful companion for a 4-channel recorder. You may mix up to four instruments or vocalists into one channel of the recorder; you may also mix three channels down into a fourth channel (called premixing); and finally, after you've recorded on all four channels, you can play them back through a 4-input mixer, and feed the output to an amplifier. Figure 3–3 shows these various possibilities. So even if you can't afford the budgetary shock of a mixing console after getting the deck, you can take care of a lot of business with a 4-input mixer.

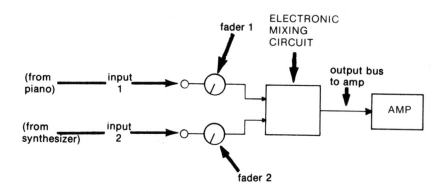

Figure 3-1.

The "mixing circuit" electrically combines the inputs with minimum interaction between inputs and negligible noise and distortion. The faders are linear or rotary motion potentiometers.

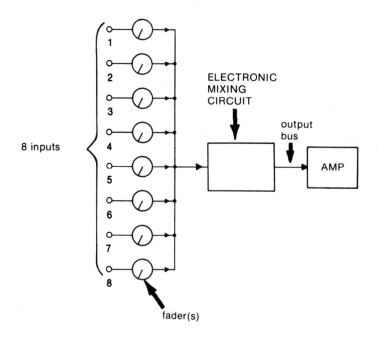

Figure 3-2.

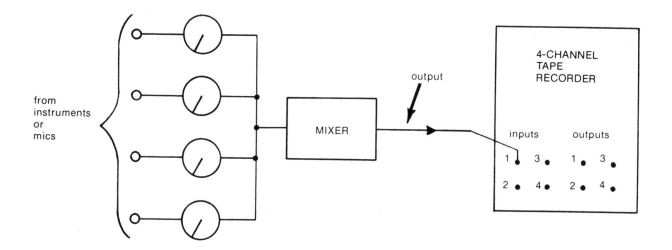

a) Patching a 4 input mixer's output into tape input 1 allows you to mix up to four instruments into track 1. You can, of course, patch into any other input.

Figure 3-3a.

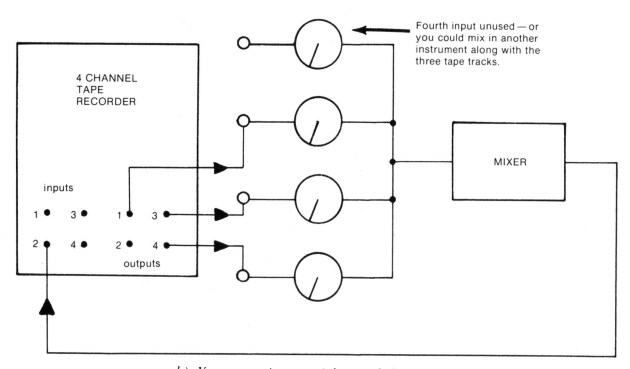

b) You can mix material recorded on three tape output channels down into a vacant track; you could also use the fourth input to mix in another instrument, or it can be left unused.

Figure 3-3b.
(Figure 3-3c: overleaf)

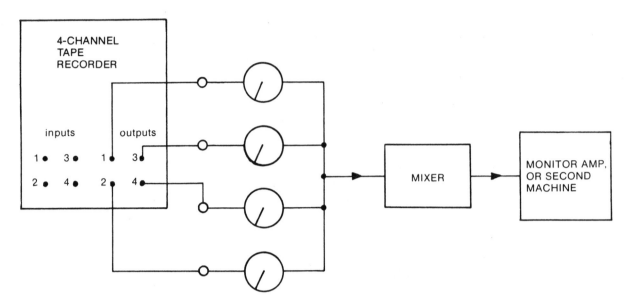

c) Patching the tape recorder output into a mixer allows you to mix down into a monitor amp or second tape machine.

Figure 3-3c.

For some applications, you'll want to have a stereo mixer. Some groups set up PA sound in stereo, which means that they have a different mix going into the left channel than the right. Figure 3–4 shows a 4-input, stereo mixer; notice that we've added some more faders for the second output channel. So, we can use the first set of faders to set up the right-channel balance and the second set to set up the left-channel balance. In the example shown, input no. 1 is feeding only the right channel—so all of its signal appears in the right channel. Input no. 2, on the other hand, has all of its signal going into the left channel. Typically, these might be vocalists, going into opposite channels for maximum separation. Input no. 3 is a little different: it has equal amounts of signal going to both channels. As a result, it appears in the center of the stereo field. Input no. 4 is almost the same as no. 3, but it has a little more output going into the left channel. Thus, the sound seems to come from left of center.

Now this whole idea of being able to set up separate mixes on different output busses opens up many new dimensions of flexibility. For example, you don't have to use the mixer in Figure 3–4 to set up a stereo mix; you could just as easily connect the 'right' output to a monaural PA system, and the 'left' output to a cue or monitor system. Then, you could have one mix set up for what the audience hears through the PA, with another completely different mix set up for the musician's monitor system. Perhaps you need to have more vocals in the monitor than in the PA; fine, simply adjust the mix accordingly.

Now let's take the process one step further. So far we've covered a 2-input, 1-output mixer; a 4-input, 1-output mixer; and a 4-input, 2-output (stereo) mixer. Some bands have quad mixdown for live performance, which necessitates four separate output busses, one for each channel. Again, we can have a separate set of faders for each output channel so that we can set up different mixes on different output channels. We end up with something like Figure 3–5, which is now a 4-input, 4-output mixer. But maybe we need a separate monitor bus for a hired string section so they can have their own monitor system. Now we're up to six outputs. But you can see that even though we've dramatically increased the number of functions and knobs, we're still dealing with the same basic principles as before. And, we can extend the inputs as well as outputs; you'll typically see 8, 12, 16, 20, 24, and even 36 inputs tied to a

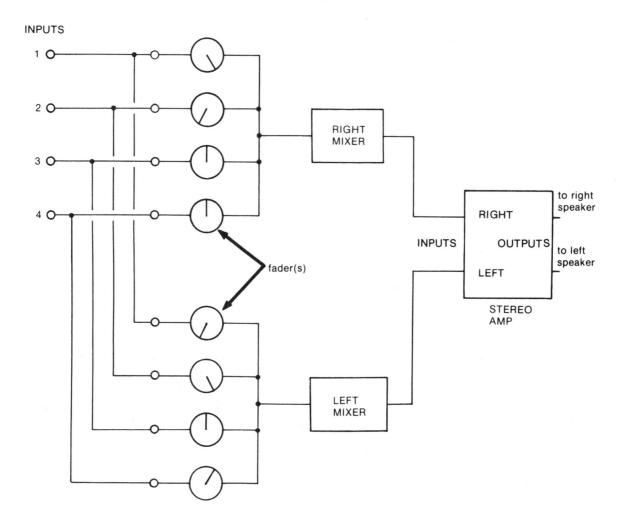

INPUTS

1

2

3

4

fader(s)

RIGHT
MIXER

LEFT
MIXER

INPUTS

RIGHT

OUTPUTS

LEFT

to right
speaker

to left
speaker

STEREO
AMP

Figure 3-4

common output line. This output line, you'll remember, is called a *bus;* but usually we'll also add a little more description—for example, one speaks of mixing instruments onto an *output* bus, *monitor* bus, or whatever.

In the real world of consoles, though, all those knobs would begin to get unwieldy very fast, so there are a variety of ways to eliminate some knobs and replace them with switches. This happens frequently with reverb and effects channels on inexpensive consoles. Also, there are devices called *panpots* which can shift a signal between two channels with a single knob. Typically, the two channels involved are right and left, so that shifting the signal between these two channels defines a

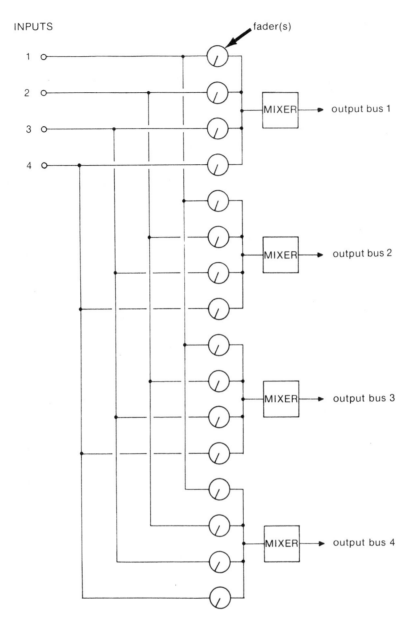

INPUTS

fader(s)

MIXER → output bus 1

MIXER → output bus 2

MIXER → output bus 3

MIXER → output bus 4

*4-input mixer with 4-output busses, each of
which can have its own mix.*

Figure 3-5.

placement for the signal in the stereo spread (see Figure 3–6). In quad, you not only have the option of panning a signal from right to left, but you can also pan from front to back. This is done either with a *joystick* (Figure 3–7) that moves in two directions, or with two knobs.

All in all, the way that the output busses are used and accessed forms some of the major differences between boards. Let's investigate another very important function of an

output bus: namely, how to use it to add effects like reverberation to the sound of an instrument.

Let's go back to a simple 8-in, 2-out mixer, where we're going into a mono PA system, and thus have no use for the second output bus. Since it's there, we should figure out something to do with it. Well, we could use it to add reverb, by taking it and feeding it into the input of a reverb unit. Then, we take the output of the reverb unit and feed it back

48

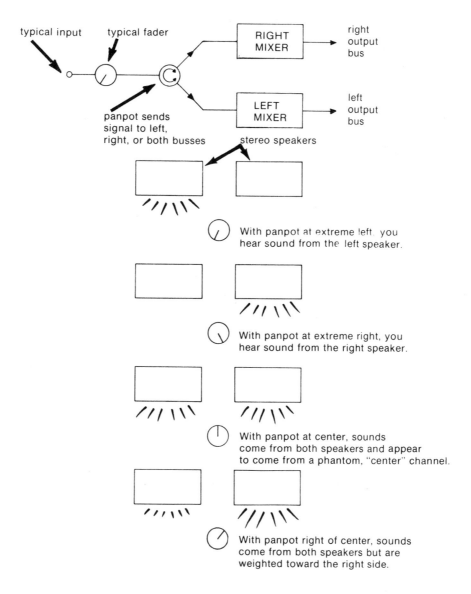

Figure 3-6.

into a spare input on the first bus (by the way, now you see why it's nice to have more inputs than you need; you'll find yourself plugging into 'spare inputs' a lot). Referring to Figure 3-8, we can now send a portion of any signal to the reverb unit. If we turn up the faders feeding the reverb system for channels 1, 4, and 5, then we'll have reverb added to those channels. Remember that each bus is independent of the others, so that we can have

separate reverb and master mixes. Since the output of the reverb goes to input eight, turning the fader down on channel 8 removes any reverb, and turning it up gives the reverb effect. This is sort of a master reverb control, whereas the other faders are reverb controls for the individual channels. The individual faders are called 'echo send' or 'reverb send' controls, because they send signals to the reverb. The master control is called 'echo

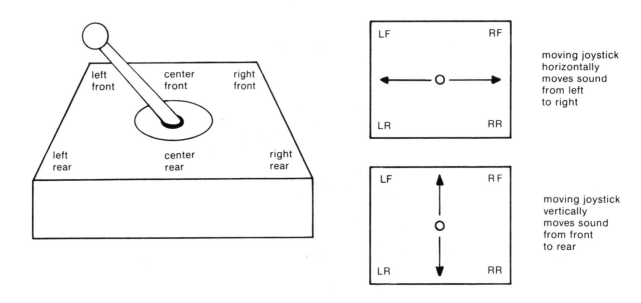

left front   center front   right front

left rear   center rear   right rear

LF   RF

LR   RR

moving joystick horizontally moves sound from left to right

LF   RF

LR   RR

moving joystick vertically moves sound from front to rear

Figure 3-7.   *A joystick is continuously variable, and can put sounds at any place in the 4-channel sound field.*

return' or 'reverb return,' since the reverb returns through the control.

A side note: Although echo and reverberation are not the same, in common usage the terms are used interchangeably. Strictly speaking, echo is composed of discrete sounds, repeated in a specific way, whereas reverberation is the diffuse effect that comes from the scattering of sound waves, as you experience in a large concert hall.

Once again, we can get as complex as we wish. With a typical stereo mixer, you might have two reverb busses, one for the right channel, and one for the left. This allows you to include stereo reverb effects, like having an instrument coming through the right channel with its reverb appearing in the left channel. A particularly effective trick with two vocal parts is to put the parts in opposite channels, with the reverb signals reversed. Naturally, you aren't limited to reverb; you could place

any other effect, like phase shifting, in the reverb path.

So you can see that multiple output busses are useful to have; a studio console will commonly have 8, 16, 24, or even more output busses. In addition, these busses are more or less interchangeable, and if you only need one cue bus, you can press another cue bus into service as an extra effects bus. Conversely, if you don't need quad and are only mixing down in stereo, that frees two more busses for use in other applications. The point of this is that, although mixers are designed with a certain application in mind, they can be custom tailored to provide many other, different, functions. Most of the time, implementing these different functions simply means changing a few patch cords around, which certainly isn't too hard to do. It is a little harder to recognize how to utilize this hardware to

50

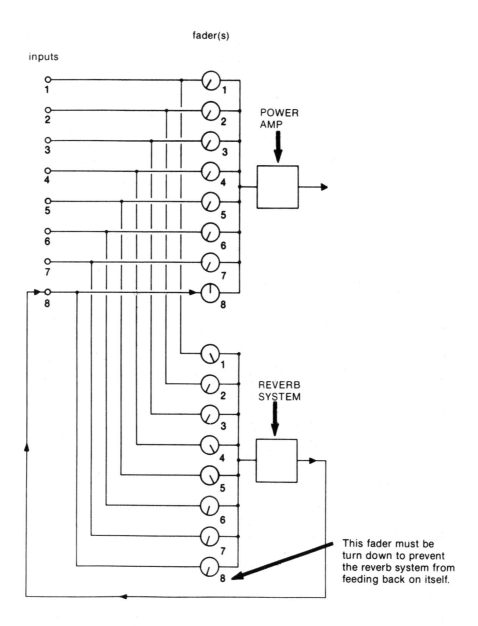

inputs

fader(s)

1
2
3
4
5
6
7
8

POWER
AMP

1
2
3
4
5
6
7
8

REVERB
SYSTEM

This fader must be
turn down to prevent
the reverb system from
feeding back on itself.

Figure 3-8.

maximum advantage. That comes with experience, and explains why creative engineers are
worth a lot of money to the record business:
they can operate the same console as other
engineers, yet have the imagination to apply it
in different and novel ways.

To recap, we now know that a mixer has
a variable number of inputs (the more the
better), and a variable number of outputs (the
more the better). But there are still lots of

knobs left over that we need to explain, and
for this we need to look at the *input module*.

Each channel of a mixer has its own
input module, which connects between the
input of the mixer and the fader. For example,
in Figure 3-9, we see where the input module
goes on our 2-input, 1-output mixer. As you
may have guessed, the placement of this
module allows modifications to a signal before
it is committed to the output bus. This module

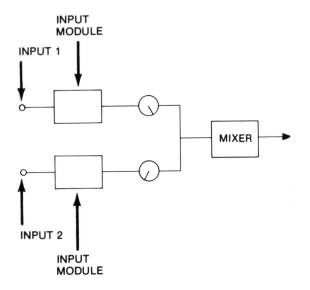

INPUT
MODULE

INPUT 1

INPUT 2

INPUT
MODULE

MIXER

Figure 3-9.

may be a single unit, or it may have a collection of submodules making up a super-input module. In any event, as the signal works its way from input to fader, it's going to encounter several signal processing options, along the general scheme given in Figure 3-10. It is the choice and implementation of the 'options' that makes one board radically different from another. Let's look at those options for a fairly sophisticated input module; remember that we're talking about a representative example so don't expect to find any mixer that has these exact same features.

MICROPHONE PREAMP

A mixer is designed to accept relatively high-level signals called *line-level* signals. However, there are other types of signals in the world, called *microphone-level* ('mic-level') signals. These are much, much weaker, and need to be amplified before they are strong enough to be used by the mixer. Enter the microphone preamp. The preamp may have variable *gain* (the ratio of increase of output over input), or it may have switch-selected gain in discrete steps, to accommodate microphones with different level outputs. Now we run into another requirement: not all mic signal levels are the same—some are high-impedance, unbalanced signals; some are low-impedance, balanced-line signals. High-impedance signals are very common in the musical world; guitar pickups and amps are designed to work with this type of system. But the professional audio world revolves around the balanced-line system due to its superior noise and hum cancelling characteristics (we cover this in much greater detail in the section on microphones). However, the preamp needs to interface with both the balanced and un-balanced signals, so frequently you'll find a switch that selects between a high-impedance input and a low-impedance, balanced input.

Another option for the preamp section is a *phase reversal* switch, which works in conjunction with the low-impedance microphone input. We talk some more about phase changes

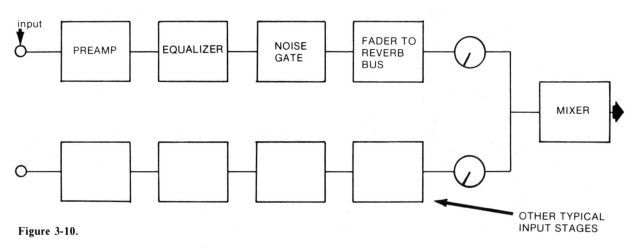

input

PREAMP   EQUALIZER   NOISE
GATE

FADER TO
REVERB
BUS

MIXER

OTHER TYPICAL
INPUT STAGES

Figure 3-10.

in the section on microphone applications, but for now let's just say that it is possible to place two microphones so that, when they are listened to simultaneously, destructive effects occur to the signal. The phase change switch minimizes and sometimes eliminates this problem.

Other options include an *overload indicator* that flashes if you are overloading your preamp, forcing it to distort; another is an *input attenuator*. This control adds an *attenuation pad,* or volume-loss network, between the microphone and preamp, to take care of problems that can occur when miking very loud singers, amplifiers, and other loud sounds. Mic preamps usually have a fixed, high-gain stage to amplify the microphone, which is then followed by a volume control. Although this type of design gives the best performance in terms of noise, a very strong signal can force the high-gain preamp to distort. Switching in additional attenuation solves this overload problem.

So we can feed just about any signal into the preamp, and, by selecting the right combination of input and gain, can make any signal look like any other signal in terms of level; now we're ready for more processing.

EQUALIZATION

An *equalizer* is a device that allows you to make precise tonal adjustments to a signal as it works its way towards the tape recorder; think of it as a fancy, flexible tone control. The term 'equalizer' comes from the concept of using this device to even out, or equalize, overall frequency response, making it flat. However, nowadays equalization is also used as an effect, to create a super bass sound and shimmering highs in a normally uninteresting signal: in this case we're concerned with creating a sound in its own right, not trying to faithfully reproduce a previously existing sound. Equalization (EQ) may be used while recording, while mixing down, or sometimes at both points in the recording process.

Here are some examples of what you can do with equalization: if a vocal is thin and brittle sounding, you can boost the bass somewhat and roll off the highs a bit. On the other hand, if an instrument is 'boomy' and lacks crispness, you can do the reverse—increase the treble and pull back on the bass. Or let's say you have a dual lead guitar part, over-dubbed by the same musician using the same guitar. To make the sound of the guitars 'bigger,' you can boost the treble slightly on one and the bass slightly on the other. The net effect of this is a slightly larger than life sound.

Equalization is to recording as spices are to food; if used properly, the results are delicious. If abused, the overall effect is unpalatable. Unusually large amounts of boost added with EQ can exceed a tape recorder's dynamic range and negatively affect listenability. Too many high, low, or midrange frequencies can overload your tape and produce a nasty, gritty, distorted sound.

Equalizers can be very simple or very complex, but they all have one electrical characteristic in common: they use *filter circuits* that isolate some desired portion of the sound. This facilitates cutting or boosting the desired signal, while leaving all the other portions intact. The simplest type of filter found on audio equipment is called a *passive* filter. In this case, there are no amplifying circuits; rather, various electronic components (resistors, capacitors, and inductors) are arranged to form a frequency-selective circuit. However, these types of passive filters can only remove parts of a signal; they can't boost or provide gain. A good example of a passive filter (of the *treble cut* variety) is the kind of tone control found on the majority of guitars. Turning the control counterclockwise cuts out treble, and appears to make the bass more prominent. Similarly, there is an analogous passive circuit which cuts bass out of a signal path, leaving the treble response essentially unchanged. Passive circuits can also be configured to give a midrange boost, or a midrange cut.

Despite the low cost and lack of flexibility, these simple passive filters can be very helpful in eliminating hiss by removing unwanted high frequencies, and in eliminating rumble or hum by removing the unwanted lower frequencies. The midrange boost can add presence to signals; the midrange cut can give a flat kind of dryness. But, using passive circuits produces an unavoidable amount of loss unless you either precede them with a preamp, or follow them with a postamp, to boost the signal. The advantage of passive circuitry is that you don't introduce any noise in the filter itself. Unfortunately, it is often the case that you have to use an amplifier to try to get back to a suitable level, and this adds noise. Also, the type of response obtainable with a passive circuit is inflexible; you can achieve greater filtering effects only at the expense of much greater loss through the circuit.

For these reasons, professional equalizers are usually built around *active* filter circuits, which use frequency-selective components, in conjunction with a low-noise amplifier. With this arrangement, the amplifier can not only provide boosting, but can also isolate frequency-determining circuits so that they are not loaded down by subsequent audio amplification stages in the amplifier.

Before we go any further, we should talk a bit about filter characteristics. Figure 3–11 shows an ideal *low-pass* response. This circuit is said to *roll off* the high frequencies, at a rate specified in decibels per octave. In our representative curve, each octave rolls off the high frequencies by a factor of two (the frequency ratio of an octave is 2:1), which turns into a 6dB per octave rolloff. The point at which the rolloff begins is called the *corner frequency.*

Figure 3–12 shows a *high-pass* curve, which cuts off low frequencies at a rate of 6dB per octave. Again, the corner frequency is where this action begins.

Finally, Figure 3–13 shows the response of a *bandpass* filter, which amplifies one part of the audio spectrum. The frequency where this boosting appears is called the *center* or *resonant frequency;* the degree of boost is called the *resonance* of the filter. The resonance is also specified in decibels; we could have a 3dB boost, a 6dB boost, a 10dB boost, or whatever (within the limits of the circuitry). In this particular instance, the boosting happens at 1kHz; but there's no reason why it couldn't happen at 3kHz, 80Hz, 20kHz, or at any desired frequency. The inverse of this band-pass response is a *notch* response, which puts a dip in the response, and is very handy for taking out one specific 'problem' frequency such as 60Hz, where hum can occur.

The simplest type of active equalizer you'll encounter is similar to the type found in a typical hi-fi amplifier, which can shape

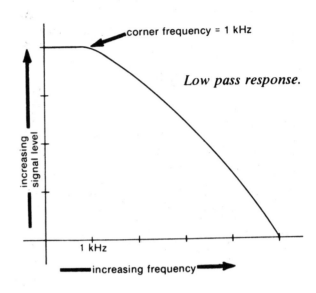

Figure 3-11.

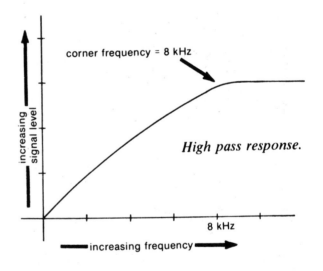

Figure 3-12.

response in four different ways: it can boost the treble, cut the treble, boost the bass, or cut the bass. Additionally, the bass and treble controls can be adjusted independently. Figure 3-14 shows the type of response you can expect to get from this type of equalizer; note that the corner frequency is not selectable.

54

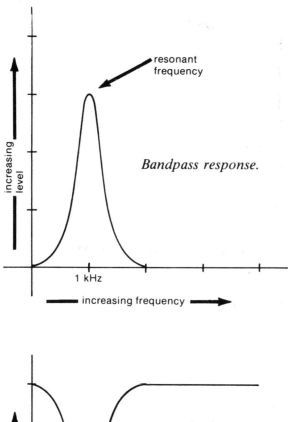

resonant
frequency

Bandpass response.

increasing
level

1 kHz

increasing frequency ➡

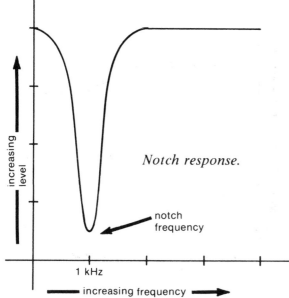

increasing
level

Notch response.

notch
frequency

1 kHz

increasing frequency ➡

Figure 3-13.

A somewhat more complex variation allows you to change the corner frequency for both the bass and treble controls. Commonly, this is done with a pot that, in center position, does not affect response; when it is turned to the right, it boosts, when turned to the left, it cuts. Then, a stepped, concentric switch selects

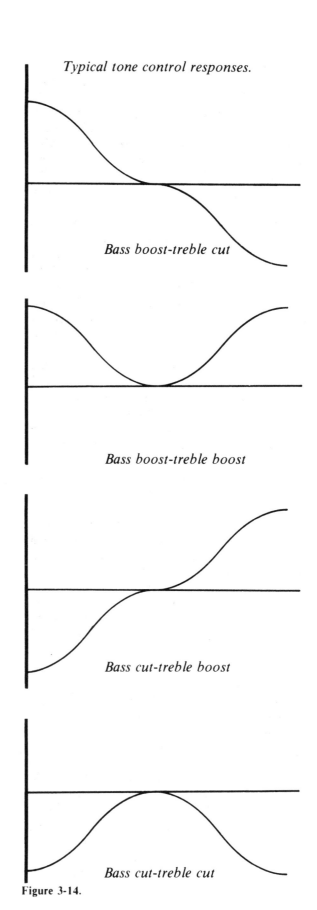

Typical tone control responses.

Bass boost-treble cut

Bass boost-treble boost

Bass cut-treble boost

Bass cut-treble cut

Figure 3-14.

55

the corner frequency, where the boosting or cutting should start (see Figure 3-15).

The next step up in complexity is to add a midrange control, which allows you to boost a given number of decibels at (hopefully) a selectable place in the audio spectrum. The resonant frequency location is usually selected with another stepped switch, with the pot giving the desired amount of boost or cut. The resonant frequencies are usually spaced an octave or so apart; Figure 3-16 shows an equalizer front panel for this type of unit, and some of the responses you can obtain.

If you wanted to get fancier, usually your next step would be to add another adjustable midrange position. But we can change over to a different type of equalizer, the *graphic* equalizer, and get even more interesting frequency responses.

The graphic equalizer is made up of a number of bandpass filters—the more steps it has, the more precise the tonal adjustments it can make to an audio signal. Some inexpensive types may only have five steps, which don't do much more than one of the simpler types of tone control we've already covered. On the other hand, you'll see 24-step equalizers used in critical applications like room-tuning, or in flattening out the overall response of a studio. These units have 24 little bandpass filters, spaced one third of an octave apart, so you can get quite a range of response. In fact, with most of them, you can boost, as well as cut, up to 12dB or so per section. Figure 3-17 shows some of the characteristic response curves you can expect with a graphic equalizer. Note how much flexibility we can get with this type of setup. But you might also note that a high-quality, low-noise graphic equalizer costs a fair amount of money. So, although you seldom see a graphic equalizer built into every channel of a mixer, studios will often have one or two super-high-quality units floating around for special applications.

One final class of equalizer is the *parametric* equalizer. It gives an amazing amount of flexibility by spacing several versatile active filters throughout the audio spectrum; you will typically see three or four filter sections in a parametric equalizer. Each of these filters is optimized for a specific frequency band (like low, midrange, or high), and has its own separate cut-flat-boost pot, resonant-frequency

selection, and *bandwidth*. Bandwidth is a term that's new to our discussion; Figure 3-18 shows both the response of a typical parametric equalizer and the concept of bandwidth. Not suprisingly, different parametrics offer different features.

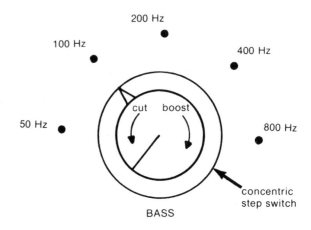

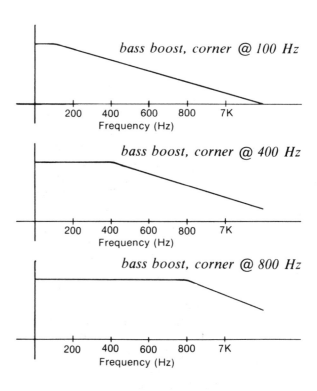

Figure 3-15.

Panel view of common equalizer.

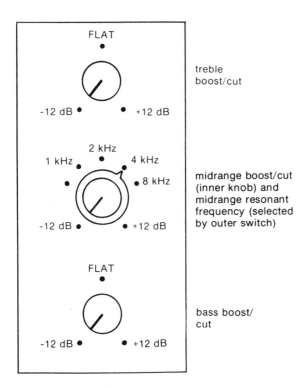

Figure 3-16.

It may seem like we've gone overboard on this subject—but the altering of tonal quality is vital to the modern recording process. The uninitiated might wonder how any person could ever use such an incredibly subtle and sophisticated system, and some people wonder if you can actually hear such small differences in sound. Well, you *can* hear the difference. A truly good engineer will hear remarkably small sonic changes because he's trained to hear them, but even a person with an untrained ear can still *perceive* differences, even though he may not be conscious of the exact nature of them. For example, an engineer might encounter a situation where a bass guitar and bass drum sort of 'mush' together on mixdown, where there's a lack of differentiation between the two sound sources. The engineer might feel the appropriate remedy is to roll off a little bit of deep bass from the bass drum and accentuate the lower midrange very slightly to give the sound more punch. Addi-

tionally, he might roll off some upper midrange and high frequencies from the bass to give a sound that's more muffled and laid back in the overall mix. An untrained listener might compare the equalized and unequalized versions and call the equalized version 'less muddy' or something similar; the engineer goes a step further and knows the technical translation—where to do the boosting or cutting, and how much to use. Of course, this isn't a universal situation by any means: if the bass part were sort of choppy and trebly, with a funk type of feel, then making it bassier and further back in the track could destroy the character of the part. In a case like this, it might be better to soften the bass drum to acquire a proper balance and leave the bass as it is, or maybe even boost the midrange on the bass a bit for more punch. In any event, different situations require vastly different control settings, and that's why equalizers have developed such a high degree of precision and refinement.

A final note: Equalizers generally have an in-out switch, so you can compare the equalized and unequalized sound. However, this feature also comes in handy when using EQ as an effect: a guitar can be churning along doing a rhythm part, and then you can cut in the equalizer to modify the sound during a lead guitar part. Cut in on the beat, though, so that if there are any glitches or clicks they become covered by the music. If you're lucky, any click that's accidentally generated may sound like a percussive accent.

BUS ACCESS CONTROLS

This is where boards exhibit some of the greatest differences. Busses may be *normalled,* or pre-patched into specific locations. Thus, to put a signal on to a reverb bus, you simply turn up a control that connects to that bus. With other boards, bus outputs and other strategic board locations may be brought out to a patch bay. In a case like this, the board is set up in a general way, and is tailored to specific applications through appropriate patching. Some boards combine the two approaches: points are usually normalled together unless you insert a plug, which breaks the normalled connection and allows you to add patch cords.

5-point graphic using slide (linear) pots:

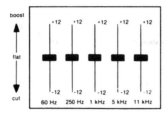

Some possible responses:

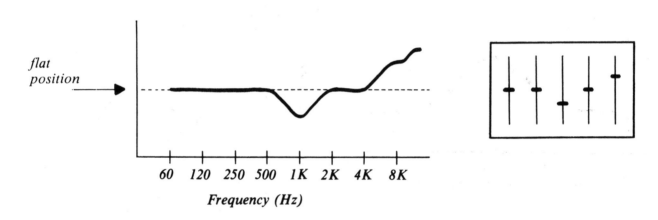

Frequency (Hz)

Bass unaltered; midrange slightly dipped; upper midrange boosted, treble very boosted.

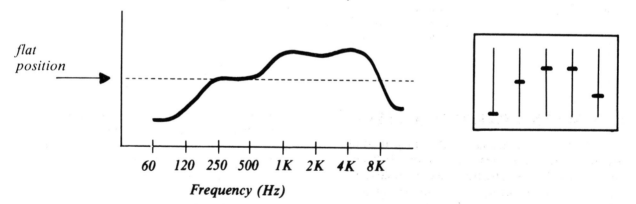

Frequency (Hz)

EQ setting used to salvage guitar track played through bad amp. Low bass cut gets rid of hum; extreme treble cut removes hiss. Slight midrange boost gives a presence that helps compensate for the loss of very high frequencies and makes the guitar stand out a bit more.

Figure 3-17.

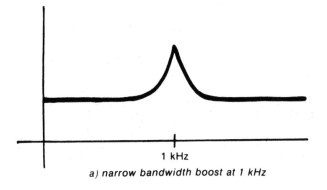

a) narrow bandwidth boost at 1 kHz

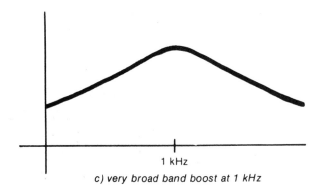

c) very broad band boost at 1 kHz

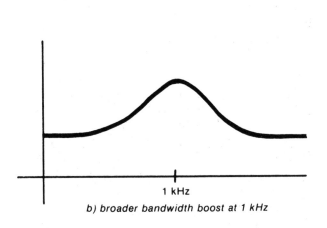

b) broader bandwidth boost at 1 kHz

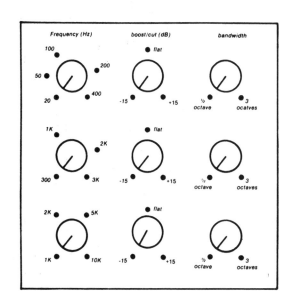

Representative front panel.

Figure 3-18.   *A parametric can typically boost or cut, with variable bandwidth, at several different places in the audio range.*

BUS ACCESS, PATCH BAY STYLE

With systems using a patch bay, including many large consoles, you can patch different output busses into different destinations, and patch tape recorder inputs and outputs to the board. For example, while recording, you may patch one bus into a cue system, another bus into a separate cue system, and run another bus as an 'effects bus,' with two busses dedicated to stereo control-room monitoring. Then, for mixdown, since you don't need cueing busses anymore, you can patch those bus outputs into the reverb system. With a patch bay, the various points are (hopefully) clearly labeled, and if you understand what you're trying to do with your signal (e.g. trying to get it to a tape recorder, or to the mixing board), then you can patch accordingly.

BUS ACCESS, NORMALLED

In a *normalled* patch arrangement, you have your options selected with switches and pots, not with patch cords. A good example of a normalled arrangement is a self-contained synthesizer like the mini-moog; a big synthesizer with lots of separate modules uses the patch cord approach. Every board has its own configuration. You will often find:

1) *Bus selectors*. Each input has a row of pushbuttons, which connect the signal in the input module to the selected bus(ses). Frequently, these have a mechanical locking action so that more than one button can be pushed down at a time.

2) *Panpots*. These are used in stereo mixdown, and place the signal from the input module into the left, right, or center (or anywhere in between) of a stereo field. Stereo requires two busses (one left, one right), and sending a signal to both channels makes it seem to come out of the center, so sometimes the panpot will pan between two specific busses—between, say, all odd-numbered and all even-numbered busses.

3) *Reverb-send controls*. Earlier, we talked about adding a reverb-send pot, and having an echo return to put the reverb output back into the system so that we could hear it. Sometimes, you'll see a single echo-send control for each channel; but studio consoles usually have stereo reverb systems that require a couple of controls to send the signal to either, or both of, the right and left reverb busses. Stereo reverb can give some very pleasing effects. One of these is 'cross-echo,' when you have, for example, a vocal part placed in the left channel with its associated reverb going to the right channel; and another vocal part in the right channel, with its associated reverb going to the left channel.

4) *Cue control*. Sometimes you'll find this control on the input module itself; sometimes it's off to one side to avoid cluttering up the board. In any event, it puts some of the signal going through the input module on to the cue bus, which leads, through the cue amp, to the musician's headphones. Frequently, you'll find two or more cue controls per input for different cue busses.

5) *Direct-to-tape switch*. While this doesn't actually put a signal on a bus, it does send the input module signal directly to an equivalent channel of a multitrack tape recorder. For example, channel 3 would go to track 3 of an 8-track recorder; channel 7 would go directly to track 7 of the tape recorder, and so on.

OTHER CONTROLS

There are many other controls that are not necessarily universal, but you may find them on your board; some of these are:

1) *Preview (or solo) pushbutton*. This isn't on all consoles, but it is very nice to have. By pushing a button associated with an input, *all other* input modules are muted so that you only hear what's going through the input module with the solo button depressed. Pushing two preview buttons gives you two inputs, and so on. These are very handy for balancing tracks relative to one another, and for making delicate equalization changes in one track when the others are a wall of sound. Because the preview button often hits the signal path before the fader does, you can still preview on most boards even with the fader down.

2) *Mute switch*. If you don't have a preview button, hopefully you have a mute switch, which automatically cuts out, or mutes, its associated channel. Again, you can mute more than one channel by simply activating more buttons.

3) *Reverb pre-post switch*. This switch determines whether the reverb send from the input module comes before or after the fader. When the signal to the reverb bus is sent after the fader, it goes down when the fader is turned down. Otherwise, the level going to the reverb bus remains constant, re-

gardless of the setting of the fader, even if it's all the way off.

4) *Rumble filter.* This is usually a simple, passive, low-cut filter, which cuts out frequencies below about 100Hz. Another option will cut down frequencies from somewhere around 40Hz instead, giving a less drastic cutting action. This switch is useful for getting rid of microphone pops, hum, room rumble, air conditioning drone, and seismic activity.

5) *Echo-return control.* We mentioned this earlier; in stereo consoles you will have a right and left return control, sometimes with simple equalization to shape the reverb sound. Many engineers agree that rolling off the extreme high and low ends of a reverb unit improves the quality of the reverb sound.

6) *Talkback controls.* These are also separate from the input module area, and connect a microphone within the *engineer's* control to an audio or cue bus (or both). With this microphone, the engineer can cue musicians, identify takes on the tape, and so forth. Sometimes, a tone will be available instead of the mic, and some consoles will allow you to choose either one. Popular sine-wave, test-tone frequencies are 400Hz, 1000Hz, and a high-frequency tone somewhere between 7kHz and 10kHz (helpful in setting bias controls, when accessible).

The only other controls that are fairly standard are *submaster* controls that mix down several busses into a smaller number of busses.

ACCESSORIES TO THE BOARD

No board is complete without some external accessories and special effects, so many boards will have patch points at the input modules where you can patch in different effects or additional modules. Here are some of the most popular and useful add-ons:

1) *Compressor.* A compressor is a form of amplifier that reduces the dynamic range of a signal. Unlike a normal amplifier that produces more output when you feed it more input, a compression amp produces *less* gain as you *increase* the input, and produces *more* gain when you *lower* the signal (see Figure 3-19). The result is that any signal fed into it stays relatively constant in level, as peaks are attenuated and valleys brought up. One drawback of the compressor is that it will bring any low-level signal up to the average level desired, and those low-level signals include noise. Therefore, compression offers the least problems, in terms of noise, when used with microphones, guitar pickups, and other transducers that don't feed through an amplifying stage whose noise can be inadvertently compressed.

Compression is a valuable tool in the recording studio. We've already seen how tape recorders can only handle a limited amount of dynamic range that appears all the more limited when compared to the huge dynamic range of many instruments. The compressor evens out these differences, making basses sound smoother, voices more consistent in level, and drums less of a problem for the tape. With stringed acoustic instruments, compressors give greater sustain since they amplify the decaying sounds of strings. Compressors also help with pianos, increasing the richness and sustain while, at the same time, evening out response over the full keyboard range.

But compression, if overused, can produce some very 'squeezed,' unnatural sounds. Although these can be used as effects, they can become obnoxious if overdone. It's best to compress enough so that you can see a difference on the tape recorder's meters, but not so much that you audibly color the sound.

2) *Tuning standard.* Not enough studios have this device, but every one should have it. Stroboscopic kinds are prob-

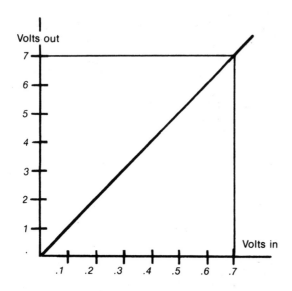

Graph of normal amp with gain of 10.

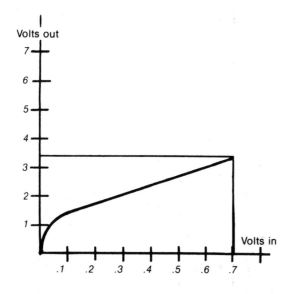

Graph of compression type amp.

By amplifying output of this compression amp, you can boost the compressed signal up to full output.

Figure 3-19.

ably the most useful, because they don't rely on a good ear for accurate tuning. Otherwise, a piano kept regularly in tune is as good a standard as any.

3) *Limiter.* A limiter is similar to a compressor in function, but it only evens out the peaks of a signal, leaving the valleys essentially unchanged. Limiters can give a more realistic, uncolored sound than compressors; I think they are also harder to abuse. Figure 3–20 shows the way that a limiter affects a signal.

4) *Expander.* This is—you guessed it— the opposite of a compressor. Although less popular than compression, expansion takes noise that is present along with a signal and expands it downward as the dynamic range increases (see Figure 3–21). So, expanders are frequently used to get rid of noise from something like a noisy or hissy electric instrument. As we will see later, under noise-reduction techniques, expansion is a key element in most noise-reduction systems.

5) *Another tape deck.* Since there's probably a second machine sitting around idly while tracks are being made, it can be pressed into service as an echo unit by feeding some signals (say, from a reverb bus output) into the record head, then picking up delayed sound from the playback head and going into an input. For multiple echoes, some of the signal from the playback head can be fed back to the record head to create a feedback loop.

6) *Variable-speed oscillator (VSO).* If you're really lucky, the second deck will have a built-in variable-speed control, or perhaps a variable-speed converter. This means that you can vary the actual speed of the capstan by a small percentage, thus changing the speed at will (within the limitations of the motor and cooling system). When used with echo, you can create echoes that ascend or descend

in pitch. We'll encounter the VSO later in the section on special effects.

7) *Digital-delay line or analog-delay line.* These are devices that process a signal by giving it a selectable time delay, so that the output of the line is delayed with respect to the input of the line. The analog-delay line uses a process that is inexpensive enough to offset its somewhat mediocre performance; the digital type offers excellent performance and has a price tag that matches. Take your pick. The amount of delay is usually adjustable from 1 millisecond (ms) or so, up to about 15ms, 100ms, or even one second. This may not sound like much of a delay, but it can create many of the same effects, such as flanging (see the section on special effects), previously attainable only through the use of a variable-speed recorder. Also, a delay line is excellent for doubling and thickening sounds; if you have a weak vocal, put it through a line set for a fair amount of delay, and the vocalist will sound almost like two vocalists singing very tightly together. Delay lines can thicken the sounds of saxophones, guitars, pianos, and other instruments. Generally, the delay is continuously variable, which means that you may obtain excellent flanging sounds by splitting a signal between

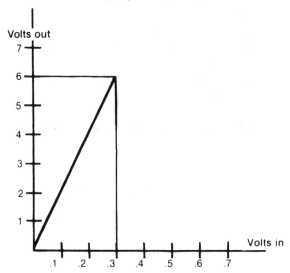

In the example shown, a signal that only has a dynamic range of 0-.3V acquires twice the range (0-6V) after being expanded and amplified.

Figure 3-21a.

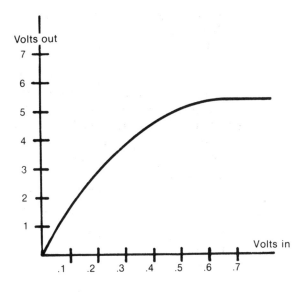

In this example of limiting, the limiting takes effect at about .6V.

Figure 3-20.

Example of expanding noise downward.

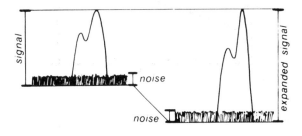

The expanded signal hits the same maximum level, and sounds just as loud — but expanding the signal increases the signal-to-noise ratio and extends the dynamic range downward, making the noise less obvious.

Figure 3-21b.

the delay line and a normal channel, and then listening to the combined outputs (see Figure 3–22). By varying the delay time, you will create cancellations and reinforcements of harmonics that give a characteristically 'spacey' sound. This effect is particu-larly effective with cymbals and drums. Like an echo unit, many of these devices provide for recirculating some of the output back to the input, producing an effect very much like tight echo or a super-short-spring reverb unit (without the 'boings' you

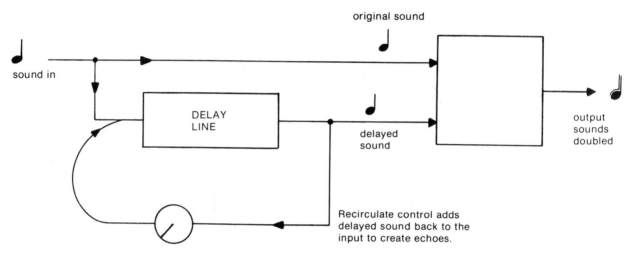

original sound

sound in

DELAY LINE

delayed sound

output sounds doubled

Recirculate control adds delayed sound back to the input to create echoes.

Figure 3-22.

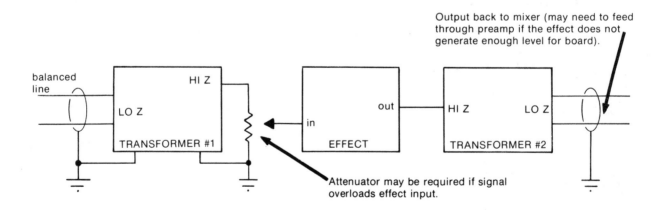

Output back to mixer (may need to feed through preamp if the effect does not generate enough level for board).

balanced line

HI Z

LO Z

TRANSFORMER #1

out

in

EFFECT

HI Z

LO Z

TRANSFORMER #2

Attenuator may be required if signal overloads effect input.

Figure 3-23.   *Putting guitar-type effect in low-impedance line.*

have to cope with in a spring reverb design).

8) *Using instrument effects boxes and synthesizers.* By using matching devices in some cases, and with no modification at all in many other cases, you can patch guitar- and keyboard-effects boxes into the board, and apply those effects to an input or track. Sometimes, however, you may need to add attenuation or matching transformers to mate the effect with the board, as shown in Figure 3–23. Synthesizers can also process sounds in very versatile ways, and some progressive studios are starting to regard synthesizers as an extension of the recording console.

To sum up, the console is amazingly sophisticated, but a lot of that is due to engineers constantly searching for *more*. What else can you offer to a jaded engineer who regularly sits behind a board that costs upwards of $10,000?

You probably won't have many of these features available on your first board, but don't feel too bad. You can always build some of the effects yourself, make continual additions to your board, and add modules to your system as you grow musically and technically. You'll likely end up with something that is not just useful, but very individual as well.

Chapter 4:
Microphones

IMPEDANCE

Microphones are surrounded by mythology as well as by sound waves. Both engineers and performers place a tremendous amount of emphasis on selecting the 'right' microphone ('mic'), but this may be a bit old-fashioned. Recent advances in microphone technology, coupled with large demand and high-volume manufacturing techniques, have minimized the differences between microphones and have brought prices down to a reasonable level. Additionally, equalization can help reduce the differences between different mics, but there's more on this later in the book.

Microphones have different physical constructions, different sound pickup patterns, and even different ways of connecting into your mixer. This last difference is probably the hardest to understand for many musicians, as it involves the concept of impedance (Z), so let's get that out of the way first.

You have undoubtedly heard of high-impedance and low-impedance systems; you may have also heard that they are incompatible. In other words, if a mixer has inputs designed to accept a high-impedance device, it cannot accept a low-impedance mic without some modifications; also, the opposite holds true, although there are some (very few) instances where you can violate this rule.

Most stage electronic setups, involving electric guitars and pianos, guitar amplifiers, and the like, are high-impedance systems, and we'll cover these first. Impedance is the amount of resistance a signal will encounter on its way into, or out of, an electronic device or amplifying stage. For example, your stage amplifier has an *input impedance* (see Figure 4–1). This is just like having a resistance across the input to ground, even if there isn't an actual physical resistor in that part of the circuit, which shunts part of the signal away to ground, thus diminishing the signal's power.

An *output impedance* is like having a resistance in series with the output of your amplifier; this also acts to diminish the signal strength. This is illustrated, in the case of an instrument amp, in Figure 4–2. The input impedance acts like a shunt across the input; the output impedance acts like a resistance between the output of the amp and the speaker.

A device like a microphone also has an output impedance. The unit of impedance is the *ohm,* and a lower number means a lower impedance. Thus, a 50-ohm microphone would be a low-impedance, and a 10,000-ohm microphone would be a relatively high-impedance output unit. Most guitar pickups are of the high-Z variety.

Remembering what we said about an output impedance being in series with a signal, then we can see, from an electrical point of view, how a microphone would look (Figure 4–3). Now, let's see what happens if you take a high-Z microphone and connect it to an amp with a low-Z input (Figure 4–4). You are no longer getting all of the signal from the microphone, but are picking up the signal at the *junction of two resistances,* namely, at the output impedance of the mic and at the input impedance of the amp. Now, put that thought 'on hold' for a second as we look at a volume control.

A volume control is called a *voltage divider* because, as you move the knob, you're actually tapping off a point along a piece of

66

resistive material (see Figure 4–5). If you hook up that volume control between a guitar and an amp according to Figure 4–6, in effect, you turn down the volume by progressively adding more resistance between the guitar and the amp, while simultaneously shunting more and more of the signal to ground through the other leg of the volume control. Turning it up

This resistor represents the output impedance of the mic.

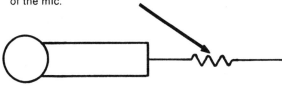

Figure 4-3.

Most of the input signal goes to the amp, but some shunts to ground. The less resistance there is to ground, the more signal gets shunted to ground.

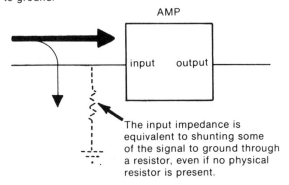

The input impedance is equivalent to shunting some of the signal to ground through a resistor, even if no physical resistor is present.

Figure 4-1.

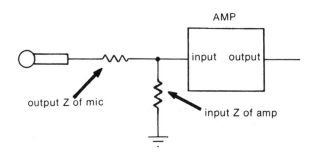

output Z of mic

input Z of amp

Figure 4-4.

Output impedance acts like a phantom resistance at the output.

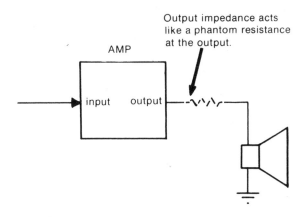

Figure 4-2.

does the exact opposite: less signal is shunted to ground, and more is allowed into the amplifier. Thus, for maximum transfer of sound, we want to have as high a resistance as possible between the signal and ground, and the lowest possible resistance between the signal and the amp it is feeding.

Now let's relate this back to impedance. The combined output and input impedances form a sort of involuntary volume control, as shown in Figure 4–7. Thus, if an output impedance is many times greater than the input impedance, a lot of power will be shunted to ground. If, on the other hand, the input impedance is much higher than the output impedance, very little of the signal will be shunted to ground.

Before we go any further let's make one point good and clear. Many people are under the misconception that impedances must be matched—i.e. a 10,000-ohm output impedance should feed a 10,000-ohm input impedance. This is not necessarily so. I don't want to get too involved with this; let's just say that, for minimum signal loss in an audio system, in most cases an input impedance should be

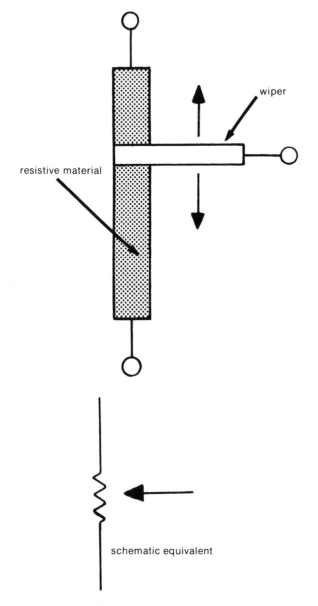

wiper

resistive material

schematic equivalent

Figure 4-5.

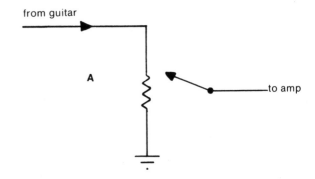

A

from guitar

to amp

With volume control up full, there is little resistance between guitar and amp. Also, there is very little resistance shunting the signal to ground.

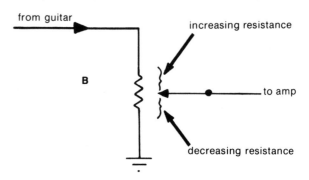

from guitar

B

increasing resistance

to amp

decreasing resistance

With volume control up halfway, there is resistance between the guitar and amp; additionally, the resistance that shunts the signal to ground is getting smaller, which shunts more signal away.

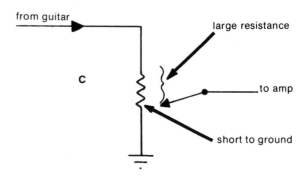

from guitar

C

large resistance

to amp

short to ground

With volume control all the way down, there is maximum resistance between guitar and amp; plus the signal is shorted directly to ground. Thus, no signal passes from guitar to amp.

Figure 4-6.

approximately ten times greater than the output impedance feeding it. There are exceptions (aren't there always?) but this rule generally holds. Thus, a 10,000-ohm microphone would like to feed at least a 100,000-ohm input Z; sometimes with guitar pickups and other coil-based devices, a 1,000,000-ohm input impedance is required to keep loading of the signal to an absolute minimum.

Are you still with me? Let's sum up. A microphone with a high-Z output, like 5,000 to 10,000 ohms, must 'see' an input Z of at

68

least 50,000 to 100,000 ohms to transfer the maximum amount of signal to the next stage. A low-impedance device, on the other hand, can feed a much lower input impedance; a 50-ohm output Z mic, for example, can feed a 600-ohm line and still fit our "input Z should be at least ten times output Z" requirement.

But we aren't finished yet, because a few more problems creep in. High-Z inputs have a far greater sensitivity to noise and hum. As less and less of the signal is shunted towards ground by the input impedance, the input cable can act like a long, floating antenna that picks up a lot of garbage as it winds its way across a stage or studio. Additionally, the cables tying the various units together have problems: as the output Z of a device goes up, requiring that it feed a higher input impedance, the cable starts acting like a tone control and shunts away high frequencies ('treble') to ground. This is because the cable acts like a giant capacitor, but let's not open that can of worms. Instead, we'll jump immediately to the solution for the problem: a low-impedance, balanced-line system.

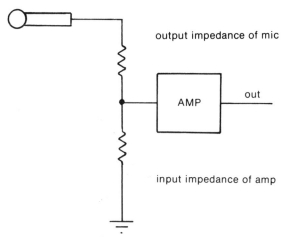

With a high output Z and a low input Z, most of the mic's signal shunts to ground. With a low output Z and a high input Z, most of the signal goes straight to the amp — the action is similar to an involuntary volume control.

Figure 4-7.

The high-Z system we were talking about earlier had two wires, just as musical instrument cords do. One wire is the ground line, which can also be called common, earth, shield, or DC return; the other is the signal line, which is often referred to as the 'hot' line. The hot line carries the signal, and the ground acts like a voltage reference. This is called an unbalanced system, and uses two-wire $\frac{1}{4}''$ phone jacks and plugs as shown in Figure 4–8.

A balanced system uses three wires; it adds another signal line to the signal-line-and-ground combination that we find in an unbalanced system. The basic principle here is that the two hot leads carry signals that are *identical, but 180 degrees out of phase* (see Figure 4–9); thus, as a signal increases in voltage along one line, its mirror image on the other line decreases. This type of signal has to feed a special type of input that responds to the *difference* between these out-of-phase signals. These *differential inputs* can be either the winding of a transformer or a special class of amplifier. The differential input is a mighty unusual beast, but it comes in very handy here because it rejects signals that are in phase. Let's look further into why this happens.

The simplest way to explain the concept of a differential input is by the analogy that is illustrated in Figure 4–10. The balanced signals arriving from the previous stage feed the input, and are 'differenced' to produce a final, unbalanced output (we'll explain why we need to get back to the unbalanced form shortly). Fine. But the real strength of this approach is that signals that are in phase are cancelled. If you think back to the beginning of this book, you'll remember that when you have two sound waves meeting so that the crest of one is at the trough of the other, then the net result is no wave at all. Luckily, the kinds of noise and garbage that get into a line are not produced by a nice, controlled, balanced output; instead, the signal spills over both signal lines, and, carried along in phase, these spurious responses are rejected by the differential input. Since the differential input responds only to the differences between the two signal lines, when you have the same signal present on both lines, then there isn't any difference, and the differential input does nothing. Some differential amplifiers can reduce these interfering signals (technically

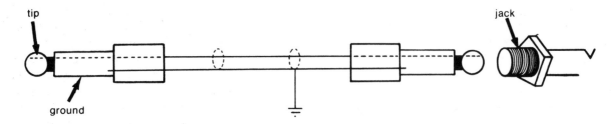

tip

jack

ground

The inner, hot conductor, is surrounded by a grounded shield that fences out hum and interference.

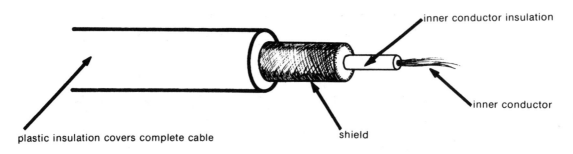

inner conductor insulation

plastic insulation covers complete cable

shield

inner conductor

Cross section of shielded cable.

Figure 4-8.

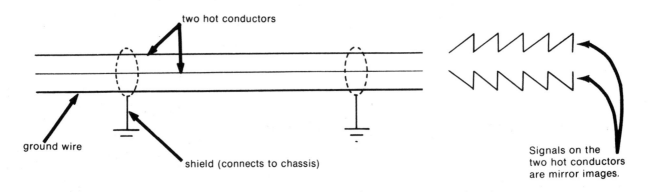

two hot conductors

ground wire

shield (connects to chassis)

Signals on the two hot conductors are mirror images.

Figure 4-9.

called *common-mode signals*) over 30,000 times—that is, an interfering signal, as strong as the desired signal at the input of the amp, can be reduced so that it appears to be only 1/30,000th as strong at the output of the differential amp. That's about 90dB worth of rejection. How's that for a useful trick?

Now we have a way to run really long cables without having them act as antennas, and we're beginning to see the end of all this orgy of theory. We now have a nice, low-Z mic, say with a 50-ohm output Z, feeding a 600-ohm line, which terminates in a differential input that rejects any of the common-mode noise picked up along the way. As an added bonus, if you're feeding a circuit with a transistor input, you can also keep the noise level lower (by keeping the input Z down) than you could with a higher-Z, more sensitive input. An input impedance of about 10,000 ohms for a transistor amplifier produces the least amount of noise, and this is why many mixers have a 10,000-ohm input impedance if they are the high-Z input type.

And now it's time to return to why we want to convert back to a high-Z signal, and then the puzzle will be nearly solved. As you can see, using a balanced-line system requires all these differential inputs and transformers; high-Z systems use only two lines, are easier to deal with, and are less expensive. Additionally, once you get inside the console, your cable runs are much shorter and less prone to pick up interference; also, the signal levels are

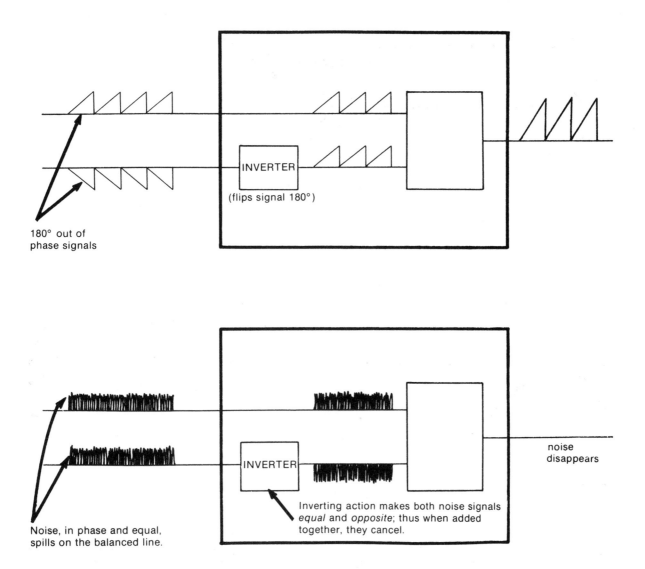

180° out of
phase signals

INVERTER
(flips signal 180°)

Noise, in phase and equal,
spills on the balanced line.

INVERTER

Inverting action makes both noise signals
equal and *opposite*; thus when added
together, they cancel.

noise
disappears

Figure 4-10.   *Conceptual equivalent of differential amp.*

line-level rather than mic-level, and don't need the sheltered environment that those weak mic-level signals require. So, the usual procedure is to use a low-Z mic, feed a balanced transmission line with that weak signal to the mixer, and then convert that balanced signal back to a two-line, far stronger, unbalanced signal for further modifications.

In most cases, the conversion back to high-Z uses matching transformers. These are wonderful little devices that can match to a three-wire, balanced system at one end, and to a two-wire, unbalanced system, at the other. You can use this type of transformer either way—so if you have a high-Z instrument output and a low-Z board, hook the instrument into the high-Z end and the mixer into the low-Z end and you're ready to go. Sometimes these transformers are wired into a device called a *direct box,* which allows you to plug the instrument directly into the board without going through a microphone. Conversely, if you have a high-Z input mixer but a

low-Z mic, then you plug the mic into the low-Z end of the transformer and the mixer input into the high-Z end. Simple? Mixers featuring low-Z inputs almost always have a matching transformer built inside the console. If you have a mixer with high-Z inputs, you can buy audio matching transformers and connect them to the inputs, though, at about $15 each, they are not cheap. Another alternative is to use little matching devices that insert in the line, such as the TEAC 109A. Transformers, however, are not perfect devices; due to their coil construction, they can pick up hum and introduce a small amount of distortion and coloration in terms of frequency response. Sometimes, active circuits (like preamps and circuits that require power supplies) are used to perform the conversion. The only trouble is that they aren't perfect either, since they add noise as they add gain, and they must add lots of gain. On the other hand, they can be less expensive. For home setups, I'd recommend sticking with transformers. Despite the cost,

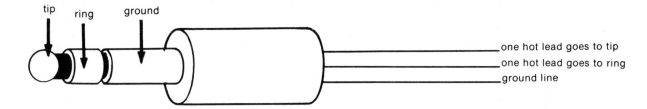

Stereo phone plug.

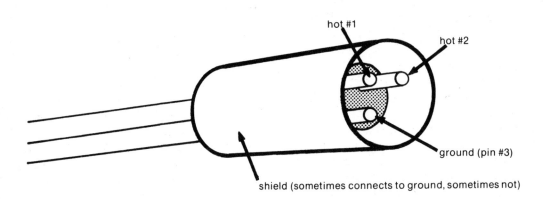

XLR connector.

Figure 4-11.

in a home environment, where noise is a persistent problem, the transformer system has an edge.

Whew! We're almost done, but we need to look at one more aspect of this whole mess—the actual connectors themselves (see Figure 4-11). The two-wire, unbalanced systems almost universally use ¼″ phone jacks and plugs. Three-wire systems present a choice: you can use ¼″ stereo phone plugs and jacks, since they have the required capacity for handling two signal lines as well as ground; or you can use XLR connectors, which are far more rugged. Also, because the ground pin is brought out separately, you can separate the signal ground line from the shield itself, which can be very handy in some circumstances. Anyway, in low-Z systems, the microphone will terminate in a male XLR connector, which then mates with a female XLR on the line. An unfortunate problem is that the three pins of the XLR connector are not always wired in the same way; either pin 1 or pin 3 can be ground, with the other two being the signal lines. Most consumer stuff won't give you any problems, but it never hurts to have a couple of adapters around to convert from one pin wiring to another. You may be tempted to figure out the wiring scheme by probing around the pins with a continuity tester like a multimeter—don't do it, as it could damage the mic element.

THE DIFFERENT TYPES OF MICROPHONES

Three basic types of microphones are used in recording: they are the dynamic, the condenser, and the ribbon microphone. Each one operates on a different principle, but they all have similarities. In each case, air waves hitting a sensitive diaphragm cause motion inside the body of the mic that is translated into electrical energy. The dynamic, for instance, is the type we talked about briefly in the beginning of the book, and its physical construction, along with the other two types, is illustrated in Figure 4-12. As the coil of a dynamic mic moves through a magnetic field, the action of cutting across this field induces a voltage into the coil, which we can then amplify and work with. The condenser microphone is based on the construction of a capacitor, and takes

advantage of the fact that capacitance changes will show up as voltage changes if the capacitor is *biased,* or permanently connected to a constant voltage. The ribbon type uses a thin metal ribbon that catches air waves, and so on. But much of this is of academic interest. Why? Because, although once upon a time these different types of mics sounded very different, recent advances have increased the versatility and usefulness of all types. Proper tone shaping through equalization (see the section on the console) can also minimize differences between different types of microphones. Dynamic mics, for instance, used to have very poor high-frequency response; lighter diaphragms have solved that problem. Condenser mics have always been good, but inconvenient, since they required a separate power supply and some heavy-duty preamplification in order to be usable. Now, new condenser materials have resulted in a modern version of the condenser mic, called the electret microphone, which doesn't require any weird, high-voltage supplies, like the old condensers did; the old vacuum tube preamps have also been replaced by quiet, simple, solid-state units. In fact, a good electret microphone is quite inexpensive. Ribbon mics were once known for two major characteristics: excellent response and extreme fragility. Now, ribbon microphones can stand up better to the kind of hostile treatment that recording equipment frequently receives.

Musically, though, what we really want to know is when we should choose one mic over another. This problem becomes even more acute in home recording, where you can't afford the luxury of investing in several microphones and then choosing the one that sounds best. You'll probably have to settle for one or two general-purpose types. Following are some observations on the different mic families, written from my biased standpoint:

1) *Dynamic.* This is a very rugged mic, the kind you'd want to take on tour, with no complications, and no power supplies; if you drop it, the thing will still probably keep on working. One disadvantage of this mic is a lack of response at either end of the audio spectrum; a dynamic microphone that does a really super job in the high-

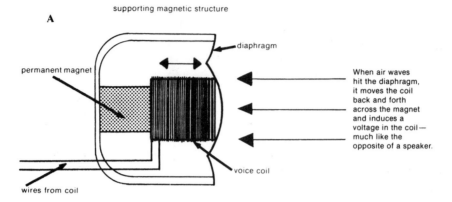

A

supporting magnetic structure

diaphragm

permanent magnet

When air waves
hit the diaphragm,
it moves the coil
back and forth
across the magnet
and induces a
voltage in the coil —
much like the
opposite of a speaker.

voice coil

wires from coil

Dynamic Mic.

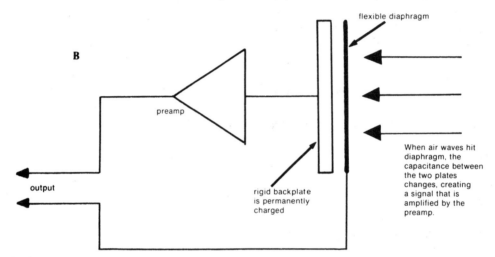

B

flexible diaphragm

preamp

output

rigid backplate
is permanently
charged

When air waves hit
diaphragm, the
capacitance between
the two plates
changes, creating
a signal that is
amplified by the
preamp.

Condenser/Electret Mic.

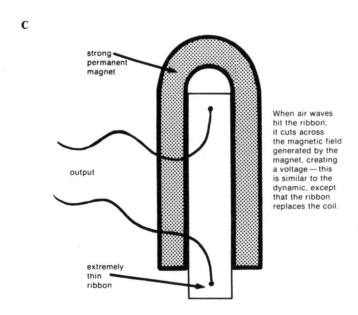

C

strong
permanent
magnet

output

When air waves
hit the ribbon,
it cuts across
the magnetic field
generated by the
magnet, creating
a voltage — this
is similar to the
dynamic, except
that the ribbon
replaces the coil.

extremely
thin
ribbon

Figure 4-12.   *Ribbon Mic.   (front view)*

frequency range costs a lot of bucks. Another disadvantage is low output, but this is something all mics have in common. There is another problem with the lack of *transient response*. In case you're not familiar with the term, transient response is the ability to respond rapidly to a rapidly changing signal. In other words (see Figure 4-13), a system with good transient response follows the sharp attack of a snare drum; one without it mushes it a bit, losing definition. The result is a less crisp, less precise sound. Dynamic mics resist overload well, and overload can be a problem; after all, microphones are physical systems and can be driven to the point of distortion, where they just don't respond in a nice, predictable fashion anymore. Since dynamic mics can handle powerful signals well, they get used a lot for bass drums and for 'screamer' vocalists.

2) *Condenser/electret*. These offer superior high-frequency response and transient response characteristics when compared to the dynamic types. Many condensers exhibit a peak in the high frequencies, giving a larger-than-life sound that is very shimmering and crisp. However, to get a more natural sound, you may have to add some high-frequency rolloff in the 10kHz to 20kHz region. What are its disadvantages? Well, condenser mics put out so little power by themselves that they need the help of a preamp stage, which of course adds a finite amount of noise and distortion. Additionally, the preamp needs power, so an electret microphone will usually have a battery that needs to be replaced from time to time, though current drain is quite low, unlike some other musical toys that eat batteries. Regular condenser mics are nice but not really applicable to home recording; condenser electret types cost less, require less external circuitry, and are easier to use. But now we have another problem: the condenser/electret can't

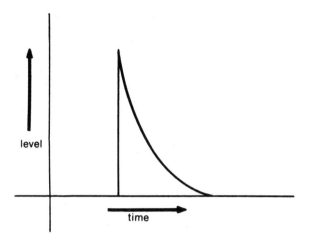

Graph of snare drum signal (rapid percussive transient) through system with good transient response.

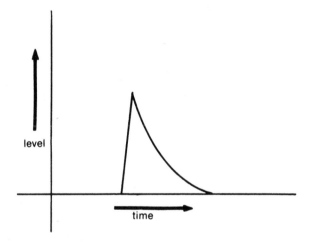

With poor transient response, a system can't respond as fast as the signal. The diaphragm of a dynamic mic, for example, has a certain rigidity that prevents it from responding instantaneously. This problem can also happen in amplifiers.

Figure 4-13.

75

take as strong a signal as the dynamic mic can—it overloads. The reason for this is that with a dynamic mic, you only have to worry about overloading the microphone element itself. With an electret or condenser, you have to worry about overloading the preamp, too, and electronic circuits have a lower dynamic range than real-life instruments. Studios generally favor condenser mics for acoustic guitar, some drums (like snare, where crispness is important), and some vocalists. However, voices vary so much that some sound better with electrets, some with dynamics, and some with ribbon mics.

3) *Ribbon mics.* I've only experienced these in the studio, because I can't afford one for my own uses—they are expensive. In general, these mics are very fragile mechanically, but paradoxically, they resist high-temperature and high-humidity environments that can cripple electret and dynamic mics. They have the best transient response of the lot, but again paradoxically, they suffer from a little bit of ringing after responding to a sharp transient (see Figure 4-14). The audible effect of this is a slight additional resonance to the sound, which gives a subtly warm feel to acoustic instruments and voices. Although not as much in demand as it was many years ago, due mostly to improvements in the other types, the ribbon mic nonetheless has a well-defined place in the recording world. No doubt, ten years from now some clever person will figure out how to make a substantial improvement in the ribbon mic, and it will again compete for favor. But in the meantime, for your home recording endeavors, I would suggest a mixture of dynamic and electret types. If you take good care of them and keep them away from high heat, high humidity, and moisture, they will give you good service.

MICROPHONE DIRECTIONALITY

Different mics have different pickup patterns: some are *omnidirectional,* meaning they pick up sound from all directions—front, rear, side, whatever; some—mostly ribbon types—are *bidirectional,* which means that they pick up sound from the front and back, but not from the sides; and others have a heart-shaped

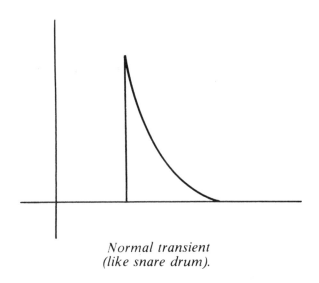

Normal transient (like snare drum).

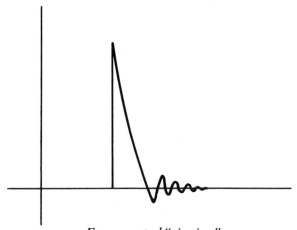

Exaggerated "ringing" added by ribbon mic.

Figure 4-14.

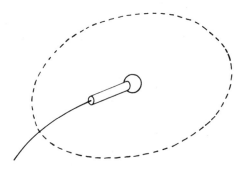

Omnidirectional response.

pickup pattern. These last are called *cardioid,* or *unidirectional,* because they tend to pick up sound from one direction only (see Figure 4-15).

Now, before we go any further, you should probably know that directionality is not cut and dried; in fact, response patterns don't mean all that much. Low frequencies are less directional than high frequencies, so even your omnidirectional mic may be 'omni' only for certain frequencies and more 'uni' for other ones.

Directionality is most important for PA or sound reinforcement work, because in these cases you have to worry about picking up signals that could cause feedback. In the studio, directionality can be used to increase separation without using extra baffles and the like. However, bear in mind that most mics use internal acoustic pathways to derive these responses, and are not necessarily precise. The point is to believe your ears, not the specs, when the two conflict.

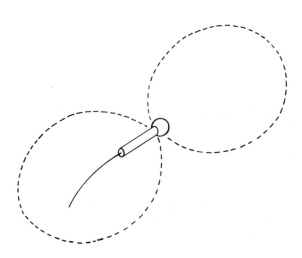

Bidirectional response.

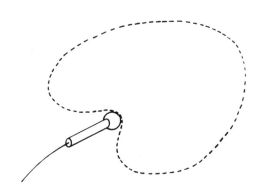

Cardioid response.

Figure 4-15.

Chapter 5:
Recording Techniques

THE TEACHING MACHINE

For me, having a 4-track recorder at my disposal has been highly educational. Almost exclusively, I do demo recording where I play all the instruments. Some, like the drums and occasionally bass and keyboards, are synthesized; others, like guitar and my voice, are traditional instruments. By having to blend all these together in an ensemble, utilizing extensive premixing, I acquired a very rapid education on the functions of the different sections of a band. Home recording is very, very different from professional recording; it requires much more sweat and craftiness, and because of this, teaches you more than you would learn sitting behind a 16-track mixing board. For example, the electronic drums that I use are unlike regular rhythm machines, in the sense that they are played via a keyboard that lets through timing pulses. I found that musical phrases requiring a nice, melodic fill on guitar usually didn't want to have a nice, rhythmic fill going along with it—there was too much clutter. A little more intensive listening to drummers really taught me that a lot of them play not just on the beat, but sort of in the holes, and if I wanted to get the same kind of feel, I had better approach percussion with this type of outlook. Not only did this experience improve my rhythmic abilities, it made me interact better with human drummers —I'd seen at least a taste of it from their side for a change.

Having a recorder around made it much easier to learn to use my voice. I had always concentrated on electronics and guitar; and though I had done some singing, because of 'vocal paranoia' I hadn't gotten around to working seriously with my voice. One day I finally got up the nerve to start, and although those first results were not exactly ego-boosting, they gave me the encouragement to go on; at least the pitch was right. But an important advantage was that I could lay down a song, sing a track along with it, listen, criticize myself by playing producer, then go back and try again. Working out harmonies became very easy; without a tape recorder or a willing friend, it would have been impossible. By this time, I was having so much fun learning how to do vocal tricks—with overdubbing, voltage-controlled equalization changes, delay line effects, and so on—that I ended up singing quite a lot and getting my voice into shape. Needless to say, the positive feedback of hearing my progress, with the tape recorder as an impartial witness, was more incentive to keep at it.

My learning didn't stop there, however. I still had lingering voice insecurities that kept me from mixing the voice to a prominent level on the tape; I sort of hedged my bets by keeping it back in the track. A friend of mine heard it, suggested that the vocals weren't up enough, and explained something very important: whether it's good, bad, or indifferent, a part, once recorded, is *there*, and you might as well give it full recognition. You can't hide something except by mixing it out totally.

A tape recorder can give you lots of almost free lessons; they may be a little bit painful (tape recorders don't edit and are quite unforgiving), but don't let that rattle you. Just learn and keep on pushing.

Now that we have all this knowledge about the equipment, it's time to apply it. By way of introduction, the basic rule of recording is that anything goes if it sounds good. There are no rights and wrongs, no 'proper' microphones, and no rule books. Engineers will strongly disagree over extremely basic points; one might say that the choice of a microphone is crucial, another will maintain that it doesn't matter if you follow it up with a good equalizer. All of this is very much a matter of taste.

This translates into more work for you, because you not only have to learn about the equipment you are using, you also have to increase your senses of music, self-analysis, and taste, and none of this is easy. In a professional studio, all the musician has to think about is making the music—the engineer figures out the equipment layout, and the producer arranges and gives direction to the music. If you're going to perform all these functions at once, you have to become proficient at them. Although it takes years of practice to become an expert—it's just like learning a musical instrument—you can enjoy your work almost immediately with studio machines: all you need to do is to master a few very basic technical rules.

You'll probably never be completely satisfied with any tape you create; while you're making it, you will learn something new that you can't apply unless you start all over again. Although sometimes it's a good idea to scrap something that's not working out in order to work in new ideas, often it's better to simply save your new pieces of knowledge for a future tape. Don't look back, look ahead. Like music, recording, itself, is also a fine art. The keys are the same that make someone a good musician: practice, experimentation, and a desire to learn from others as well as from yourself.

GENERAL RECORDING TECHNIQUES

Setting up is an important part of the studio process. The basic goal is to have everything set and ready to go so that, once you start, the recording process can proceed smoothly, without interruptions or frustrating/embarrassing breakdowns. It's helpful to do the following when you're getting ready for a session:

Clean your machine. Hopefully you did this after your last session; but if you didn't, make sure that the heads, capstan, pinch roller, and all other parts that contact the tape during its travels, are clean. You can use a magnetometer (see the chapter on maintenance) to check the residual magnetism of the heads, and then demagnetize if necessary. Do all this with the machine off. Then check that the various controls on the tape recorder are correct: record switches off; sel-sync switches off; output switches set to 'source'; and speed, bias, and reel size (depending on the recorder) switches on the correct settings. Then check whatever else applies to your machine, dust it and wipe off any greasy fingerprints, give it a pat on the head, and turn it on.

Warm up your machine. I feel that even a solid-state recorder requires some warm-up time—nothing excessive, mind you, but letting it idle for five to ten minutes lets everything get up to temperature and up to spec. I certainly don't see how it could hurt, and you can spend those five minutes or so getting the rest of your act together.

Select, leader, and thread your tape. Select the tape that's appropriate for your uses. This is a good time to introduce the handy accessory of paper leader tape. By splicing it to the head of the magnetic tape (see Figure 5-1; if you aren't familiar with splicing, see the section on assembling a tape, which covers splicing in explicit detail), you give yourself several advantages: First, using a felt-tip pen—sparingly—you can write on the leader and identify the tape. Second, when rewinding back to the beginning of the tape, you can hit the stop button as soon as the leader tape appears, before the tape has a chance to unravel. Without the leader tape, it's very easy to rewind the tape off the takeup reel; then you have to go through the hassle of threading. Finally, a paper leader tape keeps the end of the magnetic tape from getting ratty. Plastic leader tape is also available, but I think that the paper type gives less problems with static build-up.

Threading tape is never fun; luckily you only have to do it once per tape. Figure 5-2 shows how to thread tape. Make sure that when you thread the tape it lies evenly around the hub of the reel; any bumps will affect the smoothness of the tape's travel. If you have to stop in the middle of a session and you're in

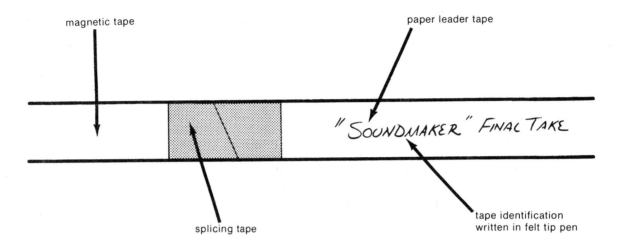

magnetic tape

paper leader tape

"Soundmaker" Final Take

splicing tape

tape identification
written in felt tip pen

Figure 5-1.

the middle of a reel, it's all right to leave the
tape on the machine overnight or for a few
days, but in that case you really must cover
the recorder with a plastic or other non-
porous dust cover, which you should do
anyway.

In any case, before you start to record on
any piece of tape, listen to parts of it and see if
there is any prerecorded material. Nine times
out of ten there won't be, but you'll be grateful
that you checked if there ever is.

THE TAPE RECORDER

Although your tape machine has input-
level and output-level controls, these are
almost always superseded by the mixer controls. As a result, the tape's controls are
adjusted to a specific point of reference so that
all channels behave the same way in terms of
level matching. Professional studios adjust to
very accurate test tapes or tones; we don't
need that much accuracy. Here's the way I
zero my TEAC 3340S:

1) Feed a constant tone into the tape
   recorder's channel 1 line input. If you
   don't have some kind of electronic
   oscillator to use as a standard, invent
   your own—e.g. place a microphone in
   front of a speaker that's tuned between
   FM stations. This area is a source of
   'white noise,' which is a very consistent
   sort of signal. Something like an organ

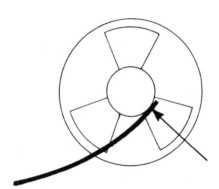

*Press finger against tape and
take-up reel hub; then rotate
hub with thumb, continuing
to hold tape against hub with
finger.*

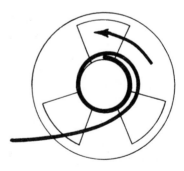

*Rotate reel counterclockwise
until tape is firmly wound
around hub. 4 or 5 turns
should be sufficient.*

Figure 5-2.

80

or synthesizer (*without tremolo or gadgets*) will also work.

2) Turn the channel 1 input control about three-fourths of the way up, and set the input selector to 'source'. Turn up the input control until the meter for channel 1 reads 0 VU.

3) Thread some of the tape onto the tape recorder, at the speed you're going to use. Turn on the record switch for channel 1, then push 'play' and 'record' simultaneously so that you're recording the test tone.

4) Switch the output selector to 'tape,' so you are monitoring directly from the tape itself, and adjust the output-level control until the meter reads 0 VU. With some high-output tapes, you may have to set this reference down 2 or 3dB to keep the pointer from banging away at the right-hand side of the VU meter during playback of program material.

5) Stop the tape, rewind back to the beginning, and run the same procedure on the other three channels of the recorder.

Check over your mixer. Make sure that everything is returned to normal, that reverb sends are turned down, preamps and EQ are switched out, and the like. While you are checking things over, look for any pilot lights that aren't working, or other symptoms of trouble.

Now the equipment is set up and ready to record. But record what? Perhaps, if you're doing the whole tape by yourself: an instrument, or maybe a band. In either case, you are going to have to make a choice between recording the signal(s) in question via microphone, or by plugging directly into the mixing console.

RECORDING DIRECT

This is the easiest way to get a signal into a tape recorder, but it only works with electric instruments. With this method you take the output of your electric guitar, electric piano, organ, rhythm box, or whatever, and simply plug it into the tape recorder line input. However, some instruments will have insufficient

level to drive the input; or they may be loaded down by the tape recorder input and give a 'dull' sound. In this case, you need to add a mic or instrument preamp. Many musicians, because they use them to overload their amplifiers and thus obtain a distorted effect, associate a preamp with a distortion-producing sound. However, a preamp by itself, unless overdriven, should be a clean device that adds no coloration of its own. It has been my experience that a gain of 10 preamp will take almost any electric instrument up to 0 VU at your tape recorder input. Preamps are available commercially, or you can build one yourself—they aren't very complex.

Recording directly from the instrument has a disadvantage: if the amplifier is part of the musician's 'sound,' then going direct, as we describe it, cuts out that part of the sound. However, you can still record direct by adding a tap from the amplifier's speaker (see Figure 5-3). You can then feed this line into the mixer. Precise resistor values aren't given because different players will use their amps at different levels, but the figures given should put you in the right range.

RECORDING WITH MICROPHONES

This is one of the most controversial aspects of tape recording. Everybody has their own favorite mic to record specific instruments, their own particular ideas of where to position microphones for best pickup, or of the correct number of mics to use with a drum set, and so on.

No one knows all the answers, and that certainly includes me. However, I have found out something important: if you know what you like, you can experiment around until you find the perfect sound for your purposes. Our rule—"If it sounds good, use it"—transcends any other rules. Here are some thoughts about how to use microphones, but first we'll have to look at some of their peculiarities and characteristics so we can use them to maximum advantage.

The proximity effect. No, this isn't a science-fiction movie, but rather a phenomenon that occurs with all mics, but is most pronounced with the dynamic types. It means that as you get closer to the mic, the apparent bass response goes *up*. Singers proficient in mic technique use this to advantage: on soft, intimate parts, they'll sing softly, holding the mic close to the mouth, to exaggerate the bass and give a warmer sound. Then, during louder parts, they'll hold the microphone further back and sing louder to compensate for the extra distance. Classical guitars can also take advantage of the proximity effect to get a warmer recorded sound. In any event, you should be aware of it and either use it to your advantage or compensate for it.

The inverse square law. This is a fancy way of saying that the further you get away from a mic, the more the sound drops off. "Big deal," you say. But it is a big deal, because the sound does not fall off uniformly as the sound source moves away; rather, the mics ability to pick up sound decreases dramatically when the sound source moves only a few inches

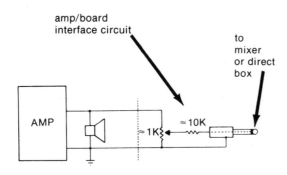

Adjust 1k pot to prevent overload of the mixer.

Figure 5-3.

away (see Figure 5–4). This can be a serious problem with vocalists who aren't really good with mic technique and who wander around the vicinity of the mic, alternately swallowing it and then backing away, without changing their volume to compensate. The electronic solution is to add compression, but it's better if you can explain to the artist that he can achieve a consistent signal only by recognizing the demands of the inverse square law and the proximity effect.

Overloading. Since condenser and electret mics have their own built-in preamp, they

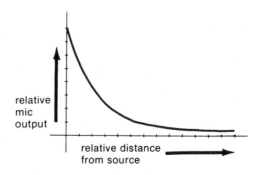

Figure 5-4.

generally produce more output than dynamic mics. So, if you find an overloaded sound, the problem may not be occurring at the mic: it may be occurring at the board, especially if the board is set up to handle the low-output dynamic mic, and not the high-output condenser types. That's why many mixers have attenuators to cut the microphone signal down to size before it hits the rest of the mixer. Alternatively, the mixer can be set up to handle the condenser mic without amplification, and to add it for the dynamic types. In any event, you may have to experiment with mic placement if overloading occurs and you can't fix it at the board.

Popping and wind noises. Microphones, particularly the dynamic and ribbon types, are sensitive to sounds that linguists call 'plosives' (*b, p,* and the like). These produce nasty pops and thumps in the output. Also, wind noise can register as interference. To cope with this problem, you can buy, if your mic doesn't have one already, a little foam cover that slips over the head of the mic and attenuates these sounds, as well as keeps breath moisture from the mic. The foam must be acoustically transparent to high frequencies, which rules out regular styrofoam—use the acoustic foam designed for the job. Again, the performer can help reduce this problem with proper mic techniques, such as singing off-center into the mic during sections containing these problem sounds.

Phasing problems. Remember in the microphone section when we talked about how two signals arriving at the same place 180 degrees *out of phase* could cancel each other out, unless they happened to be feeding a differential input? Well, signals arriving *in phase* can also *add* to each other; and if signals are neither totally in phase nor totally out of phase, other responses will occur. So when you're using two mics, you can run into phasing problems if one mic is picking up the crest of a signal while another is picking up the trough (situations are rarely this clean cut, though; I'm simplifying for the sake of illustration). Actually, the phase changes will be different at different frequencies, so that some bass notes might be reinforced while some of the treble cancels, or then again, the opposite could be true. So, although each mic might sound all right when monitored by itself, when it is combined with others, the sound can be considerably altered. Thus, if you are using two mics to record an instrument like a piano, check to hear what they sound like together as well as separately. Phase problems are particularly acute if you feed one mic into the right channel and one into the left channel

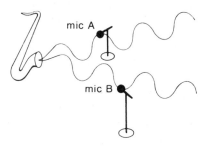

A and B are picking up the signal from a sax at points that are out of phase, which can possibly cause problems. In rooms where reflections are occurring, the problems can be even more troublesome. Moving mic B back or forth slightly can give a different sound — experiment with the placement for best results.

Figure 5-5.

of a stereo system to obtain a stereo spread, then play the recording back over a mono system; the phase changes inherent in the system could suddenly become very prominent. Figure 5-5 illustrates this kind of problem.

The difficulties are compounded when miking drums, since several mics must then be used to get an acceptable sound from the set.

The phase relationships in such a case can be horribly complex. Again, your only real option is to monitor, listen, check, and compare, until the sound is correct. If you are dealing with a stereo spread, also check the mono combination from time to time. Some boards, as we mentioned earlier, have phase switches that can change the phase of a microphone from the console rather than in the studio. But it should be emphasized that by simply flipping the mic's phasing 180 degrees, you will not necessarily solve your problems, and you may introduce some new ones. Oh well.

Mounting microphones. You should have mic stands, booms, and the like, to mount mics. You should also probably have a gooseneck extension for *close miking,* where you stick the mic right up next to your sound source, whether, for example, it's the sound hole of a guitar, or under a harpsichord cover. If you are some distance away from the sound source—say, in a live recording situation—you have a couple of options: you can place the microphone on the floor (yes, on the floor!), lying on top of lots of foam and stuff so that it doesn't pick up floor vibrations and rumble (a particular problem with dynamic mics). This gives you less chance of picking up out-of-phase signals that bounce off the floor (see Figure 5–6). Also, you can try hanging the mic from the ceiling; this will produce the same general results, and may even be better because you won't have people stomping on the ceiling; if your mic is on the floor and there are people dancing then you'll probably pick up the thumps.

Using the little switches on your microphone. Sometimes mics have extra little built-in gimmicks. One of my favorites is a low-frequency rolloff switch. This basically reduces response from below about 250Hz, and is very useful with voice recording, as it can delete many of the pops and breath sounds without forcing you to resort to the wind screen device that we mentioned earlier. Also, some voices tend to sound almost murky if they're too bassy, and in this case the low-frequency rolloff comes in handy. For musical uses, where you want full frequency response, you can take the rolloff out by putting the switch back in its flat position.

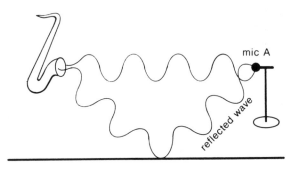

Microphone A picks up not just the main sax sound, but also a destructive out-of-phase reflecting wave at some frequency or frequencies. Placing the mic on the floor can reduce pickup of reflected waves.

Figure 5-6.

Another switch that you'll find, but only on electret and condenser mics, is an on-off switch for the battery. Use it! Even though the current drain is small, *continuous* extended use is what drains a battery. And whatever you do, don't use those cheap carbon-zinc batteries; if they leak, and corrode the inside of a microphone, you've just lost a substantial investment by trying to save a few cents on batteries. Use the better alkaline types.

MICROPHONE TIPS

Vocals. Although there are several recommended 'best ways' to use a mic (such as holding it away, holding it close, singing across it, singing above it, or singing into it), every person's voice requires a different technique because every voice is different.

For my vocals I use a dynamic mic. It's rugged, so that I can use it in as many situations and on as many different instruments as possible, and it doesn't have a built-in preamp that adds noise. My particular model also has a low-frequency cut switch that minimizes popping, and can clean up the sound of some instruments. By singing close to the mic (to take advantage of the proximity effect) and rolling off some bass to avoid sounding too boomy, I can obtain just the right balance—even though in theory these two actions should cancel each other out. But

the point is that no one would necessarily have recommended that for me; and to someone who *doesn't* need a little extra fullness, it would probably sound inappropriate. If you are recording a vocalist, make sure that he or she understands the necessity of keeping the volume level constant. It's amazing how few singers are aware of good mic technique; they could learn a lot from the engineers who earn their living by properly applying it.

Acoustic instruments. Most signals from the 'real world' of acoustic instruments are very subtle in character and hard to capture with a microphone; as an additional complication, the dynamic range of an acoustic instrument is huge compared to that of the tape recorder, so that you can easily go from a signal that can't get over system noise to one that distorts. Intelligent mic placement and sympathetic playing are both equally important in solving this problem. Some players just don't understand dynamic range, and don't realize that playing in the studio is different from playing live; with these players, engineers are forced to use extreme compression. I feel that compression is very important when you use a mic, but you should always use the minimum amount necessary to keep a steady level. Otherwise, it sounds like an effect. Of course, you may want an effect.

Some instruments are harder to mic than others. Saxophones aren't too hard: you surely know where the sound comes out, although just sticking a mic in front of the bell results in missing some of the instrument's resonant properties. But then consider something like an acoustic guitar, where the sound hole is covered by your picking hand and the whole body resonates to produce a sound. In this case, there are several options, and a good one to consider is the *acoustic transducer.* There are many models available commercially —FRAP, Barcus-Berry, DeArmond, Hi-A, and so on—and they all work with acoustic instruments by picking up the vibrations of the body and turning them into electrical signals. However, it is almost mandatory to use some kind of equalization with these. Transducers tend to accentuate peaks and deficiencies in the instrument's response, and an equalizer can smooth these out. Again, the typical signal output of the transducer is weak and requires some kind of preamp to become usable, and of course the preamp adds noise, but you can't have everything.

A better, but more complex, approach is to use the transducer in conjunction with one or more mics. I remember one session where a classical guitar was being miked; there was a transducer to pick up the basic notes and qualities of the guitar, with suitable equalization to take out a dreadful midrange peak; a condenser microphone was pointed at the strings near the guitarist's left hand, equalized with a little high-end sheen to accent the brightness of sound; and a dynamic microphone was pointed towards the end, and to the rear of the guitar, adding a deep kind of resonant, warm sound to the basic character of the guitar. These were mixed together in stereo, with the transducer in the center of the spread, the bassier mic on the left, and the trebly mic on the right, mixed fairly low. The sound was really nice, but there were probably a hundred other equally valid ways of miking that guitar. Keep in mind, though, that there is a point of diminishing return in the number of mics you use: you become vulnerable to phase mismatch and other uglies with more mics. But as we've said, you can't have everything.

Drums. Drums are a real challenge: First, they're loud, and if you want to pick up one drum without picking up the rest of the kit, you'll have to figure out how to eliminate huge amounts of leakage. Second, you have an incredible dynamic range to handle, and a very wide range of frequencies—from deep bass drum, to cymbals whose energy can extend beyond 20kHz. In professional studios, drums are frequently isolated in as dead an area as possible, and this does help give a good drum sound. For rough sounding drums, you can record in any room; but if you want maximum flexibility, the acoustics are very important. One trick that's very common is to set up drums in a corner, because the configuration of the walls tends to boost the bass and adds to the feeling of power. Although most drum miking is close miking, you will also probably want to add some overhead mics for an overall sound. For a while it was in vogue to just cover a drum set with mics, but then the interaction problems we mentioned earlier became obvious; it seems that the best approach is to use the fewest number of mics consistent with a good sound. This means a minimum of separate mics for bass drum, hi-hat/snare, and overhead (such as above the toms, slightly in front of the bass drum, or above the drummer's seat); it also helps to have another mic or two specifically for tom-toms. If you've got the money for 15 mics or so, have a good time experimenting!

SETTING UP BAFFLES AND GETTING THE EQUIPMENT READY

If you are recording a group of musicians, think a little bit about the leakage problem beforehand. Should someone be recorded in another room, for example, or will baffles be sufficient? If you are simply overdubbing, leakage diminishes in importance, but basic tracks can sometimes sound really terrible because of excessive leakage (there are exceptions—e.g. drums sounds picked up through a heavily-equalized channel can work to your advantage). People frequently need eye contact for cues; players like to hear the vocals that belong to a song as they play; and equipment may not fit in a way that allows optimum arrangement. One help is to have the vocalist do a reference vocal through the cue system only, so that the musicians can hear vocals through the phones, but they don't get picked up by the mics recording the group. Afterwards, the final vocals may be overdubbed without leakage problems. Sometimes it's easier to overdub an instrument like acoustic piano instead of trying to isolate it from other instruments through baffling. If, in this case, you're short for tracks, perhaps you could mix in another overdub so that, say, harmony vocals or an acoustic guitar part, would be recorded at the same time as the piano.

ROUTING WIRES

Now you have to get AC to all those musicians and headphones. It's important that you make sure that all the wires are not underfoot and are out of danger's way; be especially wary of damp cellar floors, which can be lethal. There is nothing more frustrating than having someone blow a take (or a fuse) by walking on a wire or tripping over it.

Figure 5–7 shows a good miking scheme for a jazz quintet consisting of electric guitar, electric bass, piano, drums, and sax, including AC and headphone cords.

This is where the VU meters do their number. Your task is to learn how to read and interpret the meter and use this knowledge to set your levels. Unfortunately, it's very difficult to describe this subject fully in words, so we've included some exercises to perform with your VU meter so that you can get to know it better.

The easiest way to learn a tape's character —how much signal it can take before it distorts, how much noise is occurring, how the hiss level changes when you record a signal— is to find a consistent live music source; perhaps you could press someone into practicing their guitar or piano into your tape recorder for a half hour or so. Put on your headphones for this one; you want to hear every little sound on the tape and block out the sound of whoever is practicing. Drums are probably best for this purpose if you can isolate yourself completely from the drum sound; vocals aren't that good because they don't cover enough range.

Send your test sound source into channel 1, and switch the meter for that channel into the 'source' position. Turn up the level until the meter indicates a signal that seldom, if ever, *pins.* Pinning (when the meter pointer swings all the way to the right-hand retaining pin on the meter face) should be avoided to prevent damaging the meter. Now, run the tape in record mode and switch the output selector to 'tape'; listen to the sound coming from the tape itself. First of all, you'll notice a delay compared to the sound source as soon as you start running the tape—it's bothersome, but try to tune it out and concentrate on the tape sound. Make sure, incidentally, that you are not in the sync mode. Most recorders, in one way or another, prevent you from recording when you attempt to use a synched channel.

After you've tuned in to what's going on, decrease the input level and notice how much the noise seems to increase. From time to time, switch into the 'source' position so that you can see what type of input signal is going into the recorder. Then, turn up the input— very slowly—until you start getting audible distortion, and note how the quality of the

sound changes from clean to progressively 'gritty.' Also, with very loud low-frequency signals (e.g. bass and bass drum), you will hear, along with your signal, a swishing sound, like white noise. This is called *modulation noise,* and can be minimized with certain types of noise-reduction equipment. Signals with lots of high-frequency content tend to block out the noise; it's still present, but it's hidden. Sometimes you can counteract hiss problems by boosting the treble on an instrument when you record it, and cutting the treble on playback. Not only does this remove the highs that were added artificially, but also the bulk of the modulation noise and hiss.

Another excellent source to get a feel for levels is an electric rhythm box (you know, with all those buttons—foxtrot, cha cha, rock, etc.). These traditionally put out very clean sine waves (which are 'pure' signals with little harmonic content) for the drum sounds, and white noise for the cymbals. These machines cover a very broad band of frequencies, from low to high. The bass 'drum' is particularly good for hearing how the tape reacts to low frequencies; the cymbals are good for checking out high-frequency saturation characteristics of the tape. Here's one tip: Sometimes, like on bass and some drum tracks, you can use to advantage the tape's overload characteristic if you want to obtain a grunching, straining type of sound. However, you do increase the chances that some sound will spill over into the other channels (*cross-talk*), and that the extra level may change the magnetic fields imprinted on neighboring portions of tape when the tape is wound on its reel (*print-through*). Also, the modulation noise can become pretty nasty. Nonetheless, I have used this technique a few times; the effect is similar to that of an amp being pushed, yet it is different. To prevent any really terrible accidents, make sure that you are in the tape monitor mode when you do this and monitor the sound like a hawk. Since you're in this mode, you should also turn down the channel's output-level control to keep the meters from self-destructing.

By doing all this, you've hopefully got some idea of how the VU meter readings correlate with tape sounds. You perhaps noticed that your meter is *overdamped,* in which case the pointer has some inertia which

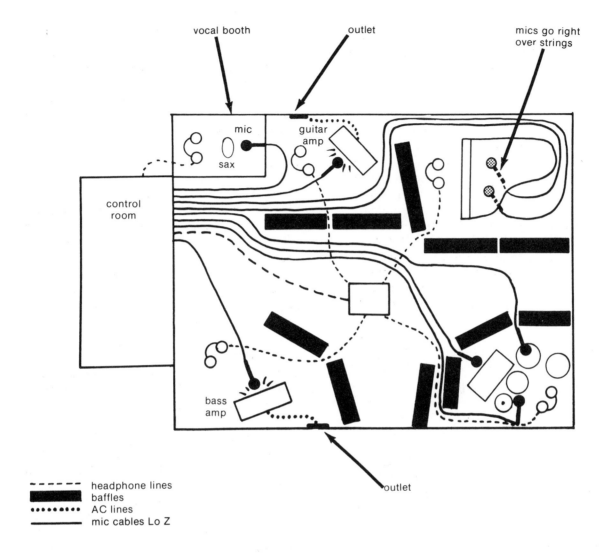

vocal booth   outlet   mics go right over strings

mic

guitar amp

sax

control room

bass amp

outlet

- - - - - headphone lines
▬▬▬ baffles
●●●●●●● AC lines
――――― mic cables Lo Z

Sax: Put in vocal booth to prevent leakage during spaces between solo passages. Like many vocal booths, this one has headphone jacks built in the wall that are permanently connected to the control room.

Guitar amp: Located near outlet at wall. the mic is aimed at dead center of the speaker for bassier effect; placing the mic more to one side can reduce the bass by using the proximity effect to advantage, if required.

Bass amp: Also located near wall outlet. Actually, a direct line might be the best approach; that way, the bassist could sit in the control room and not have to use an amp at all.

Baffles: Baffles are arranged around drums and piano to keep sounds from hitting their mics; but they also keep the drum and piano sounds from getting out.

Headphone cords: A line comes from the control room to a master headphone box, then separate headphones are distributed to the various musicians.

Piano: Two mics are located over the sounding board; but try one above and one below the sounding board for a very different sound.

Drums: Drums have three mics, one for bass drum, one for snare/hi hat, one for overhead, mounted mostly over the toms.

Figure 5-7.

prevents it from following sharp, fast signals; or it may be *underdamped,* where the pointer follows every little nuance of the music, to the extent that it overshoots the correct level when a strong signal hits it suddenly. In either case, learn and cooperate.

An additional problem is that tape recorders are very sensitive to high-frequency overload, due to the internal pre-emphasis and to some of the new noise-reduction systems. So, with a guitar you may be able to register a +3dB signal without any noticeable distortion; but try that with a tambourine, whose metal-to-metal contact produces tremendous high-frequency energy, and you'll probably get a grossly distorted sound on playback that actually sounds 'crunched'—and to make matters worse, it will probably have leaked onto other tracks of your tape. Be very careful when you set levels with any kind of very trebly instrument; you will have to monitor and play with the input level to control the effects it can produce.

The following doesn't really relate to setting levels, but it's another instructive exercise: with the tape recorder running in the record mode, and with headphones on, listen to the tape output from one of the channels when its associated input control is turned all the way down. Turn the output all the way up so that you are only hearing the noise and 'glop' that the machine-plus-tape combination produces. At this high amplification, dropouts on the tape will cause little sounds like corn popping; the familiar tape hiss becomes a wonderland of constantly changing white noise. You'll probably pick up a faint bit of hum, too. Listen to the character of the tape; for comparison listen to a cheap tape (if you have any around—it's better if you don't, actually). With cheap tape, the clicks will sound like explosions and the tape hiss will sound 'gritty' and unorganized. You will also notice that the head contact, or the tape quality, or something, is not quite as good on the outermost tracks of a piece of tape; compare tracks 1 and 4 to tracks 2 and 3. Listen to your recorder through the audio equivalent of a microscope and you'll learn many interesting things, and probably feel a little closer to it.

LOGBOOKS

When you are playing multitrack games, you really need to keep track of what's·going on as you record. You need to know the tracks for the various instruments, and the timings and tape counter numbers for introductions, solos, and so forth. Take notes on what you do and how you obtain certain sounds. There are two reasons for this: First, so that you can concentrate exclusively on the music; and second, because you will find that taking notes prevents you from getting into the situation of wondering what track you recorded something on. Also, you'll find that when you are busy working on a session, your memory isn't putting much effort into remembering all of what went down. If you decide to go back and remix a tape six months later, you will be very happy to have some notes.

TUNING, IDENTIFYING, TIMING

When you put on a tape, don't just begin immediately with the piece of music you are recording; here are some ideas on what to put on tape first:

1) *Test tone.* Begin each selection on the tape with something like an *A*-440 or other standard musical tone. Give it about 20 or 30 seconds. By recording at a level that gives 0 VU on the output meter of your machine, you have a reference level for subsequent dubs if required. When you play it back, not only will you have a good idea of what kind of wow and flutter your machine has, but, in case the speed changes when you come back in a couple of days, you will have a reference for tuning. Don't blame your tape recorder if it doesn't always come back to exactly the same pitch —even a 1% change in speed is very audible and requires retuning of instruments. Naturally, this is where variable-speed recorders shine. For this reason, first record hard-to-tune instruments (pianos, harps), or instruments whose tuning can't be changed easily (vibes, electric pianos), and then have singers and stringed instrument

players use notes from them to determine pitch. In a case like this, it's helpful to have a tuning standard that can vary a slight and predictable amount to compensate for slightly off-pitch instruments.

2) *Identification* (slate). The term *slating* comes from movie production—you know, that whole take 1, take 2, type of thing. It's not a bad idea if, after the test tone, you speak the title of the selection and the take number. The first one would be take 1. If it gets blown, you can either rewind and announce take 1 again or say take 2. In order to conserve tape, you will probably want to rewind over false takes and start anew, but there are times when you just can't do this: let's say your group lays down a basic track, but you're not sure if it's the best they can do because the piano player came in just a little late on his break. So you lay down another one. It's great, except that the guitarist blows one note in the middle—not seriously, but you might as well try one more take, and still hold on to the last two. At this point, everyone is getting tired of the song, and the third take doesn't turn out so well. You then erase the third track, and jot down in your notes that take 2 is the one you want. If you come back in the future (say, for overdubbing), you don't have to re-listen to tracks 1 and 2 to remember which one to use; it's there in your notes.

3) *Timing.* A stopwatch, or at least a clock with a second hand, is handy to have around (If you don't want to be aware of how much time you are spending in the studio, take off the hour hand!). For one thing, you can time songs when mixing and know when to begin fade-ins, fade-outs, or whatever. Also, if you send out demos, it's a nice touch to include the timings. When assembling a final tape, timings are also useful: let's say you want to record some of your material on some 45-minute cassettes, with 22½ minutes on each side; the timings enable you to combine the songs in a suitable order, without running out of tape. We will talk more about song timings later, when we discuss assembling tapes.

Sometimes, while recording demo tracks by yourself, it's quite possible to lay down a basic drum track, and then, when it's time to overdub, have no idea where verses begin and end and that sort of thing. With strictly arranged or scored pieces this presents no problem, but with anything involving improvisation, you need some kind of reference.

The most common reference is called a *click track,* where a metronome or an electronic device puts a series of rhythmic pulses on the tape. In a 16-track studio, where tracks may be laid down to follow scheduling demands rather than musical considerations, the click track can be very helpful—you could record bass, guitar, pianos, horns, singers, and *then* put on the drums. All the time, you have had that click track for tempo reference.

Rhythm units also make good click tracks. When using one of these, I usually also set up a microphone, and cue the beginnings and endings of solos, remind myself of arrangements, speak words of encouragement during difficult solos, or whatever. While doing overdubs, it can be very handy to have a narrative track that sort of conducts you along the musical trail.

RESOLVING THE "GOING DIRECT VERSUS MIKING AN AMPLIFIER" CONTROVERSY

Guitarists, in particular, consider their amplification systems to be part of the sound of their instruments. Rock and rollers, for example, often turn their amps up to incredibly loud volumes in order to realize highly distorted amp characteristics. In the studio, this can create many leakage problems, but there is an alternative: in recent years, there has been an interest in small, practice amps. These are usually about a foot square in size, and can be made to sound just as distorted and raunchy as bigger amps, but at far lower volume levels. Although they may not produce enough sound for live playing, in the studio this doesn't matter. Stick the mic up close to the speaker and, in the control room, you won't know whether the amp is one foot high or twenty feet high. Small amps can also help your cause if you are trying to record hard rock in a residential neighborhood.

RECORDING TECHNIQUES FOR SPECIFIC MACHINES

Although in this book we're mostly talking about a multitrack studio environment, there are alternative ways to record, even if your budget is minuscule. So before we get into sophisticated multitrack techniques like ping-ponging, let's pause for a bit and see what you can do with conventional cassette and reel-to-reel recorders, especially with live recording.

THE $20 CASSETTE RECORDER

The lowly portable cassette recorder is where a lot of people, including myself, have started. I don't know a magic secret that will make them turn out super tapes; the fidelity is limited, the wow and flutter are pretty terrible, they can only record in mono, and the noise is—well, they're very noisy. But these machines are cheap and plentiful. If you decide at the last minute that you want to record your band in concert, you can't very well improvise a super tape setup, but you can put a portable cassette machine in front of the PA speaker and hope for the best. Unless *everything* is being miked (which is becoming more common these days), the drums will no doubt be out of balance; the flutter will give a forced vibrato to the whole band; and the levels will probably be way off, but if there's a solo in there that cooks, *it will come through.* If the music is exciting, you will hear that too. Was the second song really too slow? Did the transition between the third and the fourth songs sound smooth? With a tape recording, you can add your own opinions to those of other people.

You can also use the cassette machine as a notebook. Got a song idea? Hum or strum a guitar, into the machine. Most of these inexpensive machines have compressors that bring everything up to a constant recording level,

so that even if you play a solid body guitar without an amp, you will still hear something. Don't overestimate what one of these machines can do, but don't underestimate it either. Here are some additional points that will improve your chances of getting something bearable:

1) *Use really good tape.* You can always erase it and use it with a better machine later; a cheapo tape may self-destruct (and gum up the recorder's works) before you've had a chance to evaluate what you were recording.

2) *Keep the machine clean.* I know I mention this every ten pages or so, but there's a reason for that.

3) *Invest in an AC adapter.* As batteries wear down, the speed changes accordingly. If you record with low batteries and play back with fresh batteries, you will get a sped-up effect because the tape will play back faster than it was recorded. AC adapters keep the speed more constant, but make sure that you always have a set of fresh batteries inside the recorder, in case you forget an extension cord.

4) *Always use an external microphone.* Even if it's an inexpensive type, it will be better than the internal mics (built into many cassette machines) that pick up motor noise and other garbage as well as sound waves. Keep the cord short to avoid picking up hum. If you can use a really good mic, you will hear the difference—even with inexpensive cassette machines. Many recorders have an auxiliary input jack (called AUX IN or LINE IN) that can accept an output from, say, another tape recorder or a simple mixer. When you feed into this input you will be able to bypass the (usually noisy) mic-preamp section of the machine.

Though they are portable, don't knock these machines around too much, as the heads can go out of alignment and give recordings of inferior quality.

BETTER LIVE RECORDINGS

If you plan to do a lot of live recording, a little cassette machine isn't good enough, and it really is impractical to lug a multitrack machine around with you all the time, but there is a compromise: look into one of the many excellent cassette field decks, generally available in the $200–$300 range. While they can be battery operated, and are usually not too much bigger than a cheap machine, several refinements put this kind of unit head and shoulders above your average cassette deck: generally speaking, they will have much more rugged and precise motors to control wow and flutter, an integral AC adapter, some external microphones of an acceptable quality level, and Dolby or some other form of noise reduction; stereo recordings are possible as well as mono; and there will be more attention paid to the electronics, to decrease your noise level. JVC, Sony, TEAC, and several others make nice machines along these lines. One type I wouldn't recommend are those machines that include foldout speakers and fairly decent audio sections, to let you listen back with reasonable fidelity; this means that more money has gone into playback than into recording. You want a good recorder. The speaker should only serve as a monitor; if you want better fidelity, plug a small hi-fi speaker into the external speaker jack and you will be a lot better off. All the other earlier comments that we made about optimizing recordings are also applicable to this breed of machine.

So now you have a tape machine, you're at a small club, and you want to record some music. If you are recording solely for educational value (such as listening to a rehearsal), you don't have to be too careful. Stick the mic in front of the group or PA that you are recording and let the internal compressor do the rest. If the system overloads, put it farther away from the sound source.

Much has been written and conjectured about live mic placement, and it is true that every situation is different; but the similarities between them make it possible to take advantage of the knowledge you've gained in previous recordings. One rule to remember is that you should make sure that you have a couple of foam pads with you. If you just put the microphone on top of a table, you will

hear every little floor vibration, and every time anybody taps a finger against the table, you'll have a resonant 'thump.' Cradling the microphone in a foam pad (see Figure 5–8) helps isolate the mic from shocks and noise. It is even better, if you can do it, to hang the microphone. But this brings up the problem

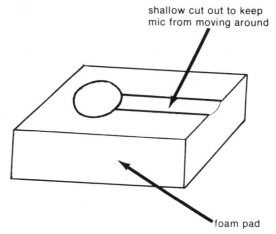

shallow cut out to keep
mic from moving around

foam pad

Figure 5-8.

that the run of microphone cable has to be longer, so you will generally have to go to a balanced line system (as we discussed earlier in the section on microphones), and carry around with you an extension cord for the microphone. Figure 5–9 shows two ways to hang a mic. The 'pointing at' works well for groups, but don't overlook the overhead position. Many times this will give good results on instruments such as drums. Again, experimentation is most helpful.

With a stereo recorder, you have some extra latitude. In addition to making stereo recordings, you can also consider that you're recording two separate mono tracks, and place the microphones accordingly. Let's say that one mic goes in front of a PA, and picks up vocals and some background; the other mic can go overhead on the drums; and when you play back, in mono, you can vary the levels of the two channels for the best balance.

The type of operation we have just described is not limited to cassette recorders. Reel-to-reel (R-T-R) machines work just as well, but they are heavier, larger, and more difficult to thread in a dark club. As a result, many people who wouldn't carry around a

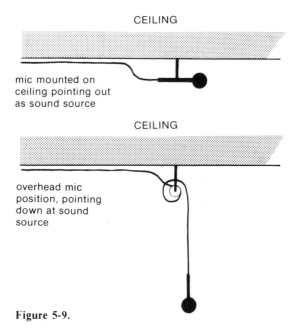

CEILING

mic mounted on
ceiling pointing out
as sound source

CEILING

overhead mic
position, pointing
down at sound
source

Figure 5-9.

R-T-R recorder can easily deal with carrying around a cassette machine. You want to make the recording process as easy as possible on yourself, or you'll lose interest. For this reason, I recommend cassettes when you want to hear your group sound, or to make some live tapes of stuff that you like.

Serious, high-quality, live recording is another matter entirely; this is where R-T-R really shines. For the price of an adequate quality multitrack machine, you can buy a truly excellent R-T-R unit and obtain low-noise tapes from live sources. But you are also going to have to take the time to do a really good job, and that means setting up secure mic stands, doing level checks, watching the VU meters extremely carefully to prevent saturation, and lots more. You might as well use a machine with the best quality possible, but this means that it probably won't have gimmicks like auto-level circuitry so you have to set the record levels very, very carefully, or else use a compressor whose quality matches that of the tape recorder. Also, you will probably want to use several mics, and since most tape recorders have limited mic input facilities, you will need some kind of quality mixer to let all these mics work together. Since using lots of mics tends to produce several long runs of cable, balanced, low-impedance mic systems are mandatory. Since you now (via the

mixer) have control over the levels of the various mics, you will also need a headphone monitor to hear what you're actually putting on the tape, and to monitor the output of the mixer or the input of the tape recorder (many machines will have a built-in headphone monitor, but if yours doesn't, you can add one yourself). Those machines with separate record and playback heads are very useful for live recording, because you can monitor the sound directly from the tape, so you know for sure if your levels are right, or not. These have a disadvantage, though: There is a delay between the live and the monitored sound.

Making live tapes that sound good is an art, because you frequently have to work against crowd noise, improper acoustics, difficult-to-mic stage setups, and other problems. But, as in the case of a musical instrument, once again, practice is the key element in making successful tapes. As long as each tape is an improvement over the previous one, you are doing all right. And if it isn't an improvement, you've just learned something not to do, which is sometimes more valuable than knowing what to do.

HOW TO GENERATE OVERDUBS WITHOUT A MULTITRACK RECORDER

I know of two ways to do multitrack recordings without a multitrack machine, using either two-head or three-head models. But first, let's have a little review.

A two-head machine presents two heads to the tape as it slithers past: first an erase head, to wipe away any signal left on the tape, and then the record/playback head. We have already pointed out that using a head for two different purposes requires a compromise in fidelity; but it also requires a compromise in terms of versatility. You cannot, for example, play back one channel while recording another. You can either record on the tape or play it back, but that's it.

However, if you have *two* two-head machines, it is possible to layer tracks, and you can even do it in stereo if you wish. For this you need the two tape machines, a stereo mixer that can handle *at least* two line inputs and two microphones, and two cassettes or reels of tape of the highest possible quality.

Dolby certainly wouldn't hurt either. The two decks can be cassette or reel-to-reel—it doesn't matter, but the cassettes will build up noise faster.

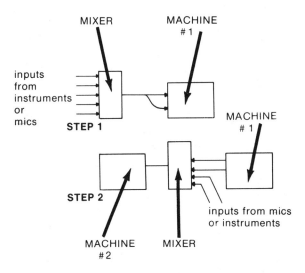

With a stereo mixer and stereo machines, you can do stereo tapes.

Figure 5-10.

Probably the best way to get the idea across is through an example: referring to Figure 5-10, let's suppose you have a five-piece band, and all the members sing. If you try to get both the vocals and instruments down on tape, you've got problems. For one thing, having a vocal mic for each member is going to give you a lot of leakage from the instruments. Also, it is a lot easier to sing when you are not holding an instrument and counting measures at the same time. So here's a solution: for step one, we record only the instruments of the band (using a single mic, a couple of mics, or a batch of mics—whatever your budget dictates) into both tracks of machine 1. After getting a satisfactory instrumental track, you play that tape back into a mixer, which also has some microphones feeding into it. The output of the mixer goes to machine 2. So, start recording on machine 2, then push 'play' on machine 1, and sing along with what you hear from it. If someone blows a note, just rewind the tape on machine 1 and re-record the vocals. The instrumental track remains intact during all this.

One detail we've kind of glossed over is how to monitor the output of machine 1. The simplest way is to have a Y-cord split off the tape 1 output and connect to a hi-fi or guitar amp, as shown in Figure 5-11; although, to avoid leakage, headphone monitoring is preferable.

You can even continue the overtracking process; i.e. now you play back the combined vocal and instrumental track from machine 2, mix it with, say, a lead guitar part, and then go into machine 1. But the problem is that every time you do a transfer, or *dub*, you lose quality. You will find that there is a practical limit to how many overtracks you can make, and this depends on the quality of the machines in question. With some, after two dubs the quality will be terrible; with others, you may be able to get up to five or six tracks (but don't count on it!).

If you are doing demos by yourself and playing all the instruments, you can record, say, an electronic drum unit and bass part into machine 1; then sing and play rhythm guitar, mixed in with the output from recorder 1, into recorder 2; then take the output of recorder 2, mix in a lead guitar part, and dub that on into machine 1. You now have taped drums, bass, rhythm guitar, lead guitar, and a vocal part all generated by one person with two tape machines.

As with all the other techniques we've discussed so far, this one again requires optimum everything: the cleanest heads, the best tape, the quietest mixers, and so on.

Earlier we looked at big mixers, which are vital for multitrack recording. However, when you can't afford a mixer, you can sometimes take advantage of a feature on some tape recorders, called *mic/line mixing*, which provides two separate sets of inputs— one for mic-level, and one for line-level signals. The manufacturer's reason for including this feature is to let you add voice-overs to tapes as you record them. But this type of machine is ideal for what we've just been talking about; if machine 2 in our previous example had this feature, we could record an instrumental track on machine 1, then play that back into the line inputs of machine 2 while singing into the mic inputs. A

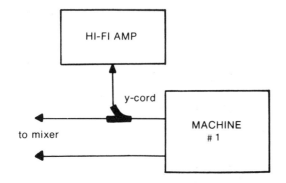

Figure 5-11.

machine with mic/line mixing will have separate level controls for each set of inputs.

The disadvantage of ping-ponging back and forth between these two recorders is that you need two separate recorders. There is, however, one type of recorder that can do all these marvels by itself. I'm referring to a three-head recorder, where the tape first hits an erase head, then a record head, then a playback head. Since the record and playback functions are now separate, *we can use them both at the same time.* Now this may not sound earth-shattering, but let's check out the implications.

The majority of three-head machines have only one set of output jacks per channel; a front-panel switch chooses whether the output will connect to 'source' (the signal that's feeding the record head) or 'tape' (the playback head). The input, of course, goes to the record head.

As we discussed earlier, one of the most vital steps in tape recording is to set the levels correctly; and the only way to know for sure that you are not saturating the tape is to monitor a signal directly from that tape as you record it; and a three-head recorder allows you to do this. However, this arrangement is also capable of generating sound-on-sound recording, a variation of the multitrack approach. The catch here is that you must have either a machine with sound-on-sound capability built in, or you must have a machine where the record mode can be initiated *selectively* for either channel, to allow recording on one while playing back on the other. Some

consumer-oriented, three-head machines do not have this feature, so be careful. You will also need a mixer if there is no sound-on-sound control.

Figure 5-12 shows an example of the sound-on-sound technique, where you first record a rhythm guitar track in the left channel. You now put the left channel on playback and the right channel on record; then, mix your next part (say, a vocal) and a bit of the left channel into the right channel. Now, in the right channel, you have a composite of your vocal and the rhythm guitar. So, you then put the right channel into the playback mode and the left channel back into record, feed a harmony voice part and a lead guitar part, along with the right channel, into the left channel, and there you have it: two guitar parts, a vocal, and a harmony vocal. Of course, you've destroyed the previous tracks along the way, but those are the breaks.

I have used this method many times when I was desperate to get some sounds on tape, and, with a reasonably good machine, have put down four or five tracks without much trouble. But you have to be good at it, because you are destroying older tracks and can't go back and make changes in original tracks. In the example, we did a guitar part, then mixed in a vocal part. If that vocal part is wrong, or mixed too high, we can always replay the guitar track and recut the voice until it sounds right. Upon ping-ponging, since we're recording into a channel where the guitar used to be, if, after listening to the final result, we decide that the guitar level is too high, there's nothing that can be done since the original track is erased and gone forever. What we had to do here is called *premixing,* where some tracks are mixed together before the tape is complete. In fact, *every* track is a premixed track with this method. If, after putting on five or six tracks, you decide that track 2 needed a little more treble or bass, then that's tough luck. Premixing is a delicate art to say the least, and it can reach true heights of sophistication with something like a 4-track machine (more on this soon). But if you want a crash course in mixing sometime, try making a few demos with a sound-on-sound, three-head recorder; you will learn a lot.

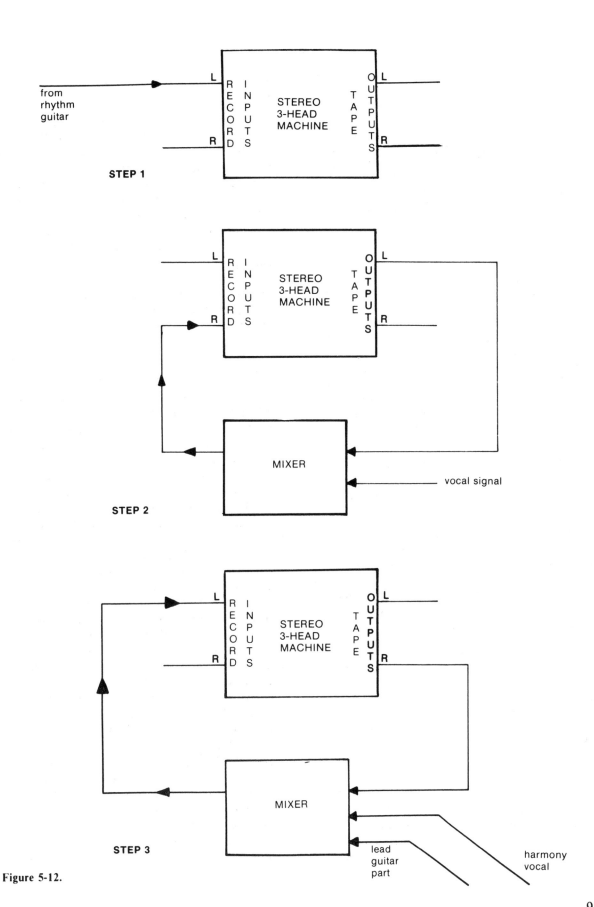

Figure 5-12.

95

MULTITRACK RECORDING TECHNIQUES

You aren't limited to only four tracks with a 4-track machine; I've been able to generate clean 9-track tapes without noise-reduction units, and you can too.

Premixing. One easy way to generate six tracks is to mix together the first three recorded tracks into the machine's fourth track, thus leaving the first three tracks available for re-recording with new instruments or parts. However, premixing can be used in many situations to solve problems. Let's look at some examples for clarity.

Assume that you are recording a guitar-bass-drums-piano group, with two vocalists, and a synthesizer solo played by the keyboard player. You would record the drums, through microphones and a mixer, into track 1; then, to avoid leakage problems, you could take the guitar and bass directly into the board and into tracks 2 and 3 of the machine. As it stands, you have track 4 left over for everything else. But, you can mix the first three tracks together through your mixer and record the results in track 4. Now track 4 has the composite rhythm section; when you're satisfied with the mix, you can now erase the first three tracks. There's more to the art of mixing than just saying "mix it," but we'll cover that in the chapter on mixing.

Your next step would be to record the piano into track 1 (since it's an overdub, you have the additional bonus of eliminating leakage problems), the synthesizer solo into track 2, and the two vocal parts, mixed together, into track 3. So, there you have six tracks.

The only problem is that you had to generate the composite track, not from live signal sources, but from signals already present on the tape; so the composite track is a second-generation signal. Thus, not only do you have the hiss and distortion that accumulated during the original recording of the basic tracks, but you generate more hiss by re-recording those tracks into another track. Also, if you have any distortion on the original tracks, and you pick up more of it re-recording into track 4, the effect is multiplied, so you have to be very careful of tape saturation. If track 4 were to be recorded along with some other tracks into yet another open track, then it would be a third-generation signal with even less fidelity.

Let's look at this more closely: say that, in the previous example, after everything was recorded, it was decided that the vocals were a little off, and you wanted to add a lead guitar solo, and include a couple of horn parts. The only problem would be some added noise: you wipe the vocals from track 3, then premix track 4 (the rhythm track) and tracks 1 and 2 (piano and synthesizer lead) into track 3. Now, you have the guitar, bass, and drums present on track 3, along with two second-generation signals, i.e. the piano and synthesizer. Notice also that the premix is once again critical, since it's far too late to go back and alter the balance of the bass or drums. However, we have achieved the objective of opening up a few more tracks: we can recut the vocals into track 1 and clean them up, put the lead guitar solo into track 2, and the horn parts into track 4.

Unfortunately, though, you don't get something for nothing. The quality of second-generation material is far inferior to first-generation material, and third-generation signals (without benefit of noise reduction) are all but useless except under the most favorable conditions. As a result, it's best to minimize the number of times you have to ping-pong, something we can do with intelligent track management.

Perhaps a better way to handle the session just described would have been to record the drums into track 1, the bass into track 2, and the guitar and synthesizer parts—mixed together—into track 3. Then, while mixing these into track 4 through a mixer, add the piano part (see Figure 5-13). This does require someone to play the piano and someone to mix, though, so it isn't all that applicable to a single artist doing demo work. Now you have drums, bass, guitar, synthesizer, and piano all in track 4. Then, record the vocals into track 1, the lead guitar line into track 2, and the horns into track 3. There you have it—the exact same number of tracks as in the first example exist on the finished product, except that we've bypassed having to do any third-generation overdubs, and have thus managed to maintain a higher level of quality.

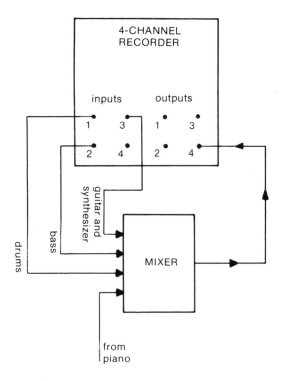

Premixing along with an instrument.

Figure 5-13.

The two-to-two bounce. What sounds like a dance step is actually a variation on the two-machine bounce we described earlier in this chapter. Again, the best way to illustrate this is with an example: a rock group wants to make a stereo demo that's as impressive as possible; suppose this is a group with guitar, bass, drums, keyboard, lead singer, and, additionally, all other band members sing backup. The first step is to mic the various instruments through a good mixer and set stereo locations for all the instrumental tracks. At this point, we don't include any vocals. After getting this mix, we send the left-channel output of the mixer into track 1 and the right-channel mixer output into track 2. So, we now have the full instrumental section residing in tracks 1 and 2. We then take those outputs and feed them into a mixer; also, we feed the four backup-vocal mics into this mixer and give them an appropriate stereo spread. We then bounce tracks 1 and 2, along with the vocals, into tracks 3 and 4. Now we have instrumental plus vocal backups, in stereo, in tracks 3 and 4, and we haven't gone beyond the second generation. We still have two tracks left: in

one we put the lead vocalist, and in the other we can put in lead guitar, plus maybe a couple of other sounds. We mix these four tracks down into a good machine, and end up with a good stereo mix of the band. If you want to get really fancy, you can add extra modifications, such as flanging effects, mixing in another lead guitar part to double the first part, and so on, as you mix down into the other machine.

A sticky problem you can find out about now rather than discover it by yourself at an embarrassing moment, and a way around it. After all this talk about ping-ponging, you might ask a very logical question. It seems that you could record on tracks 1 and 3, and premix them into track 4. So far, so good. **How about then recording into tracks 1 and 2, and premixing those into track 3?** That would give us three second-generation takes in track 4, and two more second-generation tracks in track 3, and we still have two tracks left over. But, unfortunately, we can't premix 1 and 2 into 3, and still have them remain in sync with the composite track in 4. Figure 5–14 shows why: We record into tracks 1 and 2 by monitoring from the record head (sel sync mode) on track 4, so that tracks 1 and 2 are recorded in sync with track 4. But when we switch to the playback heads on tracks 1 and 2 in order to take those signals and mix them into track 3, we run into a problem. While these signals hit the record head for track 3, the signal that we're synched to on track 4 is hitting the track 4 playback head. So, we have an out-of-sync situation: on playback, when both tracks 3 and 4 are in the play mode and are being monitored from the playback heads, track 3 is going to play back a fraction of a second later than track 4. The only way around this (which isn't too satisfactory but it's the best I can do) is to put track 3 in sync when you mix down on to your other machine after all the tracks are filled up, so that it remains synched to track 4, which should *not* be in the sync mode.

If you want to record additional material in tracks 1 and 2 after having mixed their previous contents into track 3, then monitor track 4 in the sync position, but don't listen to track 3 at all—it will be out of sync and will throw you off. After all four tracks are full again, mix down on to another machine with everything coming from the playback head

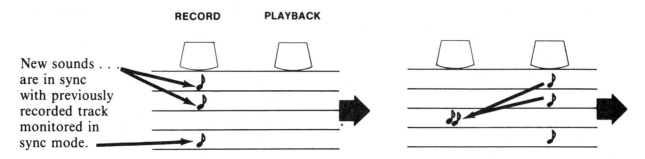

RECORD   PLAYBACK

New sounds . . . are in sync with previously recorded track monitored in sync mode.

By then mixing tracks 1 and 2 into 3, when we listen to track 4 on playback, track 3 is delayed.

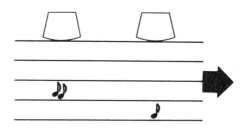

First track 4 hits the playback head, then track 3. However, playing track 3 back in sync mode (monitoring from record head) preserves synchronization with track 4.

Figure 5-14.

directly, *except for channel 3 which should be in the sync mode.* Although this puts track 3 in sync with the rest of the tracks, there is a price: the response and level in the sync mode is rather poor compared to direct monitoring from the playback head, so you will lose a fair chunk of frequency response. But it's a way to get seven second-generation-or-better tracks, unassisted by other people and without recording an instrument along with a premix.

Recording along with a premix. When you are premixing these various tracks together through your mixer, you are perfectly free to mix in another instrument along with the various tracks; this gets you another part without using another track. A problem arises, however, when you're doing solo artist material and you can't mix and play at the same time. Nonetheless, even under these conditions, you can probably add some drones, fills, percussion, harmonies, and other parts during lulls in the mixing; if you keep the mixing requirements simplified, you may even be able

to add a fairly complex part. Probably the best example would be playing a right-hand keyboard part on a synthesizer while doing the mixing with your left hand. Doesn't sound easy? Well, it isn't, but practice does make perfect, or at least a little more proficient.

SPECIAL EFFECTS

There are many ways you can manipulate your music in the studio; some of these methods, such as tape speed changes, are applicable *only* in a studio environment. I've demonstrated some of the most common methods on the sound sheet, and you will also probably recognize them from recordings.

Punching in. This trick sort of bridges the gap between simply using the tape recorder to advantage, and creating an actual 'effect.' With recorders that allow this operation, you can run the tape and, at any time during its travel, hit the record button and throw any tracks switched to 'record' into that mode. For example, say you have a vocal, and the

98

first verse is excellent but the chorus is a bit off. You run the tape and set up the mic; when the chorus comes in, punch the record button, have the singer do the part, and then stop the recorder to punch out again before you erase the rest of the track. The only problem with punching in is that it usually occurs when you are listening to tracks in the sync mode. Therefore, to monitor the track you want to punch in on, in time with the music, you must be in the sync mode, but then if you press the record button, the machine won't let you while you are in sync. So, you cannot monitor the track you are going to punch in on without a bit of difficulty, especially since its output selector must be set to 'tape,' whereas for recording it must be set to 'source' or 'input.' If you are monitoring a track, you will have to set both the output selector and sync buttons properly before punching in.

Punching in can be used in other ways: for example, let's say you have a song with two vocal parts—the singers sing a verse, go away to make room for an instrumental solo, then come back again into the verse. In a case like this you may be able to punch in another part while the vocals are out, sort of like a time-sharing arrangement. When a vocally oriented song ends on an instrumental fade-out, you can always use the vocal track to add another part and deepen the texture.

Here's another use for punching in: if you use effects boxes, unless you have the dandy, computerized kind, it probably takes you a bit of time to change sounds, turning all those knobs and all that, right? But with punching in, you can record the first part of a solo, change your settings, go back to the beginning of the solo, play it, and finally punch in where the second half begins. This is the technique illustrated on the soundsheet, and can be used very effectively: you can have vocals punch into guitar notes, and all kind of other special effects.

Crossfading. Crossfading usually applies to a situation where one cut segues into another cut; in other words, as one is fading out, the other one is fading in. In professional studios, this effect is usually implemented with multiple recorders; in a simple 4-track setup, you could have the basic track of one song recorded on one track, and the basic

track of the next song recorded on another track. If the beginnings and endings overlap, then with proper mixing you can accomplish a crossfading effect.

Backwards tape effects. The early pioneers of electronic music were very much into using tape modification to create new sounds, and much of what they discovered has been adapted into normal studio routine; backwards tape is an example of this. With early tape recorders, the recording head recorded over the full width of the tape, and therefore, the tape could only be recorded in one direction. If you turned the reels over (see Figure 5-15) and played the tape, the sounds came out 'backwards'—for example, a decaying note when played backwards, sounded like it was

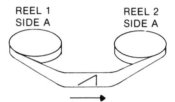

A sound that decays in level . . .

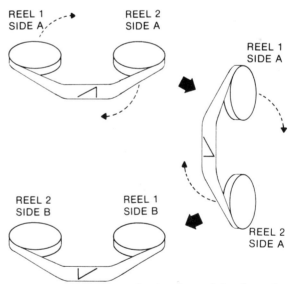

. . . sounds "backwards" when the tape reels are flipped over in the manner shown.

Figure 5-15.

coming up from nowhere to full volume. On relatively recent albums, Jimi Hendrix probably used backwards tape effects more than any other electric guitarist, although the Beatles' albums pretty much introduced the technique to popular music.

Pianos, guitars, voices, cymbals, and drums all sound quite unlike their normal selves when played backwards. Once you get your head adjusted to thinking of a melodic line, or rhythm, backwards, you can start playing with this technique.

With a 4-track recorder, you must be careful not to erase tracks accidentally when attempting backwards tape parts, as the position of the tracks changes when the tape is flipped over. Referring to Figure 5-16, let's say we have a multitrack tape with guitar, bass, and drums recorded in tracks 1, 2, and 3; we want to add a backwards guitar solo on track 4. Let the tape run through to the *end* of the song (start thinking backwards), then flip the reels over so that this ending now becomes the beginning of the tape going in the backwards direction. But notice that what we had recorded on track 1 is now being picked up as track 4 as far as the head is concerned, due to flipping the tape. Also, track 3 is now being picked up as track 2, and track 2 is being picked up as track 3. Therefore, we want to record our solo into what the machine sees as track 1, so that it turns into track 4 when the tape is flipped back over to its normal position.

Are you with me? Now, set up to record into track 1, and put all the other tracks into sync mode. Start the recorder. You will notice that the song is going by from end to beginning, so that when you lay down your part, you should start with the climax and end with the introduction. Although it may be hard to catch the exact meter of a song, the tempo will probably be pretty obvious, even when played backwards. Play along with the music as best you can; it's difficult, but luckily, upon playback, the backwards effect is so startling that it usually sounds like it's in time with the music, whether it actually is or not! Probably the best way to master this technique, like anything else, is to practice.

I'm a real fan of backwards effects. I use them all the time, and have developed a trick for cueing backwards parts: before flipping over the tape, if you have an extra track

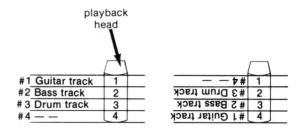

When the tape is flipped over, we hear the guitar through track 4, the bass through 3 and the drums through 2. If we record into track 1 or the record head, then it plays back through track 4 of the playback head when the tape is flipped back to normal.

Figure 5-16.

handy, record some type of sound to cue where the backwards part should begin and where it should end. You will like having those markers when you begin the actual solo itself. Make the sound percussive—like clicking drumsticks—so that the beat is easily recognizable when played backwards.

Preverb. This is reverb that builds up to a sound rather than decays away from it, and again takes advantage of backwards tape techniques. It's a little difficult to implement with a budget studio and 4-track machine, but you can still add preverb to tracks *if* there are other tracks open and if you don't have to sync the preverbed track to other tracks.

The procedure is as follows: Let's assume that you have a drum track in channel 1, and want to add preverb. You take that recorded part, flip the tape over, and listen; the drums should be picked up as track 4. Listen from the playback head, out of the sync mode, for best quality. Now, take that signal and add regular old reverb to it—lots of it, within the bounds of reason—and record that composite sound (backwards drums-plus-reverb) into another channel of the tape recorder, say track 2. Flip the tape over again. Track 3 (which we recorded as track 2) contains the re-recorded drums coming out straight this time, but the reverb is reversed, giving the preverb effect. Track 1 still has the original drum track, but it's out of sync compared to the new track 3. Either erase it to get it out of the way, or use it as an echo-type reinforcement for the preverbed drum track.

Tape echo. Although a tape recorder is limited in its abilities as a tape echo unit, it does do the job with a minimum amount of noise; the capability is built in to any three-head machine, whether you want it or not. The idea is to take some of the signal from a playback head, and feed it back into the record head of that channel. Say you have a situation where you have a guitar plugged into input 6 of a 6-channel input mixer, which goes to an output bus of all the channels that feed track 1 of the recorder. Now, by simply monitoring the tape output of track 1 and connecting it back into the mixer through another input (say input 1), you can regulate the amount of echo by working the channel 1 fader. Be sparing, though; too much echo sounds muddy and amateurish. Even a little bit of echo can add depth; but too much is impossible to deal with. The only disadvantage to this process is that by feeding the signal back onto itself, you also feed some of the noise back, resulting in a net increase in noise.

Since the echo-delay time depends upon how long it takes a signal, recorded at the record head, to hit the playback head and get into the loop again, faster tape speed means faster echo. The soundsheet illustrates both 7½ ips and 15 ips echo. Since 15 ips is usually used for quality home recording, that's the echo you usually have to work with. Although not good for long, slow, 'spacey' effects, echo at this speed does a good job of adding depth to instruments and voices.

Speed changes. Since tape speeds are related by a 2:1 ratio, a recording at 7½ ips, when played back at 15 ips, will be compressed into one half the time frame and will sound an octave higher. This fact can occasionally be put to good use in creating special effects. In one instance, when I was producing a guitar album, a harpsichord was required in a certain place; the only problem was that there was no harpsichord to be found. However, by slowing the tape down to 15 ips from 30 ips (this was a professional studio), I recorded a guitar part which, when sped up, had a timbre very similar to that of a harpsichord. Since many people have never heard a really good acoustic harpsichord, the illusion was all that much easier to create, especially with a little added reverb. Adding a 12-string guitar part in-

creased the apparent brightness of the sound until it actually became larger than life.

This effect can work the other way too, by slowing down sounds instead of speeding them up. Cymbals become gongs when dropped an octave; guitar parts become bass parts. If you only have a guitar and want to do a demo that includes a bass part, you can always start off at 7½ ips, speed up to 15 ips, lay down the guitar part, then slow back down again to get it into the bass range. But be forewarned: If you miss a note by a fraction of a second, that interval will be twice as long when slowed down. For this reason, it's usually easier and cleaner to speed up parts rather than slow them down.

If your recorder has a variable-speed gizmo, then you are in luck—you are no longer limited to simple octave changes. Some studios have outboard variable-speed adapters for their tape recorders, but I don't know how viable these are for home recording. Since the speed of a tape recorder is locked into the 60Hz signal generated by your power line, then by changing the line frequency you can make the motor speed up or slow down. However, to do this requires a separate source of variable-frequency sine waves to imitate a varying line frequency, which isn't too hard to find; but then you have to bring up this signal enough to power the tape recorder motor —i.e. 117 volts AC with enough current to handle the motor load. That is the hard part, as it requires a high-wattage, low-distortion amplifier that can handle an inductive load like a motor. As it so happens, a good hi-fi power amp will do the job, but this is a very expensive route to take. Additionally, using variable-speed devices, you can have overheating and stalling problems that can shorten your motor's life, or end it right there on the spot.

But if your machine already has variable speed, then that's another story. Slight alterations of sounds can create some stunning effects: if you add a drum part to a track that's sped up about 3%, then on playback, the drums will be slowed down by 3%. This means a lower tuning and a slightly longer decay, which can sound super with drums (particularly snare drums). Vocals, on the other hand, respond well to speeding up, if the difference is slight. For this, sing along with a track going at a slightly lower than normal speed. When you bring the track back up to speed, the voice will go up, too.

Using instruments with a variable-speed recorder is a little more difficult, since the tuning changes as the tape speed changes. This requires either transposition of the piece, or retuning, both of which are messy. Also, you have to 'tune' the track to the instrument. But this can have its advantages: if you are laying a piano track onto a piece of tape and the piano is flat by a quarter-tone, then slow the tape down to match the piano, and record along with that.

Phasing or flanging. This effect is almost impossible to achieve in a budget studio, but for the record, here is how it works in a professional studio (see Figure 5–17):

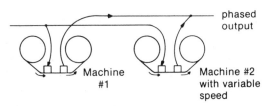

As speed changes, time delays and advancements create phasing.

Figure 5-17.

First, we need two tape recorders with identical distances between the record and playback heads; one of them must have variable speed. Then, we feed an audio signal into both tape recorders at the same time, with both recorders in the record mode. We then monitor, simultaneously, the outputs of both recorders. By slowly changing the speed of the variable-speed recorder, we create a time delay between the two outputs. One tape alternately lags behind or leads the other; when these two signals are added together, some frequencies are in phase and reinforce; others are out of phase and cancel. As the time delay changes in a continuous manner, the phase relationship changes in relation to it, giving rise to that ethereal, liquid, airplane-like, phasing or flanging sound.

Although it is expensive and time-consuming to accomplish this effect with two tape recorders, there is an alternative. In recent years, semiconductor technology has developed the no-moving-parts delay line. There are two ways to implement this type of system, drawing on two differing electronic technologies. The *digital delay line* employs computer parts and concepts, offers excellent performance, and is used in most professional studios to create predictable and stable delays without variable-speed machines; and the price is expensive. *Analog delay lines,* on the other hand, employ a technology that's noisier, less efficient, and more distortion-prone; but the advantage is its extremely low price (presently about 20% as costly as digital techniques).

The delay line accomplishes some of the same effects as a variable-speed tape recorder, but overall, it is more precise. Although you can implement simple time-delay games (like varying the delay of a signal to create flanging effects), you can also set the delay line to delay for a specific time, to counteract phase shift problems with microphones, to add a pseudo-reverb or doubling effect, and to create other sound modifying techniques.

Double-tracking. The purpose of double-tracking is to thicken recorded sounds, such as lead instruments or voices; this can only be accomplished in a multitrack environment (you can use delay lines to get similar effects, but it is just not the same). Again, an example illustrates the point best: If you have a basic track recorded in track 3, and nothing else on the other tracks, you have enough open tracks to do triple-tracking if desired. Let's say you add a vocal to track 2. You can then double-track it by re-recording another vocal, as identical as possible to the first one, into track 1. By playing these two back in unison, if the voices are together, the sound will appear to be one big voice rather than two little ones. This technique has been used for years to help give voices a push. And, you still have track 4 left over for something like a harmony line or instrument part.

The same principle can be applied to, say, lead guitar. By recording one memorized solo and then going back and duplicating it, the guitar sounds thick and big. You can even throw a few changes into the second part, although, in many cases, strict doubling sounds best.

You will note that many of the special effects we have dealt with so far involve the idea of making the sound bigger, fatter, thicker, and larger than life. This is one of the main reasons why professional tapes shine over amateur ones: the amateur doesn't give too much thought to this kind of enlarging process. But for music to come across the somewhat flat medium of a loudspeaker, then it has to really sparkle or it will get lost. For this reason and others, now is a good time to re-emphasize that playing in the studio is completely different from playing live.

Tape loops and using other machines. On one song I did, there was a basic track just waiting to have a solo on it, but I didn't feel comfortable with any of my solo ideas. Then, I thought of using a sound-effects solo instead —having a jet plane taking off during the spot previously held open for the solo part. I got out a sound-effects record and recorded it onto my cassette, hooked up the output of the cassette into the mixer, and cued up the tape. When it came time to record the plane onto the master tape, I switched the cassette deck into playback and transferred the sound.

Some electronic music fanatics I have met would use several tape recorders and drape tape from recorder to recorder, with the supply reel located on one recorder and the takeup reel on another, and would add a little help along the way with their hand to keep the tape running smoothly. When a sound was recorded on the first machine and played back on the second, there was a huge delay, limited only by how far apart the two recorders could sit and still handle the tape.

Another option is to create a tape loop with a certain repetitive sound on it (see

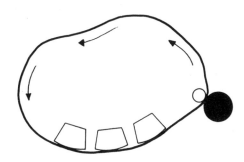

Tape loop creates repetitive sounds that repeat whenever they hit the playback head.

Figure 5-18.

Figure 5-18). By fitting the length of the loop to work with the transport of your specific machine, you can have an endlessly repeating rhythmic structure that lasts as long as it's playing. You can cut two measures of drums on a piece of tape, for example, splice one end to the other to form a loop, and there you have it—a constant drum track, which can be faded in and out. I've often thought it would be nice to have handy a loop of a really hot snare drum roll, so it could be faded in when desired. As you can probably tell, it's easy to let your imagination get carried away with tape recorders.

A NOTE ABOUT PURISTS

Although this type of attitude is becoming less common, for many years people looked contemptuously upon electronic devices as 'gimmicks,' which were somehow devised solely to mask a lack of technique. I remember once many years ago when I came up with a phase shifter and figured I had the world by the tail: at that point, there were no commercially available models, and I was sure that the first company I approached would get highly excited. So I set up an appointment and demonstrated it; after the short demonstration, I strode expectantly over to the company officials. One of them said, "That's the worst thing I ever heard. Why, it makes your guitar sound like an airplane or something." I never bothered to take it anywhere else. A similar event had happened several years before with a different company, when I had tried to convince them that a compressor was a really neat toy for guitarists. The point is that many people don't like being faced with something unfamiliar, or strange-sounding. Those who do seek the unfamiliar are the ones who thrive best in a studio environment.

A concert uses acoustic, or acoustic and electric, media, but the recording studio is a *purely* electrical medium. As such, it is somewhat remote and distant. A superb, acoustic, live concert, such as one featuring a string quartet, will always sound different from the way it sounds on tape, since the studio microphones react poorly to signals, subtleties are lost in the acoustics, noise creeps into the process at every stage. It strikes me as funny to hear a recording of an acoustic band, and then be told that "no electronics were used."

Wouldn't a tape recorder and mixing board be called 'electronic'?

I am not down on any particular type of music; it's very difficult to find music I don't like, whether it's classical, electronic, rock, or jazz. If the players are sincere and real, and sometimes even when they aren't, the music comes through. Don't exclude yourself from any alluring possibilities because of a misplaced sense of tradition. Baroque composers used phase shifters, extensive reverberation, and effects in their compositions. Sound incredible? Well, listen to a pipe organ in a cathedral sometime. The various standing waves and resonating pipes create an effect like hundreds of phase shifters, with the body of the building giving excellent and lush reverb characteristics. Different organ voicings are just like synthesizer presets.

So, don't just treat the studio as a static *reproducer* of reality, or your sounds will be static, too. The studio is a *processor* or reality; use the studio and work with it as an extension of your music, not as a barrier to it. If something hasn't been done before, go ahead and try it; Bach might very well have used sequencers, had they been available. The effects that may be *passe* years from now are still waiting to be discovered; you might as well contribute to, and share in, those discoveries.

NOISE-REDUCTION TECHNIQUES

Multitrack recording, without the parallel development of noise-reduction systems, would never have achieved the popularity that it has. Because adding another track of program material adds more noise, with a 16- or 24-track recorder, the noise contribution is substantial. Although we're not talking about 16-track machines for home use just yet, noise reduction is still highly beneficial to us, since consumer-type recorders offer inferior signal-to-noise ratios compared to professional products. In fact, I doubt whether anyone could have considered the cassette a high-fidelity medium if the tape industry had not adopted the Dolby B noise-reduction system to reduce unpleasant background hiss.

Let's see how noise creeps into the system: in Figure 5-19, we see a large (high-level) signal about to be superimposed on a piece of tape. The residual noise level, or hiss, of the tape, is shown in crosshatch, and shows up on playback. Luckily, with this large signal, the noise is small enough so that it is swamped by the signal, and we can't perceive the noise.

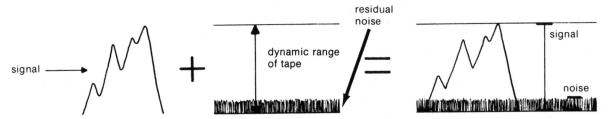

Large signal, small amount of noise yields favorable signal-to-noise ratio.

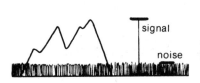

Smaller signal, with equal amount of residual noise, gives a much worse signal-to-noise ratio.

Figure 5-19.

104

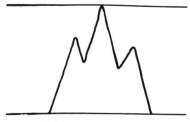

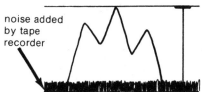

A signal with the dynamic range shown . . .

can be compressed to decrease dynamic range . . .

which can then be recorded more easily, since it fits within the tape recorder's dynamic range.

noise added by tape recorder

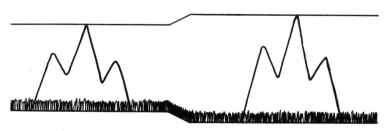

Expanding the signal on playback restores the original dynamic range and pushes noise further down, thus improving the signal-to-noise ratio.

Figure 5-20.

Now observe what happens to a low-level signal: when it gets played back, the noise represents a significant part of the signal, and we hear it as an objectionable, non-musical part of the sound.

In the early days of recording, recording engineers used to 'ride the gain' to offset these effects. This meant that during low-level passages, the recording gain was turned up to change the low-level signal into a high-level signal. As a result, on playback, the noise would be less noticeable; but the disadvantage, of course, was in decreased dynamic range. Although the passage may have *sounded* soft because the players were playing their instruments softly, *electrically,* the signal level was the same as when the instruments were played loudly. If this sounds familiar, that's because we're describing a sort of manual compressor, where low-level signals are raised, and loud peaks reduced, in order to match the dynamic range of the tape, and tape recorder electronics. Riding gain requires an alert engineer who knows every nuance of a piece, however. If the gain is turned way up in order to bring a low-level passage above the noise, and a

sudden peak occurs when the engineer is napping, you can have tremendous tape overload. This problem stimulated the development of the compressor, which rides gain automatically.

But although we've improved the signal-to-noise ratio a bit, we have seriously interfered with the dynamic range, and hence the musicality of the original signal. Wouldn't it be nice if, upon playback, a complementary amount of *expansion* could be added to offset the effects of compression, thus making the soft passages soft again, and giving back the full musical peaks that we had to eliminate to prevent tape saturation? The good news is that this is possible, and it forms the basis of every professional noise-reduction system. The bad news is that is is very difficult to get the expansion to exactly track the degree of compression, and therein lies the high price tag, and sophisticated engineering, behind present-day noise-reduction systems.

The expansion that we add also has a very desirable side effect: it cuts down substantially on the noise, as Figure 5–20 indicates. When our low-level passage is expanded to bring it back up to proper volume, the tape hiss it picked up along the way is *attenuated by an equivalent amount.* So, we have managed to restore the original dynamic properties of the music, but along the way, the noise got ditched. That's pretty slick.

You will note, however, that there is a catch: a piece of music must first be modified through precise compression, which we can consider as encoding the signal, and then it must be equivalently decoded (expanded) through very sensitive circuitry. Thus, using this type of two-ended noise-reduction system, we cannot improve non-encoded tapes that happen to have noise; we can only reduce the noise on tapes that have been encoded using the noise-reduction system of our choice. There are ways of dealing with noise reduction for tapes that have already been recorded; although these are not as popular for professional recording as those using the double-ended approach, these single-ended systems are useful, and demonstrate some of the concepts of noise reduction. Now, let's look in detail at various ways of reducing noise:

1) *Manual noise reduction.* There is a lot that you, as the operator, can do to reduce noise build-up, without using any elaborate, commercial devices. One rule is to keep your signal sources as clean as possible. For example, let's say that you are recording an electric guitar through an amplifier that has a fair amount of hiss. By feeding the guitar directly into the board, you can eliminate that amp hiss. If the player insists on using the amp to get a certain sound, then you can do a variation on the old 'gain-riding trick,' and turn down the recording level during moments when the guitarist isn't playing. Then, you can hope that while he is playing, his notes will mask the noise; when he isn't playing, you've got the fader turned down so that the amp noise doesn't leak through. Again, this requires an alert engineer. And again, you can see a possible problem: there is a limit as to how fast you can cut the fader in and out. If you only have to shut it off on certain passages, that's no problem. But if you want to turn

the fader on and off between notes, then you have to have nimble fingers and a high degree of skill, or, you can use a noise gate.

2) *Noise gates.* A noise gate (see Figure 5-21) consists of a mutable amplifier and appropriate trigger circuitry. The amplifier is like a normal amplifier, except that it may be easily muted or squelched so that it gives no gain. Thus, the amp has two possible states: full on and full off. The trigger circuit controls when the amp is full on ('gate open') and full off ('gate closed'). This trigger circuit has an input that connects up to the signal you are processing, and is *level-sensitive.* If the signal appearing at its input is greater than a certain reference level (which is controllable), the trigger tells the gate to open. If the signal is below the level you set, the trigger tells the gate to close.

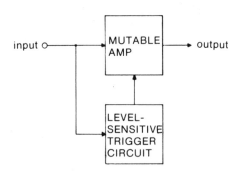

When input is above a certain level, trigger turns on amp. Below a certain level, trigger turns off amp.

Figure 5-21

Let's observe the system in action. In Figure 5-22, we have a repetitive snare-drum signal, which we represent as one with a rapid attack and fast decay. Superimposed on this signal is some noise; it can be any kind of noise: hiss, room rumble, leakage from another instrument, whatever. With the noise-gate effect switched out, the amplifier stays at full gain and the total signal (noise-plus-drum) passes through the amplifier. Now, we switch the noise gate in and set the trigger input *just above* the noise level. What happens? The noise isn't strong enough to trigger the

Diagram of three snare drum beats and noise...

with noise gate threshold set above noise . . .

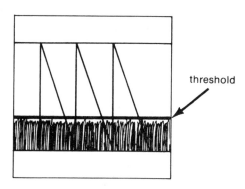

threshold

Dynamic range decreases, noise drops out because amp is off except when signal exceeds threshold.

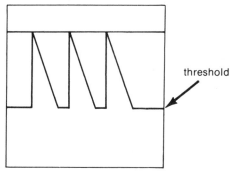

threshold

Figure 5-22.

gate into opening, so that gate stays closed and we don't hear the noise at the output of the noise gate's amp. But when a drum signal occurs, it triggers the gate, which opens up and lets the drum-plus-noise signal through. However, although we haven't attenuated the noise like a fancier noise-reduction system, we have nonetheless masked it with the intense

drum sound, so we perceive a lot less total noise coming out of the noise gate. This also has tremendous applications for getting rid of leakage.

But there are some heavy drawbacks. For one, noise gates work best on signals that don't need to be cleaned up too much. For example, in Figure 5-23, if we set the trigger control, or *threshold,* so that all noise is cut out, we don't affect the signal too much. But look at Figure 5-24, where the noise is really severe. Eliminating this noise also means getting rid of substantial portions of the signal, which would definitely sound unpleasant.

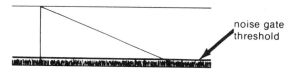

noise gate threshold

Slowly decaying piano chord.

Figure 5-23.

noise gate threshold

Slowly decaying piano chord.

Figure 5-24.

Another drawback occurs with instruments that have a long decay time. Let's say you are running a piano through a noise gate, and you hit a loud, long, sustaining chord. At first, the piano masks the noise. But as the piano decays, the noise becomes more and more prominent, until the piano's amplitude goes below the trigger level, at which point the gate abruptly closes. This switching action sounds very unpleasant, as though you had just switched something off. To further complicate matters, not all instruments decay uniformly: e.g. a guitar can, towards the end of its decay, go below the trigger threshold, then above it, then below, and then maybe even above again; and every time it passes the threshold point, you hear the signal-plus-noise, then nothing, the signal-plus-noise again, and so on. This sounds really rotten, as if someone were just switching the signal on and off in a random fashion.

The best time to use noise gates is on single-instrument tracks, rather than with complex material involving lots of instruments. In the latter case, there are so many signals going above and below the threshold that you can get some amazingly choppy effects. Noise gates are also very effective with vocals, since vocal lines are seldom required throughout a song. During instrumental passages, intros, and the like, a noise gate shuts off the microphone and tape noise. This does require a singer who understands the noise-gate process and who doesn't do something like breathe at an improper moment, thus causing the gate to open and letting the breath through.

One of the best times to use noise gates is when you are premixing three tracks into the fourth track of a 4-track recorder. If, for example, the instrument on track 2 begins two measures after track 1, and track 3 begins four measures after track 1, during those moments when there is no signal, the noise gates can shut the tracks off and prevent any noise contribution. When the tracks do come in, the noise gates can be left in or switched out. Thus, you end up with a composite track that is much cleaner than it would be without noise gates. Also (since mixing three tracks down into the fourth implies that you need to create room for overdubs), much of the choppiness of the noise gates is masked by extra overdubs and application of reverb.

Noise gates by themselves are no panacea; skillful engineering, combined with noise gates, gives the best results.

NOISE REDUCTION THROUGH EQUALIZATION

There is a moderately effective way to curb tape hiss: simply eliminate the high-frequency part of a signal, since that is where tape hiss is most obvious and objectionable. The price you pay is negligible with an instrument like bass, which has little high-frequency content; but removing all the treble from a cymbal can make it sound terrible. So, cutting back on high frequencies isn't always a solution; but in general, there is no reason to give a signal more frequency response than it needs. This principle applies at low frequencies, too;

if you have picked up some hum on a lead guitar solo, rolling off the bass will take little away from the solo (it may even help the solo to cut and sound a bit brighter), but any hum will be substantially reduced.

Using noise gates in conjunction with high-frequency rolloff can make bass, bass drum, and rhythm guitar tracks sound almost noiseless on the tape.

THE BURWEN NOISE-REDUCTION SYSTEM

As noise-gating automates manual gain riding, so the Burwen noise-reduction system automates noise reduction through equalization. This is a single-ended system that works not on encoded tapes, but on any type of signal source. In this sense it is applicable to noisy guitars, effects units, microphone pre-amps, reverb units, and so on.

The principle of operation is that if there is a lot of high-frequency content in a signal, it will mask any noise that is present. If there is no high-frequency content, then there is no point in having full-frequency response since the only signal you would hear would be tape hiss. So, the frequency response of the Burwen unit is continually re-adjusted to fit the program material. When highs are present, the Burwen unit can pass signals up to 30kHz. If, on the other hand, the energy of the signal starts to poop out at around 5 or 6kHz, then the Burwen filter restricts itself to a 5 or 6kHz frequency response, thus neatly cutting out any tape hiss above that frequency.

Figure 5–25 shows the implementation. The heart of this system is a voltage controlled, low-pass filter. If you play synthesizer, you already know exactly what that means; but remember the section on equalization? This low-pass filter is the same as the low-pass filter described there, except that it is 'tuned' (i.e. the cutoff frequency is varied) through a programmable voltage rather than through a knob. In the case of the Burwen unit, the point at which it decides to restrict the high frequencies can be varied by applying a voltage to the *control input* of this filter. This controlling voltage is derived from the actual signal through a complicated extraction process, whose major purpose is to respond to the high-frequency content of the signal, and open and close the filter accordingly. Unlike the

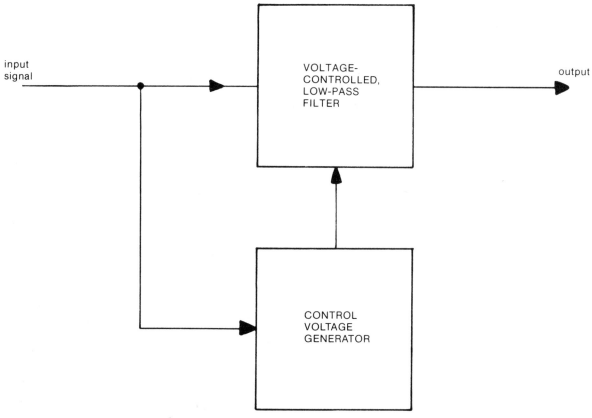

input
signal

VOLTAGE-
CONTROLLED,
LOW-PASS
FILTER

output

CONTROL
VOLTAGE
GENERATOR

The control voltage generator responds to the high-frequency content of the input signal, and tunes the filter accordingly to restrict bandwidth to the minimum necessary for full fidelity.

Figure 5-25.

noise gate, note that this is not a switched, on-off action but rather a smooth, continuous type of process that follows the signal.

Of all noise-reduction systems, the Burwen probably has gained the least amount of acceptance for reduction of tape hiss *per se,* as the dbx and Dolby systems we discuss next do a far more dramatic job. However, the ability to process signals or dirty signal sources that have already been recorded is a very valuable option to have under certain conditions.

THE dbx SYSTEM

For a while the Dolby system was the only one to grace recording studios, but in recent years the dbx system has found more and more homes. This is a straight compression-expansion system, along with some pre-emphasis and de-emphasis. In many ways, the dbx is the ultimate in automated gain riding during record and complementary expansion during playback.

Figures 5–26 through 5–28 show the dbx process. In record mode, the signal is precisely compressed in a 2:1 ratio. As a result, 100dB of dynamic range can be compressed into 50dB of dynamic range; in effect, the dynamic range of a live instrument can finally fit into the limited dynamic range of tape and disc systems. The hardware used to implement this consists of a voltage-controlled amplifier, and a precision circuit that controls the amplifier, depending on the magnitude of the input signal. In this case, as the signal increases in level, the gain of the amplifier *decreases,* and as the signal decreases in level, the gain of the amplifier *increases* (just like riding gain). On playback, this compressed signal goes through another voltage-controlled amplifier, again controlled by another precision control circuit;

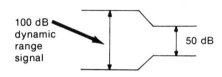

During record, the input signal is compressed by a 2:1 ratio, so that 100dB of dynamic range compresses down to 50dB—well within the dynamic range capabilities of a tape recorder.
Figure 5-26.

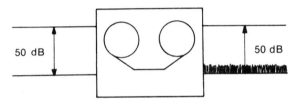

After the compressed signal goes through the recorder, it exists with the same dynamic range — but the signal has also picked up a bit of tape hiss during recording.

Figure 5-27. *The dbx System.*

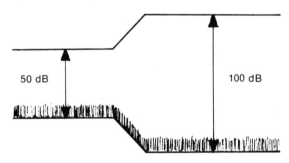

After 1:2 expansion, the original dynamic range is restored, and the tape hiss is pushed down to the lowest level possible—frequently down to inaudibility.
Figure 5-28.

but this circuit *increases* the gain of the amp for an increase in input signal, and *decreases* the gain for a decrease in signal level (thus, expansion). As long as you expand exactly as much as you compress, then in theory the output signal will exactly duplicate the input signal—and once again, as we increase the dynamic range on playback, the noise picked up as tape hiss from the machine gets expanded back down into nothingness. There

are limits to the accuracy obtainable with the tracking compressor-expander scheme; but the dbx system does a good job.

By working on the complete signal, with no attention paid to specific frequencies where hiss is most objectionable, types of noise other than straight hiss, such as modulation noise, hum, room rumble, air conditioning, and that sort of thing, disappear also. Boosting the high frequencies on record and cutting them on playback also contributes to reducing the noise problems.

THE DOLBY SYSTEM

This, the brainchild of Ray Dolby, is the one that started it all. It is actually two systems: the Dolby A, which is the professional model; and the Dolby B, the kind you find in cassette players and in equipment for home studios. We'll look at the B first, since it is simpler.

The Dolby B, unlike the dbx, concentrates on the high-frequency areas of a signal, since that is mostly where the tape hiss is a problem. The Dolby process is not a broadband, compression-expansion-type system, but rather boosts and cuts the response of a single high-frequency band. When we talk about a high-level signal, we mean a signal with lots of energy in the high-frequency band selected by Dolby. In Figure 5-29, we see that, on record, high-level signals pass through the Dolby unmodified, since their presence will mask any tape hiss on playback. But low-level signals have their high frequencies boosted by about 10dB, with the boosting starting at 5kHz and extending upwards as frequency increases. Again, like with the dbx, we rely on some precision signal-analyzing circuitry to perform the control functions necessary for this boosting to happen in a predictable way; and again, we have a similarly sophisticated detection scheme on playback. Strong playback signals pass through the Dolby unchanged; but the low-level signals precipitate a reduction of high-frequency response by acting on a low-pass filter. The signal returns to its normal, non-boosted state, and with it goes the high-frequency tape hiss accumulated during record.

The Dolby A does not use frequency-shaping, but rather is based on a principle that is similar to that used with compression-

110

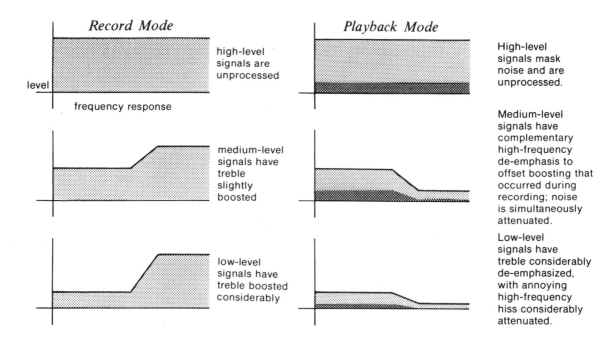

Record Mode

level

frequency response

high-level signals are unprocessed

medium-level signals have treble slightly boosted

low-level signals have treble boosted considerably

Playback Mode

High-level signals mask noise and are unprocessed.

Medium-level signals have complementary high-frequency de-emphasis to offset boosting that occurred during recording; noise is simultaneously attenuated.

Low-level signals have treble considerably de-emphasized, with annoying high-frequency hiss considerably attenuated.

Figure 5-29.

With the dbx system, which is not frequency dependent, our graphs only showed the dynamic range. with Dolby, however, which processes different frequencies in a different fashion, we need to look at the frequency response of the full signal.

expansion-type noise-reduction systems. Unlike the dbx, it splits the spectrum into four audio bands, and works on each of these separately. Each of these four bands contains different types of noise problems; the low (80Hz and below) band has hum and rumble problems; the low-mid band (80Hz–3kHz) has crosstalk and modulation noise problems; the remaining two high-frequency bands (3kHz on up and 9kHz on up, respectively) concentrate on tape hiss and modulation noise. The system gives a broadband 10dB improvement in signal-to-noise ratio, unlike the Dolby B, which only offers a signal-to-noise improvement in the upper-frequency response areas.

One tremendous advantage of the Dolby system is that it operates only on low-level signals. Thus, any mistracking between the record and playback modes is hardly noticeable, since a small percentage of error on an already soft signal is hard to detect; with a high-level signal, even a small error can sound quite obvious.

There are other noise-reduction systems, by Kenwood, JVC, and so on; but these are almost all exclusively consumer-oriented and are not in use at major recording studios. The overwhelming preference is for Dolby A and dbx systems. For home recording, both the Dolby B and dbx consumer systems have their adherents also. However, due to the dramatic results possible with dbx (up to 30dB noise improvement, compared to 10dB for the Dolby) and the less critical home environment, dbx seems to be a winner. It is also relatively affordable.

DOES NOISE REDUCTION INTERFERE WITH THE SOUND?

Engineers have endless and very opinionated discussions about noise-reduction systems: whether they color the sound, whether you can really hear the dbx while it is working, and so on. Well, any time you pass a signal through an electronic circuit, it's going to be altered—period. It just so happens that noise also goes away when altered according to the wishes of a noise-reduction unit; so if you want to get rid of noise, you are going to have to mess with the signal. I have used both Dolby A and dbx systems, and I do feel there is a very subtle coloration of sound, but in different ways for the different systems. The major complaint I hear about dbx is that you can "hear the thing working." A carefully set up and aligned unit should be undetectable, but electronic circuits are never perfect, so any mistracking—no matter how miniscule—is going to be noticed by an engineer; after all, his livelihood depends upon being able to hear infinitesimal changes of sound. Yes, sometimes you can hear it work if you are a perfectionist, but I'm willing to deal with that for 30dB of noise reduction. The Dolby has its critics too; the most common argument is that instruments lose a bit of 'life.' Possibly this is because the Dolby splits the audio spectrum into four bands, so it is conceivable that the fundamental of an instrument could be processed differently from the harmonics. Another problem is that the Dolby must be carefully calibrated before use. I have heard engineers say things like "I'd never use Dolby for rock and roll recording; dbx is best for that," and "I'd never use dbx, or Dolby, for live recording because it removes immediacy," and a lot more. But the bottom line is very simple: if you object to tape hiss, and if you want to avoid hiss build-up while overdubbing, then you must use some form of noise reduction. And although you can nit-pick them, they are really quite sophisticated, and have advanced the quality of sound tremendously, for hi-fi enthusiasts and musicians alike.

A few other comments on noise reduction: Noise problems are most acute with multitrack recorders, because the more tracks you have, the more tracks of noise you have. So if you can afford an 8-track recorder, you'll probably have to afford noise reduction too, if you really want to get the most out of the device.

Neither the Dolby B nor the dbx systems have the market sewn up, and as a result there is no 'standard' noise-reduction system (except with cassettes, which have pretty much gone over exclusively to Dolby). So, a tape recorded through Dolby will not play back through a dbx unit.

Chapter 6:
Mixing And Assembling The Master Tape

MIXING

Now that you have all these tracks recorded on your multitrack master tape, it's time to learn about mixing them down to a mono or stereo master. This process can make or break the sound of your music, and is critical. Also, at this stage you may introduce further changes and modifications that can add an extra range of effect to your music. You can subtly alter the tone of instruments to bring them further out in front (more prominence), or place them more in the background. You can add echo and reverb to soften the sound and give a sense of depth. You can fade out portions that don't fit, and do some all-important editing and cleaning up. In short, you can do a lot with a mix, whether you are premixing three rhythm tracks into a composite fourth track, or mixing all your tracks down into a master tape.

Before we go any further, you should know that mixing is one of the most delicate and intense operations of the recording process; it is also one of the most difficult, and requires the most objectivity. Now, all of a sudden, we have to drastically shift our emphasis: we are no longer trying to make signals that fit into our tape recorder, we want to make sounds that satisfy our ears and the ears of other listeners. Of course, we still need

to take certain technical matters into account, but the primary emphasis of a mix is on music. Let's examine some of the problems we face in trying to make a good mix.

THE SLIPPERY NATURE OF SOUND

If you stop and think about it a moment, hearing is a very intricate process, what with the idea of these air waves impinging on little hairs inside your head, then being translated and processed by the brain. So, it's no wonder that some bugs creep into the system. Here are the most difficult ones to deal with:

1) *Sound takes a finite amount of time to travel from one place to another.* Because the perception of a sound depends upon how far away you are from the source of it, your ears face quite a set of difficulties. Sound waves bounce off of walls, concrete, and other hard surfaces, but are absorbed by soft surfaces. As a result, if you are sitting in the middle of a room, you are hearing several sound waves: the sound source itself, some reflections that result in reinforced frequencies, some reflections that cancel other frequencies, time delays, uneven frequency response, and so on. No

matter what your listening environment, if not treated acoustically, it will color your perception of the sound.

2) *The human ear is far from perfect.* It is a marvelous and amazing transducer, but we must recognize that it has some limitations. Because of the ear's structure, sounds will have slightly different pitches at different volume levels. This isn't too serious a problem with mixing, as sounds tend to be within the same general range. A far more serious problem, is the ear's loss of bass response at lower listening levels as mentioned in the beginning of this book.

Studies show that virtually every person has a different hearing response; one aspect in common is that, at very high listening levels, bass response will almost be the same as response to trebly sounds; as the volume gets progressively lower, the loss of bass response becomes more severe. As a result, when you mix you can never be sure of the actual bass content because *it changes almost every time you listen to it.* The best route is to take an average reading of the sound: see how a mix sounds at low volume levels, high volume levels, from another room—does the bass boom through and shake the walls, or is it still balanced compared to other instruments? It doesn't hurt to listen through other speakers on other people's systems. Do make sure that a system is as flat as possible when you listen, though—some people may have the loudness button pushed in, or the treble cranked all the way up.

3) *The human ear hears less treble as it ages, or if it is abused.* Delicate mechanism that it is, the ear dislikes prolonged exposure to loud volume levels. This can cause problems not only with the highest frequencies that you hear, but with the midrange as well. Some studies have shown that engineers who mix at very high volume levels develop an uneven hearing response, which certainly seems to be detrimental to the cause of good music! Also, after a person reaches the age of about 25, treble response of ear goes down, whether it is abused or not. I wonder if some of the new albums have so much treble because it is the vogue, because the performers are getting older, or because all concerned have had their ears blasted for years by loudspeakers. You should take good care of your hearing.

4) *Playback systems do not all have the same response.* If you play a recording on a kid's record player, you probably won't hear much bass or treble and the distortion will be terrible. The example is extreme, but the comparison is valid: studios spend thousands and thousands of dollars on a product that is frequently played over a two-dollar speaker and listened to by someone who cannot differentiate between a synthesized instrument and the real thing. Therefore, in addition to all the minute details of sound that you must attend to while mixing, you must pay particular attention to the overall effect that you are creating, to the general mood and character of the piece. Even if a playback system is inferior, the mood can come through. If your music must be played on only the finest equipment in order to sound good, it's probably not mixed or recorded well enough. It takes a *really fine mix* to sound good on anything from an AM transistor radio to a superb stereo. Very few producers have this knack; those that do have it command very high fees, and deservedly so.

THE MIXING ATTITUDE

Now that you have some background on what we are up against, let's generalize a bit more and talk about the mixing attitude. If you, without being seen, could look at an engineer during a mixdown session, you would most likely see someone with a totally glazed look on the face, staring at a couple of meters. The average mixdown engineer does appear to be in a trance while his hands make extremely precise and gentle movements with faders, equalizers, and various controls. Actually, mixing is almost like a form of meditation; your concentration on the music has to be so outstanding that you, in essence, become one with it, familiar with every little tiny segment and nuance. Mixing can be a very draining experience, requiring unwavering concentration over a period of several hours; figure that every minute of final product translates into at least 30 minutes of mix time.

Before you even begin touching dials, put on your mixing head and remember a few points:

1) *This is going to take a while.* Get comfortable, have a glass of water handy, but not where it can spill into the equipment, and have a notepad to take notes on the mix as it progresses.

2) *Don't just take the first mix.* Mix and mix until you get something that feels right. Then, listen to it as if you had a magnifying ear. Is there anything you don't like? If there is, you had better deal with it now or live with it every time you listen to the piece of music. Listen on a variety of systems, under a variety of circumstances; one trick used in many major studios is to switch between their normal pair of super-speakers, and some smaller, car-radio-type speakers, for comparison. All of this will help give you the feedback necessary to make yet another mix that is better. Listen as critically as possible. Now is the time to make changes. Don't be satisfied with less than the best; if you are, you will probably regret it later.

3) *There are a lot of dials to turn.* If you have a friend or assistant who can help you, it might not be a bad idea to get into the habit of working with a helper. Even mixing a simple 4-track tape always seems to require more than two hands.

SETTING UP FOR THE MIX

Start off by getting back to ground zero with your mixer: remove any equalization, any reverb, effects, preamps, everything—just listen to the signal from the tape machine. Make sure that you don't have some tracks in sync and some not, and that all other machine switches are correctly set. Let's limit ourselves to premixing for now, and assume that you have recorded drums, bass, and rhythm guitar, in tracks 1, 2, and 3, and you want to mix them into track 4 so you can re-use tracks 1 through 3 for other instruments.

The general progression is to listen to the sound of each instrument by itself, and make the proper adjustments for a 'good sound' (now there are two poorly-defined words); then listen to the instruments in various combinations, attempting to set up the best possible balance. Here is a typical scenario:

Listen to the drums alone. How do they sound? Do any of the drums boom, or sound dead? Does the bass drum sound too prominent? Do the cymbals dominate? Maybe you made some mistakes when you set up mics on the drums, and the high hat was too prominent. Luckily, many of these problems can be eliminated through proper equalization. Equalization, as we have mentioned before, is a very delicate process, so be careful not to overcompensate. With a sophisticated equalizer, you might be able to place a controlled amount of cut at a frequency that's almost identical to the bass drum's, (or any other drum's, for that matter), and eliminate over-prominence. Cymbals may be trimmed by cutting back on the high-frequency response, although this removes much of the beautiful sheen.

While you are setting up the equalization, bear in mind that the drums are not going to exist in a vacuum, but will need to fit in with the music as a whole. Some effects, which might sound super on the drum track alone, may sound horrid when combined with the rest of the track, so be on the lookout. Don't overdo things, and if you don't *need* equalization, then leave things alone.

After equalizing the straight drum track so that it sounds just right, turn your attention to the reverb. Bring up the reverb-return fader and advance the reverb-send for the drum channel(s). Listen carefully to strike a compromise between too little reverb, which sounds dry, and too much reverb, which sounds muddy and indistinct. Also, try to keep the reverb-send level as high as possible, to optimize your signal-to-noise ratio.

Run through the drum track again, and perform any minor control tweakings, until everything sounds just dandy to your ears. Now, switch off the drums, rewind the tape, and start in on the bass.

With the bass, once more we work for the 'right' sound. But bass is a very powerful low-frequency instrument, and must be carefully handled. Compression or limiting is often used with bass to keep the bottom end in line; also, modulation noise tends to be more of a problem with bass than with other instruments, because there is so little high-frequency content to mask any noise. In my experience, the best route to take with bass is to mix it with the idea of obtaining a smooth, uniform sound, free of excessive dips or peaks in level. In this way, you create a relatively constant bass that, along with the drums, serves as a good rhythmic reference throughout the track. You can try adding reverb to bass, but don't be surprised if you don't like the results. Bass is diffuse enough as it is, way down toward the lower limit of our hearing, and reverb just tends to muddy things up more.

Having dispensed with the bass, we can now turn our attention to the guitar. For the sake of argument, let's say that, after listening to the guitar, it sounds just fine to us. It's supposed to be somewhat mellow to fit in with a sort of jazz feel, and since it does that, we simply leave it as is, with only a trace of reverb added for warmth and depth.

Now, we come to balancing the tracks relative to each other. This is the key to premixing. Once the tracks are mixed in the *correct* balance, then in the final mix, the drums/bass/guitar combination can be raised or lowered in level as required, and the instruments will (hopefully) still maintain the proper balance relative to each other.

Now you want to set up the drums and bass at the same time. How do they sound together? Like a good, tight, bottom end? Or mushy and flaccid? Perhaps the bass drum now sounds too prominent with the addition of the bass, in which case you just have too many low frequencies. So, maybe you should pull a little bass from the drum track and keep them from fighting. Listen to these two tracks, making sure they don't overwhelm each other. Now, try for a balance between bass and guitar. Aha! When they are combined, we get hit with a surprise: the mellow guitar part gets kind of hidden by the bass, and some of the guitar's low notes also get swallowed up. One possible solution is to add a little midrange boost to the guitar, to make it stand out a bit more; perhaps a slight cut in bass response does the trick. The possibilities are endless; listen to them all and choose the one that's best; and remember that every change you make involves some kind of tradeoff.

So you got your bass and drum balanced, then your bass and guitar; now try listening to all three at once. Maybe you will have to make a few more changes, like adding a little more guitar level to get out over the drums; maybe you will want to pull back a bit on the bass and replace some of the bass EQ, which we removed from the drums a while back, to bring out the bass drum more, thus accenting beat over melody. You have a tremendous variety of options, and don't expect to choose exactly the right one the first time you sit down to do a serious mix. It takes practice, lots of feedback listening on other systems, comments from people who preferably *don't* like your music, *and* very critical self-analysis. If something doesn't sound like you want it to, keep trying. If a track doesn't make it, replace it now—before you go any further—or maybe scrap the thing entirely, and start over with a different outlook.

A final point: On my board, part of the mixing ritual is to set the noise gates for the various tracks. You may not use noise gates, but if you use any kind of noise-reduction system, make sure you press the right buttons for record and the right buttons for playback.

So now you have your premixed rhythm track sitting there in track 4, and you are ready to erase the first three tracks to do some more recording (making sure track 4 is in sync when you listen to it, of course). But, don't do any erasing quite yet. Let the mix of the basic track sit around for a day or two, and listen to it carefully. Picture it in the context of the song as a whole, listen to it under different circumstances and at different times of day (you respond differently to sound at different times of the day and night). You should only continue when you are completely satisfied with your premix. If you are really hot and you just can't wait, at least listen to the basic track several times before proceeding. Once you erase the first three tracks, they are gone forever.

With an 8-track machine, premixing can be even more fun: you can record percussive stuff exclusively on the first seven tracks, then mix them into track 8 and still have seven tracks left to go. Incidentally, you can see one reason why stereo is a problem with 4-track machines; when everything has to mix down into two tracks for the left and right channels, you seriously limit the number of overdubs you can get away with before the noise becomes intolerable. With an 8-track, though, we have a different story: we can mix six tracks of drums into tracks 7 and 8, with track 7 representing the left channel and track 8 representing the right channel, for a stereo drum field, and still have six tracks left. There's more on 8-track machines in the section on stereo mixing techniques.

So far, we've been talking about premixing, where we mix together portions of a tape onto a track located on the same piece of tape. After we fill up the rest of the tape, it's time for a final mix, where we blend together the basic tracks and the overdubs we have done. The concept is the same, but the execution is slightly different. For one thing, a mix is something you have to learn: it's not just a static setting of level controls. You have to learn when certain instruments come in, when you have to begin a fadeout, and so on. So, the first step in preparing for the final mix is to do several rehearsals. Run the master tape several times, manipulating the faders and equalization controls until you have a good balance and have learned the song; then, run through the song again, but this time, have your second machine set up (reel-to-reel or cassette, whatever you're using), and record the mix on this second machine. If you make a mistake or a bad mix, or if you think you can come up with a better mix several months later, it's no problem. All your original tracks are intact on the master reel, so it's just a matter of remixing into your second machine again. While recording your mix, in fact, you

might want to record two or three different 'takes' on your 2-track machine, and then choose the one that feels best. A mix will very rarely come out exactly the same way twice, so the chances are good that if you take several mixes, one will be somewhat better than the others.

Like premixing, the final mix is time-consuming and perhaps even tedious. You still have to set up each track individually, get a 'good' sound for that track, do the same procedure for the other tracks, then listen in pairs, combinations, or whatever, all the time checking the levels for the best possible sound. It will take several passes of the master tape before you'll feel comfortable with the song. Don't worry about it; it takes time to mix. Now that we have looked at the basics, here are some specific thoughts to help obtain a better mix.

MASSAGING THE BASIC TRACK

Remember that premixed rhythm track that we have sitting in track 4 of our recorder? Well, after all the overdubs are on, you will probably wish that you had mixed the basic track differently. Unless you can foretell the future, there is no way of knowing for sure how much drums you're going to want in your finished product; the best you can do is guess (well, maybe 'estimate' is a more encouraging word). But there are some ways you can change the *apparent* mix of the rhythm track; some examples would be the best way to illustrate:

1) *Bass dominates over guitar part.* Let's say you have a basic track with bass and guitar, and the bass is just too loud. By using proper equalization, you can remove the low frequencies where the bass notes reside, while leaving the guitar part (which is higher in frequency) relatively unaffected. You can even boost the treble a bit to bring the guitar out.

2) *Guitar dominates over bass.* You pretty much apply reverse thinking: remove some treble to take the 'edge' off the guitar, then gently boost the bass. Of course all these maneuvers are changing the carefully constructed

117

tonal characteristics of the instruments, but remember that we're talking about salvaging a track, so anything goes.

3) *Drums dominate over both bass and guitar.* I encountered this recording an electronic drum set; its artificial, highly percussive character wasn't obvious until the time came for the final mix. To complicate matters, the guitar part was not compressed, and varied considerably in amplitude. The solution was to add a little bit of compression to the *entire track.* This took down the percussive peak of the drums, evened out the guitar response, and the only price was a tiny bit of added noise.

4) *One drum dominates over the other drums in the kit.* This is sticky! But there is hope. Using proper equalization, you can set up a notch response that is tuned to the exact same frequency as the drum that's causing the problem. Although, in most cases, you can't notch something out completely, in this particular example, the notch response does a good enough job to bring the errant drum back into proper perspective.

5) *Cymbals are recorded too far back in the track.* Here, boosting the extreme high frequencies a bit helps give some edge to the cymbals, without overly affecting the drums (which are predominantly low-frequency in character), save for the moment when the stick hits either the skin or rim. However, you have to be very careful, when boosting treble, not to pick up other sounds like ticks, pops, and noise.

6) *The entire basic track lacks 'punch.'* Here is where a bit of midrange peaking equalization works wonders. It brings out the string noise of the bass and the dominant guitar frequencies, and increases the impact of midrange-frequency drums, such as snare and some of the higher toms.

7) *Adding effects to the track.* Although composed of three separate signals, the track may be thought of as one unit, and as such, can be phase shifted, delayed, echoed, or whatever is appropriate.

Now that the basic track is squared away, let's get more general. One point that's worth repeating is that mixing is *not* a static process. You don't just let the various faders sit there unless you are doing a *reference mix.* (This is a mix in which the studio lets a multitrack master run onto a second machine with no level changes. The producer usually takes this home to become familiar with all the parts, *exactly as they are on the tape,* before going in to do the final mix.) Various instruments can fade in and fade out, and also, there is a chance to recapture some of our lost dynamic range by manually fading out constant signals. Sometimes, you may want to eliminate a track completely, say to build a beginning. You can fade in drums first, then bass, then guitar, and so on. On one particular demo, I was using an electronic drum set to establish the song's tempo. I had it going all the way through the song, but intended on mixdown to cut it out for the verse and leave it in for choruses only. That not only worked out fine, but while mixing, I added rhythmic manual variations to the level, which imparted a less mechanical feel to the drums.

One engineer I worked with (and he had a few hits, too) used to work really hard getting his levels and EQ and reverb set just right; then, when it came time for the final mix, he closed his eyes and had his hands riding the faders; he was mixing 8-track, and had each finger independently riding a fader and giving it a slight motion in time with the beat. The difference was not obvious, but overall, it made the song appear more rhythmic. Another trick I like is something I call 'complementary motion.' I do this most often with bass and drums, or bass and guitar, where I will vary them in opposing ways in time with the beat. For example, drums slightly forward for one measure, with bass slightly back, and on the next measure the bass goes slightly forward and the drums move slightly back. With mono, this is the closest you can get to simulating the 'placement' of stereo;

118

you can place a sound either more up-front, or further back in the track. The rhythmic variations build interest and have a somewhat hypnotic effect (which some people think is the reason we like music anyway).

But you don't just have to restrict your playing to the level controls. Changing equalization during a piece can be nice; you add a little treble or midrange 'bite' to an instrument during a solo. On fadeouts, sometimes you can make an instrument appear to fade out faster than other instruments, by adding progressively more reverberation to its channel via the 'echo send.'

Another reverb trick is called 'exploding,' or 'splashing,' and is very effective. When a signal cuts off sharply and there is a lot of reverb on it, you hear a certain amount of reverb spillover after the sound has stopped. For a neat effect, just after the sound cuts off, crank the reverb way up to accentuate that spillover or splash. This is particularly nice with vocals, percussive instruments, and backwards tape effect.

Whatever you do, keep the mix lively and interesting, but keep it subtle, too. Even minute control changes can make a *big* change on playback. Don't just add gimmicks for the sake of effect, but add them for the sake of making a more varied and musically interesting piece of music. Keep the levels dancing. Finally, don't be afraid to be creative, or to experiment. Sometimes stopping a tape and letting the reverb spill over can get you out of a jam. Break the tape at a point and insert a spliced piece of tape with something else. Don't ignore fadeins, either. I think the real goal is to know so many sounds and effects that you never have to overly rely on a single one.

FADEOUTS

It seemed right to devote a separate mixing section to fadeouts, because a good fadeout is a joy forever. The big secret of a good fadeout is to *key it to the beat of the song.* Let's suppose that you end a song with a long instrumental. You might leave the instrumental section at regular volume for four measures, then fade out over three full measures. Also, a fadeout doesn't have to be continuous. You can also turn a fader down a tiny notch, say, every two beats.

It is a nice effect to keep fadeouts from being completely linear (see the top drawing in Figure 6-1). A concave fadeout, especially on a somewhat long, instrumentally-oriented piece, can leave listeners hanging on for more. The initial rapid decay tells them to listen closely; once they're hooked, you stretch out the ending. Convex fadeouts, on the other hand, usually don't sound very good, as the music feels like it's slipping away whether you want it to or not.

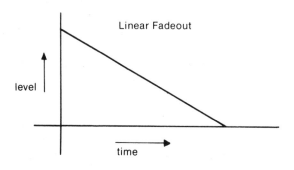

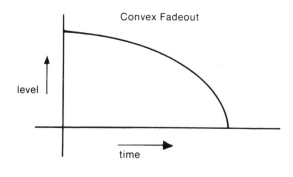

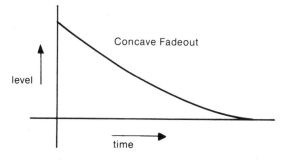

Figure 6-1.

A return fadeout is when you fade something out, only to have it fade in shortly and then fade back out again. This is the kind of trick you can use once every two albums or so, and it does add variety. But probably the best implementation I've heard was one where a song modulated up a full key during the brief instant that the fadeout had gone to zero volume. Thus, when the song came back, it had moved up a notch in terms of overall energy.

AUTOMATED MIXDOWN

You hear a lot about automated mixdown these days, and why not? Computer-style memories seem ideally suited to keeping track of fader positions and EQ; thus (in theory) you can do a mix, store the control settings in a computer or on the tape, then have a computer spit out these control settings as you play back the tape. The reasoning behind this is that you can then (if you're a producer) take the tape home with you and live with it for a while. After a week of listening, you may decide that the ten hours you spent mixing resulted in a perfect product —except for one thing: the piano player hit a clinker on one section that you just can't stand, even though it didn't seem so bad at the time. You can go back to the studio, and this time, leaving the computer's memory untouched, re-program the piano channel. You play the tape through, but fade out the piano for the one clinker. For good measure, you fade the rhythm guitar up slightly to compensate for the overall loss of level during the fraction of a second that the piano is gone, and record those changes into the computer. Now you run the tape again, and you have the same perfect mix as last week, but with the two changes you wanted to make.

Unfortunately, at the present time, automated mixdown is too complex and too costly for home recording; the reactions I have heard, from engineers using professional systems, are mixed about their effectiveness, anyway. There are a variety of systems (both real and imagined), and none of them is the standard; every manufacturer uses what it considers to be the most viable approach. I have talked to some people who have loved their automated mixdown systems and some who have hated them.

Although automated mixdown is financially out of reach for home recording studios at this time, with the incredibly rapid advance of computer and memory technology, we should be able to enjoy this promising process at low cost before too long.

USING A VARIABLE-SPEED TAPE RECORDER

If you are mixing down onto a variable-speed tape recorder, then you have some extra options. If the track isn't lively enough or seems a little slow, set the variable-speed control so that the second machine is running just a little bit slow as you mix. Then, when you speed the tape back up to normal, the piece will speed up along with it. You can also very carefully and slowly speed up a piece as it progresses; this can be very useful in adding 'momentum,' when sessions have been synchronized to a metronome or click track to give a constant tempo during overdubbing. However, if you change the speed too fast it will sound obvious and out of tune.

Conversely, you can slow a song down by mixing onto a second machine that is set slightly fast. One other point you will notice: you don't have to have much of a speed change in order to produce a drastic change in sound.

8-CHANNEL AND STEREO MIXING

With an 8-channel recorder, it becomes far easier to do stereo mixes. Here, we have almost the same situation as in a mono mixdown session, except that instead of mixing everything down into one channel, we mix everything into two channels, left and right (stereo). Let's not talk about quad mixdown, which isn't really very common.

Anyway, now is when we get to take advantage of the *panpot,* which is short for 'panoramic potentiometer'—we mentioned it earlier. To refresh your memory, the panpot places a track in any position across the stereo 'panorama' in front of you. Having the panpot fully counter-clockwise places the signal 100% in the left channel; full right places it 100% in the right channel. Middle position puts approximately 50% of the signal into each channel (I have to say approximately, because in the classic panpot there is a slight amount of attenuation built into the center position so that the signal doesn't sound louder in the middle than at the right or left extremes). The panpot is, in terms of hardware, two pots ganged together on the same shaft to form a dual pot. As you turn one to full volume, the other turns to minimum volume, and vice-versa. Each pot feeds the signal onto its appropriate audio bus, either left or right channel. Figure 6-2 shows this scheme of operation, as well as a panpot using only a single section pot. This type costs less and uses an easy-to-find pot, but introduces substantial signal attenuation—you can't have everything.

Good stereo placement is an art. There are certain stereotypes: e.g. if you have a guitar, piano, bass, and drums in your rhythm section, then during mixdown, the drums and

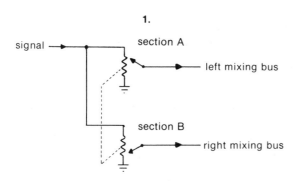

Dual ganged pot is hooked up so that when section A is full up, section B is full off and vice-versa. Smoothest panning occurs with a log/antilog taper pot.

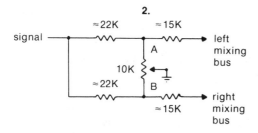

With pot turned to (A), the signal going to the L bus shorts to ground, so sound comes only from right channel. With the pot turned to (B), the opposite occurs. Other resistors supply isolation to prevent excessive interaction.

Figure 6-2. *Panning hardware implementations.*

bass will probably go to the center, with the piano going more to one side, and the guitar going a bit more to the opposite side. In some cases, signals are placed in extreme opposite channels, but they somehow just don't sound quite as substantial as signals that have a little bit of energy in the center also.

Stereo placement can significantly alter the effect of a sound. Let's take the example of a doubled vocal line, where a singer sings a part and then doubles it as closely as possible. Try putting both voices in opposite channels; then put both voices together in the center. The center position yields a somewhat smoother sound, which is good for weaker vocalists. The opposite-channel vocals give a more defined, sharp sound, that can really help accent a good singer. So placement may be used not just to place, but to emphasize and accent.

One popular panning effect is to move a signal from left to right in a rhythmic fashion, so that sounds bounce from left to right in time with the music. I agree that this is a very dramatic effect, but as such it must be used tastefully. Having instruments flying from left to right at a moment's notice can be disconcerting; but a good bent note sailing at one point in the middle of a hot break is something else altogether.

You will discover that stereo mixing is less compromising than mono mixing. You have to have your playback system balanced just right, and you have to have your head positioned just right to hear the optimum balance. And, you'd better have evenly-matched ears! Stereo is great fun, but I believe that if you know how to make a good mono mix, you have a head start when you want to make a good stereo mix. After a short period of acclimatization, you can feel at home with either one. They both have their places; for me, stereo mixdown belongs with eight tracks and more, whereas mono mixdown belongs with four tracks or less.

ASSEMBLING THE MASTER TAPE

After mixing all our pieces down onto a second machine, we have a collection of several different mixes of several different songs, some with two or three takes per song. Doubtless there are large gaps between the mixes, and the songs are probably in no special order. In the process of assembling, we select the takes that we want, splice them together in the order we want, and produce an actual finished product that you can listen to from start to finish, just like a record.

To assemble your tape, you need the following materials: your second machine, along with the tape of final mixes you have just prepared; a felt tip marker with a sharp point; a splicing block, with splicing tape and a demagnetized or non-magnetic razor blade; and several empty plastic or metal reels to hold bits of tape and specific pieces.

Like everything else we have discussed so far, assembling takes time and care. Also, this is where you really get into splicing, so let's talk about that first before going any further.

Making a good splice. A splice is what joins two pieces of tape or leader together. The general idea is to use the splicing block to

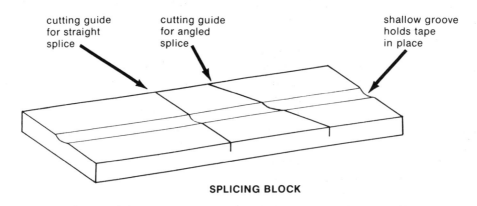

SPLICING BLOCK

SPLICING

A
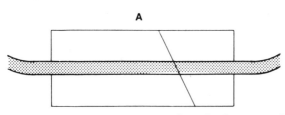

Press tape into groove, oxide side down, and cut through tape with sharp razor blade. Then do the same for the other piece of tape that splices to this one.

B
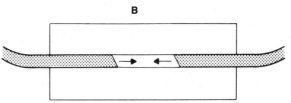

Press the ends to be spliced into groove, then slide together so that ends butt together evenly.

C
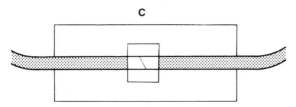

Place piece of splicing tape over splice; press down on it moderately—enough to hold it together temporarily.

D
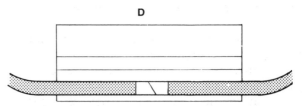

Lift tape out of groove, and place on hard sufrace of block. Use razor blade to trim away excess splicing tape. Then, run flat side of fingernail over splice, pressing firmly so that the splicing tape will adhere well throughout the recording, fast forwarding, etc.

Figure 6-3.

122

hold the ends of the two pieces of tape stationary; you then make an angled cut in the tape, and apply splicing tape to the outside of the pieces of tape in question: Figure 6–3 shows how the procedure works in detail. At low speeds, however (such as 3¾ and 1⅞ ips), the sounds are packed so closely together on the tape that you may have to resort to a straight splice rather than an angled splice.

There are a few important warnings: First, if the tool you use for cutting the tape is magnetized, you will get a nasty click as the splice goes by the playback head. Second, never use adhesive tape other than the splicing tape specifically designed for our purposes. Regular tape has an adhesive which, in time, oozes around the sides of the splice and can gum up your heads. Also, regular adhesive tape is quite thick and causes irregular winding on the take-up reel.

Some recorders are more suitable for splicing than others. The biggest problem with splicing is to pinpoint the actual location where you want the cut to occur; the usual procedure is to slowly move the tape back and forth past the playback head, until you have exactly determined the right spot. However, here we run into a problem. Many recorders, when placed in the off mode, have lifters that automatically push the tape away from the heads. This is mostly to prevent tape and head wear during fast forward and rewind; after all, there is no sense in having the tape scraping across the head at a high rate of speed if we are not going to be listening. But this type of machine is almost impossible to use for easy editing and splicing. Fortunately, many machines have either a pause or an edit feature, which disconnects the mechanism pulling the tape, but leaves it up against the playback head.

Let's say you want to make a splice at the beginning of a song, and connect it to some leader tape. First you have to find the beginning of the song, so play the tape through in its normal mode until you hear the very first few notes, then immediately hit the pause or edit button. On some machines, the pause or edit button accomplishes a different purpose, and you need to move an adjustable cueing arm to bring the tape into contact with the head; check your machine's manual for specific instructions. Now, in theory we are at the beginning of the song. While in the edit position, grasp the take-up and supply reels and move the tape back and forth across the playback head (the last head the tape passes, in case you forgot); the sound will be slowed down and unrealistic, but that is not the point. At the beginning of the song, as you move the tape back and forth, you will hear a distinct starting point. Remember that you're moving the tape past pretty slowly, so you are hearing sounds under an audio microscope, as it were. Once you've got the exact starting point determined, make a mark with a magic marker on the outside of the tape over the center of the playback head. This is where you want to cut to make your splice. Figure 6–4 shows a summary of this process.

When making splices within a piece itself, the subject becomes a little more difficult because you don't have a nice, obvious starting point. The best rule is to splice during silences, or just before a loud sound; again, you will have to move the tape slowly and surely across the head to pinpoint the exact spot. But also remember that if you move the tape too slowly, you won't hear anything, because, in effect, you are lowering the frequency of whatever is on the tape into a

Rotate tape slowly back and forth until you find the exact spot to splice on the tape. . .

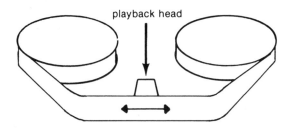

then mark the tape, and make your cut on the splicing block at that point.

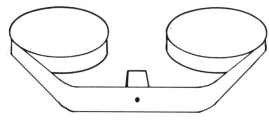

Figure 6-4.

subsonic range. In this case, a book cannot tell you what to do: you just have to make enough splices to get a good feel for the operation. A method book can tell you how to play an instrument, but to get notes you have to sit down with that instrument and practice; this is no different. Sometimes while splicing, you may find that, after several passes back and forth across the playback head, you have lost track of the point you were going to splice. This happens to professional engineers, too; don't feel bad, just start over. If you really blow a splice and cut off a beginning note, you can usually resplice, *if you do it carefully*. But try to avoid layering one splice on top of another; when this monster goes past the playback head, you will probably get a drop-out or some other inconsistency.

When splicing in spaces between songs, you have a choice of tapes: you can use paper leader tape, or blank recording tape. With paper tape in between selections, you have a slightly unusual effect since all tape hiss drops out completely during the time the paper leader tape passes over the playback head. By using blank recording tape, the noise level stays consistent from song to song, and this is psychologically less offensive. For this reason, I only use paper tape at the beginning or end of a tape.

Now we know enough about splicing to apply that knowledge to assembling a finished tape. Figure 6–5 shows in endlessly repetitive detail how to assemble a tape. We are assuming here that there is a tape with three songs on it; as the tape goes by, first you hear song A, then song B, then a bad mix of song B that you don't want to use, then song C. And, to make the example interesting, we will also assume that song C is the one you want to have *first* on your final tape, followed by song A, and then the proper mix of song B.

THE AESTHETICS OF ASSEMBLING

Assembling a final tape should take as much thought as any other part of the process; pacing is very important when listening to music. Most album sides are within a range of 15 to 25 minutes per side, and people's attention spans are sort of calibrated to this increment. For that reason, I would recommend thinking of your music in terms of blocks of time—little parts that form a greater listening whole. Albums, traditionally, are paced in several different ways: the most common is to have a strong, mostly uptempo opener, followed by something softer. The final song on a side is the equivalent of a closer when playing live; and it has to be just as strong, if not stronger, than the opener. The general custom is to put the weakest cut on a side just before the closer, the reasoning being that, if anybody has listened that far, they will already be sold, and the closer will compensate anyway. While cut and dry and perhaps a bit insensitive, this is a 'formula,' and as such is often followed religiously in the record business.

Recently, the first cut on an album has become super-important, due to the tremendous competition for the listening ear, whether DJ or record buyer. As a result, the first song is usually as universally palatable and as uptempo as possible to get people listening.

Of course, a lot of music does not lend itself to the 'formula' used with popular music. For example, much electronic music starts out fairly simply and quietly, building in intensity and then fading out again. This is directly the opposite of starting and ending strongly. Then again, some music is more poetry-set-to-music than music itself, and the words become a focal point. In a case like this, the main reason to pace is for variety. Follow your own taste, but do give the matter some thought.

A point worth remembering is that many people do not have the same passion for music as someone running a budget studio, and their ears are far less trained. The attention span of people can be very short. If you wish to pursue music as a pure art form for your own enlightenment and the enjoyment of whomever else is interested, none of these problems crop up; you satisfy yourself and that's it. But if you are making a demo for commercial acceptance, or a tape that shows off your group or your studio, or one that will get played for people with a variety of ages, tastes, and outlooks, then you may have to make some concessions to all these different tastes. A healthy sign, however, is that there are enough people interested in almost any form of music to enable a good artist to make a living in his field. Even classical music, once scorned by public and record companies alike, is making

124

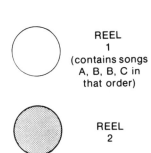

REEL
1
(contains songs
A, B, B, C in
that order)

REEL
2

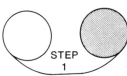

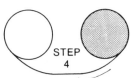

STEP
1

STEP
2

Play tape until song C hits playback head. Splice at beginning of song C. Place reel 2 aside temporarily, which now holds songs A, B, and false version of B.

Splice several feet of paper leader to beginning of song C.

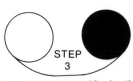

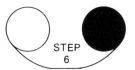

STEP
3

STEP
4

Wind leader around reel 3; play through to end of song C, then cut tape at end of song C. Splice a couple of feet of blank tape to the end of song C, then lay reel 3 aside temporarily. Reel 1 now has nothing left on it of use, and may be used as an extra take-up reel.

Rewind onto the take-up reel until you locate the beginning of song A, then make a cut and lay reel 2 aside.

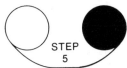

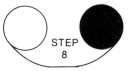

STEP
5

STEP
6

Splice beginning of song A to the blank tape following song C. Now, we finally have paper leader, song C, a little bit of space, then song A on reel 3.

Make cut at end of song A; add a few feet of blank tape, then lay reel 3 aside.

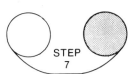

STEP
7

STEP
8

Using reel 2 as take up reel, locate proper mix of song B on reel 1 and cut at beginning of song.

Splice beginning of song B to the blank tape following song A. Now, we have songs C, A, and B on reel 3 and are almost finished.

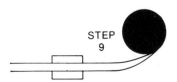

STEP
9

end of tape STEP
10

Make cut at end of song B, then splice several feet of paper leader to end of tape.

Reel 3 now contains our final assembled tape. Because the end of the tape is sticking out, this reel is called "tails out" and must be rewound before it can be played.

Rewinding tape on to other reel makes tape ready to play . . .

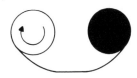

STEP
11

heads out

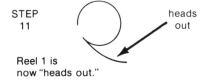

Reel 1 is now "heads out."

Figure 6-5. *Assembling a tape.*

a comeback; purely electronic albums, too, are selling better than they ever have.

In addition to pacing by mood, I also try to pace my own tapes by key. For example, if one piece is in *G* and another in *B,* all things being equal, I will follow the *G* with the *B.* Sometimes a side can almost go up the scale; the effect is subtle but it does excite people more as the side progresses. With material that is less tonal in character, I frequently pace by rhythm, alternating between slower and faster pieces.

Sometimes, after you have a tape all assembled, you will run into some problems: the most common are level changes from song to song, or changes in pieces recorded on one day, compared to pieces recorded on other days. In professional studios, which have access to all that fancy low-noise equipment, this situation usually precipitates a *2-to-2 mix,* where the master is run from one 2-track machine into another 2-track machine (or a spare 4-track, or whatever), usually *without* going through the board. Then, levels are directly compensated for with the record level controls of the second machine. Although it adds another generation to the tape, with the high level of the signals, modern noise-reduction techniques, and ultra-high-quality mastering decks, the difference is minimal. Additionally, if further modification (like overall brightening) is necessary, a single, high-quality stereo equalizer can do the job. Sometimes, adding a light amount of compression to the process will even out a tape. In any event, this all goes to explain that from the inception of a song idea, until it has been transformed into a final product, a song gets diddled with, improved, shaped, modified, and worked on at every step of the way. Then, it gets into the hands of listeners, who play with the tone controls. See what I mean about a piece of music never being static?

Chapter 7:
Maintenance

Even if you have the equipment and the knowledge, full maintenance of a tape recorder can be quite a challenge. First, though, you have to have the recorder's detailed service manual, and some very costly test equipment, just to get off the ground. Armed with this, you can buy some expensive test tapes, then match levels, move the heads around, dig inside and custom bias the machine for your favorite tape, etc.

But it's difficult to score a service manual and the required equipment. It's a lot easier just to practice preventive maintenance, and stop problems before they occur. Then, you don't have to worry as much about repairs in the long run. If something really major does go wrong, even if you're very knowledgeable about electronics, take the machine to a factory-authorized repair shop. Someone who sits at a bench for eight hours a day working on a certain family of tape recorder knows exactly what to look for and can probably fix a problem in an hour or two. It would take me an hour just to locate all the screws that remove the cabinet. Leave the fancy stuff to the people who spend their lives at it. The cost isn't that bad, and they usually have all the replacement parts on hand.

For our purposes, maintenance consists of: treating the machine kindly, cleaning the heads, demagnetizing the heads, lubricating, taking care of accessories, and treating your tapes properly.

Treating the machine kindly. This is the key to trouble-free operation. Some people feel that electronic equipment is unreliable; it doesn't have to be, although some of it is. Remember that these are precision devices; we are dealing with a machine that is calibrated in thousandths of inches. For this reason,

don't subject the recorder to unneccessary transportation or movement; buy it, bring it home, set it up gently and carefully (these things are heavy—watch your back when you lift, or get someone to help), and move it as little as possible thereafter. Don't drop anything on your machine, bump against it with a guitar neck, or use the top of it as a shelf: treat your recording equipment as the delicate and expensive system that it is.

If you're interested in field recording, get a machine designed for that job. Something like a TEAC 3340 is quite well-made and will operate well *in the environment for which it is intended,* which is a nice, peaceful, home-recording studio. Throw it in the back of your car to take to a gig, and you're asking for trouble, unless you add considerable padding and protection. A recorder designed for road-ability costs more—pay for it; it's worth it if field recording is your main interest.

Another way to treat your recorder properly is to take thermal problems into account. A tape unit generates heat, and should be cooled. Any vent holes should have complete and total access to circulating air; the fans on the back of tape recorders, which help to cool things down, should also have a clear field of operation. Blocked vents can have at least two undesirable results: a safety hazard is created, due to possible overheating of components; and component life is drastically shortened if heat sensitive components are constantly forced to run hot. For example, some of the heat comes from power resistors; if they build up excessive heat, resistance values can change and, at worst, the resistors can self-destruct and take some other parts with them as they go. There are other thermal considerations: try to maintain a reasonably consistent room-temperature environment for your recording machines. Excessive cold can crack rubber parts, or at least can age them and make them brittle. Too much heat, on the other hand, is bad for the various lubricants in a tape machine; in the presence of heat, oil tends to thin out and loses both its lubricating and heat-dissipating properties. Whatever you do, don't leave a recorder in the direct sunlight, or in a cold car overnight.

Don't throw covers over the vents. *Don't ever* put glasses of liquid on the top of a tape deck, and be careful of spills in general, as they can wreak havoc in electronic equipment. Keep out dust by covering the recorder when it's not in use, and clean the areas around controls and knobs to keep dust from getting inside the pots.

Cleaning the heads. Since miles of tape get dragged by the heads, you might suspect that little pieces of the tape would wear off as the tape goes past them. Well, they do, and that's why you have to clean the heads, and any other parts that the tape contacts on its travels. This is a simple operation, for which you will need Q-tips and head-cleaning fluid. Although alcohol is frequently mentioned as a suitable cleaning agent, it really is not that good at dissolving the various binders that hold the oxide layer to the base material of the tape itself. If you scrub enough with alcohol and a Q-tip, you can get a head fairly clean; but a head-cleaner, specifically designed and formulated for the job, does a better job, and leaves no residue on the heads. I always get the head-cleaner recommended by the manufacturer of the machine so that in case something goes wrong, I can truthfully say that I followed instructions to the letter. Tape recorders these days usually come with a small head-cleaning kit to hold you over until you hit a hi-fi store and get a big bottle of the stuff.

To clean, first make sure you don't have any tape on the machine; then locate the heads. To get at the heads, remove the head cover; usually there are a couple of obvious screws that hold this in place. Dip a Q-tip in the fluid, swab it around on the head a few times, neither lightly nor with great force (an insistent, small pressure is fine), and look at the Q-tip. Is it brownish red and dirty? Then use the other end of the Q-tip and swab again. When it comes out clean, proceed to the next head. Don't glop lots of fluid over the heads; just use enough to do the job. Contrary to societal programming, more is not always better.

While you are at it, clean the capstan. For some reason, this gets dirtier faster, so you might need to use two or three Q-tips on it every ten hours or so. In fact, you really should clean your machine after every ten hours or so of tape travel; the dirt buildup is quite noticeable even after that short a period of time.

The rubber pinch roller is a special case and *must not* be cleaned with head cleaner, as this can crack the rubber. Instead, use Q-tips dipped in warm, not hot, water. Sort of drag-scrape the Q-tip along the roller until all the dirt is off.

Cleaning the capstan and pinch roller is something you should do fairly frequently; it's better to spend one minute a day on cleaning for ten days than to do ten minutes of cleaning in one day. Another suggestion: clean at the *end* of a session, not the beginning. After all this cleaning the tape recorder should dry off; the chances are good that if you do your cleaning at the beginning of a session, you'll have to wait a few minutes before you get started, and maybe during those moments the creative impulse will take a vacation. If you start a session with everything ready to go, you start it off right.

Demagnetizing the heads. In addition to a good demagnetizer, I'd recommend getting a magnetometer (Figure 7–1) for measuring the actual residual magnetism at the head. As it so happens, there's a company out there (R. B. Annis Company, Indianapolis, IN 46202) that makes both products and is specifically into demagnetization from an audiophile viewpoint.

Unfortunately, the magnetic coating on a piece of tape is very thin and highly sensitive to extraneous magnetism. Also, iron or steel (which makes up much of a tape transport) is subject to magnetization by stray magnetic fields, such as those generated by loudspeakers and similar equipment. Exposure to stray magnetism degrades the recorded signal by erasing high frequencies and adding hiss; to complicate matters further, each time the tape

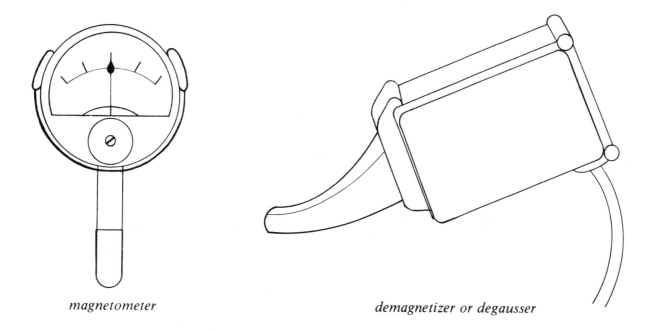

magnetometer

demagnetizer or degausser

Figure 7-1.

passes over a magnetized head, tape quality deteriorates until the head is demagnetized.

Magnetism is an unusual phenomenon, and, before I had a magnetometer, I kind of waved a demagnetizer at the recorder's heads on a regular basis, according to any instructions, and figured I had done the right thing. Actually reading the magnetism has shown me that, tape recorders don't have to be demagnetized on a schedule; they have to be *checked* on a schedule, and if magnetism shows up, then something should be done about it. You might as well do the checking when you clean the heads; it only takes a few seconds.

The magnetometer I got cost about $8, but it's pretty sensitive. Moving it relative to the earth's magnetic field can give a change in reading, so you have to consider that when you take measurements. Also, the magnetometer has a clip-on extension probe for getting at recessed heads and the like; but this reduces the sensitivity of the instrument by an unspecified amount. My general rule is that if the needle just barely moves off its little post, I leave things alone. If the movement is more noticeable, I demagnetize. I know that it sounds unscientific, but you can't totally *eliminate* stray magnetism; you can only minimize

it to the point where it doesn't cause a problem. While you're at it, check the other parts of the transport that your tape contacts as it travels from one reel to the other. Keep in mind that demagnetizers draw a fair amount of electricity, and should be limited to a 50% duty cycle (i.e. if it's on for 30 seconds, leave it off for 30 seconds before continuing use; if it's on for a minute, let it rest for a minute).

The procedure for demagnetization follows below:

1) Make sure that the recorder is off, and that no tapes are near it. This is another reason to do your maintenance at the end of a session.

2) Plug in the demagnetizer, holding it *at least* two feet away from the tape heads or any tapes.

3) Move the tip of the demagnetizer towards the head to be demagnetized, coming as close as possible without actually touching the head.

4) Wave the tip slightly from side to side across the face of the head, then *slowly* withdraw the tip from the head

129

(no faster than three or four inches per second).

5) Turn off the demagnetizer while it is at least two feet away from the tape heads or any tapes. Make sure that you don't turn the demagnetizer either on or off while it's in the vicinity of the heads, as the resulting surge of current can magnetize the heads and leave you worse off than when you started.

6) Use a similar procedure for the other heads, if required.

The Annis literature points out that it does no good just to hold the probe in front of a head and let it sit there and 'cook'; it is the slow withdrawal of the probe that accomplishes the actual process of inducing ever-smaller opposing AC fields into the head, thus leaving it (hopefully) with no residual magnetism. If you still get strong residual readings, you may have to run the demagnetizing procedure a couple of times until you get as small a reading as possible.

Lubricating. Your machine will have specific instructions for lubricating motors or other points. Make sure you follow the directions. Again, more is not necessarily better; if they say a drop of fine oil, put in one and only one drop of fine oil. Be careful not to use too much oil.

Contact cleaner for switches and pots also comes under the heading of lubrication. Frequently, as pots and switches age, the contacts become dirty and dusty; spraying contact cleaner on them will often extend their life by months or years. With pots, use the extension rod supplied with the contact cleaner to lubricate as far into the pot's case as possible. With rotary switches and slide switches, spray directly into the contact areas. After spraying, rapidly, turn the pot or click the switch in order to work the contact cleaner into the area. With sealed pots and switches, you don't have this option; but on the other hand, you're less likely to need contact cleaner for these more expensive types, so everything evens out.

Taking care of accessories. Maintenance means more than just keeping the equipment in minimum running condition. If a light bulb goes out, replace it. If a fader in your mixing board gets scratchy, replace it. If a battery in a tuning standard goes dead, you should have a couple of spares (or an AC adapter) hanging around somewhere. Fuses should be handy, perhaps taped to the piece of equipment they go with. In the world of professional studios, maintenance men and service representatives from various companies stay on top of things so that when the paying client-musician comes in, engineers don't have to hassle with the equipment. You don't have that luxury, but you still must keep things in shape; it's a drag working in an environment where something is always breaking down. Do things right from the beginning; if you're designing something yourself, make it easy to service (in my home-made mixer, the top hinges up to a 90-degree angle, exposing wiring, circuit boards, and pots—all semiconductor parts are easily replaceable). Then, follow up that care by immediately dealing with problems when they occur.

Treating your tapes properly. We've already mentioned that the magnetic imprint on a piece of tape is quite weak, and as a result, it can be upset by residual magnetism in the heads, but that's not all. Any electrical device that generates a strong alternating current or magnetic field, if close to a tape, can accidentally cause partial or complete erasure, destroying hours of work in a few seconds. So keep your tapes away from speakers, AC power cords, soldering irons, transformers, headphones, TV sets, or anything that generates a field; if you carry a tape in your car, place it away from the engine and ignition circuits.

The material used for tape has some needs too. Tape should preferably be kept in a cool, dry place. Studios are often climate-controlled so that they are always cool and dry, but you probably can't go to these lengths. The important point is to keep moisture away from tapes, as dampness fosters a mold growth on the tape which renders it useless. A high-humidity environment is very detrimental to your tapes; if you live in a rain forest, you might have to install a small dehumidifier in a closet or storage area to store valuable tapes. And of course, keep tapes out of direct sunlight; you can have warpage with plastic reels and other tape problems. Handle your tape

130

gently. Finger oils stick to tape, and any creases or folds introduced into the tape will show up as dropouts or discontinuities in the final product.

The best way to store a tape is to rewind it back to the beginning, or *head* of the reel. Then, play this tape at a slow speed (like 7½ ips) onto a take-up reel. By playing at a slow speed, the tape wraps very evenly around the hub of the take-up reel; and this protects the tape for long-term storage. Rewinding or fast forwarding onto a reel just before storage is not recommended, since irregularities in the winding can damage your tape.

Your tape is now on the take-up reel and ready for storage, but first mark the reel "tails out," so you know that the tail of the tape is facing out and the reel must be rewound before being played in the future. Return the tape to its box, and if you really want to keep out dust or contaminants, wrap the box in a plastic bag.

A WORD ABOUT PRESSURE PADS

Pressure pads are devices that you find on less expensive models of recorders; they press against the head of the recorder, so that the tape, as it goes by, is sandwiched between the pressure pad and the head, which gives better contact, which, in turn, means fewer dropouts and more consistent operation. The only trouble is that the extra pressure means extra head wear, and this is why the professional machines generally eschew pressure pads. But you might have to deal with them, especially if you're using something like an old 3-head, reel-to-reel recorder. So, if you have pads, make a note of what they look like and how thick they are when new. As the months roll by, you'll see those pressure pads wear down, just like the brake shoes on a car. When they shrink below a certain point, say 50% of their original height, replace them.

REPLACING HEADS

Frankly, I wouldn't try replacing a head. Now, I probably could learn how, but I'd rather spend the time making music. When it comes to routine maintenance, I'll do it, but this kind of operation requires patience and equipment. Besides, it takes a lot to wear out a head, especially some of the newer ferrite

types, which are quite durable.

How do you know when your heads need replacing? Probably the best way is to look at your heads carefully when new, and to re-inspect them whenever cleaning time comes around. As the months go by, you'll notice the tape wearing a flat groove across the heads; you may also hear a corresponding change in high frequency response. If the heads become worn, they may need to be repositioned (re-aligned) to insure optimum tape contact and positioning. If the head are severely worn, the groove created by the tape may be so deep that the edges of the groove tear at the edges of the tape. The only choice here is replacement of the head.

If you have questions about whether your head is up to par, or find a need for re-alignment or replacement, chances are the store that sold you your machine also has the facilities to keep it in shape. If not, most major metropolitan areas have specialty tape recorder or professional audio shops that can do an excellent job for you.

ALIGNING HEADS

The physical positioning of a tape head with respect to the tape is very important; improper positioning can cause dropouts or uneven frequency response. Unfortunately, it is not easy to check alignment unless you are conversant with test tapes and test equipment. Therefore, I feel it's a good idea to have a competent service person check the alignment of your heads, *even if the machine is brand new.* Because the long trip from the manufacturer to user, it is very likely that the heads will be somewhat out of alignment when the machine reaches you.

Also, alignment can change as the heads become worn, so have the alignment checked every year or so whether you think you need it or not.

A FINAL NOTE ABOUT MAINTENANCE

Proper maintenance is a state of mind: when you get behind the 8-ball, it's hard to catch up. Take care of your studio so that, no matter what, at a moment's notice you could go in and everything would proceed smoothly. You'll have a happier and more productive studio.

Chapter 8:
Getting More Music Onto Your Tape

PRODUCER, ENGINEER, MUSICIAN

In a professional studio, the musician is part of a team of (hopefully) experienced and musically intelligent people. Two of the people who play an important role on this team are the producer and engineer. In a home environment, the musician doesn't necessarily have access to these high-powered talents, and he must perform their roles himself. Although this may seem difficult at first, this experience is probably one of the greatest teachers you can have in learning how to be objective about your parts, your style, and your sounds.

It helps to be precisely conscious of the ideal role of each of the three participants, (musician, producer, engineer), so that you can assume those roles at will—alternately planning the course and arrangement of a piece (producer), playing it (musician), and getting it down properly on the tape (engineer). By becoming familiar with these roles, you can apply their differing outlooks to your music and obtain a more balanced perspective.

Producer. This is the person who has the Big Ideas, the one who is responsible for putting together the pieces of a successful piece of music. The producer's role depends a lot on the musician being produced; some producers go in and read a newspaper during the recording process, concerning themselves solely with the mixing. Other producers pick the songs, the musicians, arrange string and horn parts, and in general take charge of most aspects of the music. What you want to acquire is the ability to see each piece as part

of a whole, each track as part of a final composition. If you know where you are going, it's a lot easier to get there; the job of the producer is to figure out just where you are going.

However, sometimes a producer must spend much time and effort dealing with artists: with insecure musicians who have to be coaxed to get them to play; with rock and roll stars standing around telling engineers how to run their boards. Acting as a liaison between a possibly temperamental star and a record company is sometimes not the best job in the world. In your case, you don't have a producer around to keep you working; that responsibility is up to you. If you blow a recording, don't get discouraged, just start over. If someone else blows a recording, explain that it's not the end of the world and proceed.

If a session is disorganized and confused, then you'll have a harder time getting good music down on the tape. In your little studio, you can't have too many people hanging around, making noise, having a good time, and laughing; it's hard to get a good sound while competing with partygoers. So, try not to have people waiting around to play parts. If you need vocals after the basic tracks are done, don't have the vocalists hang around getting nervous; ask them to arrive at the studio a few hours after the session begins.

Don't forget that many towns and cities have ordinances that prohibit noise after a certain time. I know it's music to your ears, but it may not be to neighbors. Unless you have neighbors who understand, you'd better schedule your sessions with these ordinances in mind, unless you want to be liable for complaints. Or maybe you can work something out: maybe all the neighbors like your music, or will let you make noise, if you let them make noise.

When you schedule a session, include time for getting levels, setting up mics, and breaking down. If a group expects to record 17 songs in an hour, gently inform them it doesn't work that way, especially in budget studios.

So, don't just record music, produce it. Tie everything together cleanly, vary the instrumentation, and put a little thought into the little niceties that help make a tape sound professional.

A word of caution about producing seems appropriate here: a common mistake among beginning producers is to overproduce. Open tracks do not necessarily need to be used; past a certain point, adding sounds causes more confusion than music. Keep your sense of good taste activated, and before adding a track ask yourself whether it should be edited, or whether it actually needs to be there at all.

Engineer. The engineer is the one at the session who doesn't drink, smoke, snort, talk much, complain, or even move out of the engineer's chair. While the producer is figuring out the concepts, and the musicians are out in the studio playing, the engineer is making sure that everything is set, organized, and ready to record. Whatever happens, the tape is cued up and the record button is ready to push. Of course, the above is a stereotype and no stereotype is accurate, but every engineer I have ever worked with respected the job and took it seriously, and I couldn't have only met exceptions.

It's always nice to have an enthusiastic engineer who gets off on your music, but believe it or not, you can get some great sessions out of an engineer who doesn't care for your music at all. They are professionals, whose job is to capture the sound in the best way possible.

It is very helpful to adopt an engineer's attitude when mixing, balancing, performing critical operations, and running the equipment. Put the music, your concern about whether that last run was really so hot, and *all*

of those worries out of your mind; when you are playing engineer, work with what you've got.

Musician. After the levels are set and you know you aren't going to overload the meter, you again have to switch gears. Forget about the board, and try not to stare at the VU meters. Just dig in and cook. Unfortunately, this is kind of hard—especially when you need to punch in to a track while overdubbing, simultaneously paying careful attention to where you are on the tape so that you don't erase anything you want to keep. Nonetheless, try your best. Musicians are traditionally the dreamers, the visionaries, the artists, the children; engineers are the computer-like scientists engaged in the noble quest for the Ultimate Sound; and the producer is the conductor, arranger, parent figure, politician, and sometimes mad genius. I tend to think that there is a part of each in all of us; you can get in touch with these parts by studying and getting absorbed in the roles of these characters. It will help your objectivity, and give you better tapes; the tape recorder is a mirror that lets you see a lot about yourself.

FEEL VERSUS PERFECTION

There is no doubt that some older albums, recorded under technically primitive conditions, still conveyed a joyousness and enthusiasm—a feel—that made for great music. And some newer albums are so perfect, so automated and equalized, that the sound is sterile and somehow mechanical. There are some producers who believe that the feel is all important; if a musician does a great part but blows a couple of phrases, that's all right if the feel was good. Other producers insist on doing a part over and over and over until it's technically perfect. Both approaches have their advantages and pitfalls, so try to strike a balance. Don't fall into the trap of being so self-critical that you never get anything down on tape, and end up expending all your energies laying down the first track; but also don't get so loose that everything sounds 'great' and you lose the ability to evaluate.

Some musicians try to create a feel in the studio by smoking grass or drinking. Sometimes this is to cover their own insecurities, and the fears that they have of hearing themselves on tape. I think most people would agree that a musician is at a technical peak, in terms of physical reflexes and thought processes, while he is straight. I'm staying neutral on this, but you might wish to give the matter some thought.

Music is not all that well-defined, but it surely hasn't been taken to its limits. Make the music that comes naturally to you: you are unique, and you have your own contribution to make. Remember that no matter who you are, what you make, and how well you play, there will always be people who like your music, and people who won't like your music. Since you can't please everybody, then please yourself. If you are not a flash lead guitarist, that doesn't make you any less of a musician —less of a guitarist, perhaps, though that is certainly arguable! Play within your limits, guided by your taste; listen critically to what you do. I have heard home tapes from a variety of friends and readers of my articles— each one is unique, and some are very beautiful.

Follow your own path and don't get discouraged. You will never get to go as far as you would like musically. I don't think anyone has ever gotten as far as they would like, but that's not the point. *The point is the getting there.*

Your tape recorder makes you independent of record companies, rules, engineers, clocks, hourly rates, and all the rest. Finally, you are getting to be able to just play your music, without anyone telling you what to do, without time pressure, and without commercial pressures.

THE PERFORMER AS LISTENER

You may find that you have produced, played on, and engineered a piece, and never once did you really get to listen to it for pleasure. Well, give yourself a treat. Put on your final mixed tape, and forget you had anything to do with it. Don't listen for those mistakes you were trying to catch during mixdown, don't listen to whether the tracks are mixed right (you can analyze later); just listen to the music. Pretend you walked in someplace and heard that music playing. What would you think of it? Maybe you don't really like it. I've cut a couple of things where I would listen back and wish I hadn't wasted my time, but that hasn't happened very often. Most likely when you listen to your stuff, you'll think it's pretty good, or you wouldn't have made it the way you did in the first place.

Now that you're listening, relax, let yourself go, and just enjoy your creation. You've worked for it, you've earned it, and you probably loved every minute of making it. And now you are a little closer to that funny world of dense vibrations we call music.

Chapter 9:
Projects For Home Recording

Building your own mixing board is not something to be taken lightly. I wish I could say that anybody could do it in a few spare hours with a small initial investment, but that's just not true. In fact, in some cases it may actually cost you more to build a board than to buy one—in much the same way that it would cost you more to build a TV from scratch than it would to just go down to your local store and buy one. So before we go any further, consider some of the disadvantages of building your own console.

1) *You could end up with a pile of parts that serves no useful function.* Building a board is such a complex proposition that you are almost forced to make an error somewhere—and even if you don't, you run the risk of getting a bad IC or other component that can throw a monkey wrench into even the finest construction jobs. Unless you know how to troubleshoot, you could get in trouble:

2) *You must be experienced in working with electronics.* Good intentions are not enough; you cannot afford to randomly substitute parts, or stuff ICs into remote corners of your board where replacement, in case of a malfunction, would be impossible. You also need to know how to arrange the circuit boards behind your front panel so that there are minimum lead lengths connecting the various boards and submodules.

3) *If your time is worth a lot, you will probably lose money making your board compared to buying a commercially available product.* There are so many connections that you can easily pour hours and hours into wiring your board. If you spend $300 on parts, for example, and your time is worth $5 an hour, and you spend 80 hours building the thing, then you have laid out $700 for a mixer, and it's very possible you could have obtained a commercial equivalent for less.

I don't necessarily want to discourage anyone, but, realistically speaking, you don't want to dump your time and money into an endeavor unless you have a reasonable amount of confidence concerning the outcome. Now, let's give equal time to the advantages:

1) *If you have more time than money, you can get a mixing board off the ground with a minimum outlay of cash.* For example, after buying a tape deck, I didn't have enough left to buy a board, but I did have enough to buy some parts. Even though it took a lot of my time, I was able to get a board set up and running much sooner that if I had been forced to save enough money to buy a commercial one.

2) *Pride of accomplishment means a lot.* There's nothing quite like the creative process, whether we are talking about

135

writing a song or building a fine piece of equipment. It's much more fun to use a board that was built with your own hands and heart than to use a mass production piece of equipment that is just like your neighbors.

3) *You know your board inside and out.* This is perhaps one of the strongest advantages—if something goes wrong, if you need a replacement part, if you need to change a pot—you can deal with these problems yourself. You don't have to wait six months for a part to arrive from some obscure factory warehouse. As a big plus, by fully understanding your circuitry from the ground up, you can take advantage of many features that people might overlook in commercial boards. I have seen professionals use their boards at only a fraction of their possible capacity; yet amateurs, using home-made equipment, can often squeeze out more performance and options than you would expect out of a simple board.

4) *You can make exactly what you need.* The basis of this chapter is a mixer, specifically designed for a flexible, mono, demo-oriented studio (by the way, avoiding stereo really helps to keep the cost down). I use this mixer in my own setup, and it has several features which are there specifically for my convenience. As an example, many times with a professional board you have to go through all kinds of gyrations just to plug in a cassette recorder to make a dub of your music. With my board, I added a couple of outputs specifically for that purpose. Or take noise gates: I happen to find them very useful when using non-professional-quality tape decks that lack superlative noise figures. In professional studios, noise gates are expensive accessories; but in my board, I was able to put in six noise gates for about the same cost as a single professional-quality noise gate designed for sophisticated commercial studios.

Additionally, you can implement your studio on a modular, pay-as-you-go basis. I happened to design the unit on paper first, did some paper simulations of sessions, saw that it checked out as far as I could tell, and proceeded to build. But if you want to spread out the commitment of finances and time, fabricate a modular system—start with the basic mixer, then add cue and reverb busses, and finally build input modules such as microphone preamps, noise gates, equalizers, and so forth. In this board there are effect 'break jacks' where you can patch in other modular effects; for example, although I don't have a graphic equalizer on each channel, I can patch one in when I do need it.

5) *You can design for reliability.* It has been my experience that when something fails in a studio (which does happen) the whole recording experience becomes a little less fun. It can be very discouraging to get all keyed up for a session, plug in the power supply, play a few notes and then have something sputter and die. But with a well-designed mixer, you should be able to chase down the failing IC or whatever in a matter of minutes, especially since you built the thing and know where to look.

Speaking personally, I wouldn't buy a board (unless I had enough money to get a huge 16-track machine and a board with automated mixdown) if for no other reason than that I like to personalize everything, and am particular about having the exact features I want. If you decide likewise, and you feel confident enough to proceed, let's start.

ENTRANCE REQUIREMENTS

If you have built electronic units from scratch successfully, if you can wire from a schematic, and if you know how to troubleshoot, then you will probably have no trouble building your own mixer. I urge beginners, however, to start off with some simpler projects before attempting something of this magnitude.

I could write a book about building projects from scratch; in fact, I have. It's called *Electronic Projects For Musicians* (*EPFM* for short) and it's brought to you by the same people who bring you this book. In fact, one of the reasons for this project section is that many readers of the first book have requested mixing boards projects and circuits.

It would be nice if there were enough space in this book so that I could reproduce all the sections from *EPFM* on construction technique for the benefit of beginners, but that's just not possible. Instead, I'm going to attempt a short-form version designed to help those who are beyond the beginner stage, but haven't tackled anything of this complexity yet. If you need more background on such matters as packaging, PC boards, finding parts, and so on, check out the previous book.

Some people may feel qualified to build something like this if they have prior electronics experience in another field, such as computers. But I cannot stress strongly enough that musical/audio electronics are very different from many other kinds of electronics. Shielding and actual physical location of wiring can be important; parts are sometimes used in unorthodox ways; and troubleshooting these types of circuits is usually more challenging. If you are familiar with electronics in general but are a novice concerning musical electronics, enlist the aid of a friend who is involved with musical stuff. The job will probably go just that much easier for you.

DESIGN PHILOSOPHY

In designing this mixer, I tried very hard to hit the optimum compromise between simplicity, performance, and cost; that kind of choice is very subjective. My first priority was low-noise operation, but flexibility also counted very heavily in the design. Although there are areas that could be improved (I never did like spring reverb units all that much, for example), the various parts of the mixer are well-matched to each other. Again, this is a mixer I use in my own studio, day in and day out, and it has functioned well and reliably.

I have gone out of my way to avoid gimmicks and frills which I do not think are vital but add considerably to the cost. For example, you won't find any VU meters—use the ones on your recorder, it cost enough to put them there! There are no overload indicators on the mic preamps—use your ears to listen for distortion. The mixer is not designed for stereo, because it would have upped the complexity to the point where only a limited number of people would have had the required experience to build it, and if they already have the experience, then they probably don't need this book to recap it for them.

Before we get into the actual construction, let's look at a block diagram of the system as a whole.

The heart of the mixing board is the Basic Mixer section. It has seven inputs, six of which connect to the outside world through input modules; the seventh is the reverb-return control from the reverb section. Each input, in addition to feeding the basic mixer, also feeds a cue bus mixer and reverb bus mixer. Each mixer has its own set of input level controls, so we can have three different mixes—one for the main mixer, one for the cue mixer, and one for the reverb mixer—occurring at the same time.

The output of the basic mixer goes to an output selector that switches the output into any of the four channels of a 4-track recorder, or into two separate outputs designed for dubbing. The output of the cue mixer feeds a headphone amp; a separate monitor amp can switch between monitoring either the cue bus output or the main mixer board output. The output of the reverb system feeds into the main mixer (reverb-return) and also into the cue mixer via a separate control, should you want reverb while listening to the cue bus (not absolutely necessary, but fun to have if you want to monitor a track and hear what it will sound like with reverb added).

The six inputs of the main mixer are fed by the outputs of six input modules, which process signals before they hit the mixer. Four of the inputs would typically connect to the outputs of your 4-channel tape recorder, whereas the other two inputs are spares for adding instruments or mics. However, each input module has an input selector that can select between the tape output or an instrument output. That way, you can mix up to six different instruments or microphones into a tape recorder channel by simply setting the

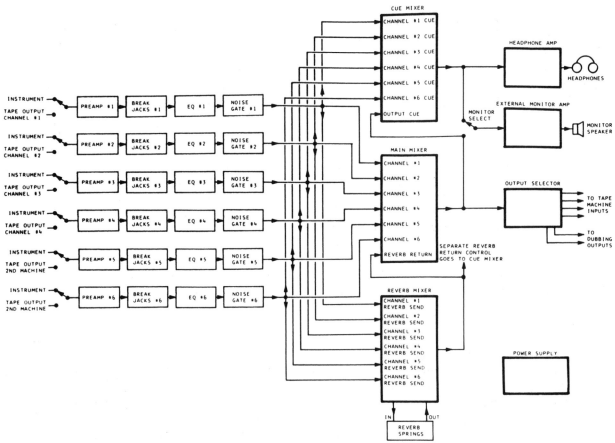

Mixer Block Diagram.

input selectors for instrument/mic outputs rather than the 4-channel tape machine outputs.

After the input selector, you have the option of using a mic preamp. Most mic preamps in studios are complicated, high-gain affairs that boast lots of switches, matched resistors, low-impedance inputs, and expense. We strip all that away to yield a basic preamp that accepts high-impedance inputs, gives a gain of 10 maximum, and has a low-frequency rolloff. The rolloff is handy to have, and only costs one capacitor and one switch. If you wish to use low-impedance mics, no problem: just add a matching transformer in between the low-Z output device and the preamp's high-Z input.

Gain of 10 may seem to be on the low side for a mic preamp; many mic preamps give gains of 100 or even 1000. However, with close vocal or instrumental miking (especially with an instrument like drums) a gain of 10 is all you will ever need. For the few times you

do require more gain, the mic preamps may be *cascaded* (i.e. the output of one feeding the input of another) to give as much gain as you want. Of course, the more gain you have, the more noise you have, so you will want to run at minimum gain wherever possible. But it is nice to know that if you need lots of gain for amplifying some very weak-output acoustic instrument, you can cascade the preamps. There is also a bypass switch for when you want the preamp out of circuit. The break jacks between the preamp and tone controls allow you to take the output of the mic preamp and route it somewhere else (like to the input of another preamp, as mentioned before). Or, you can patch in different effects —like tape echo, fancy tone controls, whatever. The reason for placing the break jacks between the preamp and EQ is so that devices requiring high-level signals may be fed from the output of the preamp; but by preceding the EQ section, changes in tonal quality may still be added. You aren't limited to plugging

138

only one effect into these jacks; you can have a string of effects, with one feeding the other, before plugging back in (see Figure 9–1). With nothing plugged into the jacks, signals flow uninterruptedly from preamp to EQ.

The EQ section is a simple treble/bass, boost/cut arrangement. This will take care of the majority of simple equalization needs, help get rid of tape hiss, rumble, and other common gremlins. There is also a bypass switch for this section. However, having the break jacks available allows you to patch in a super-complex graphic or parametric equalizer when needed, in which case you can bypass the EQ section or use it for further processing. Due to the high cost of fancy equalizers, chances are you can't afford one for each channel, but maybe you can afford one, and this board allows you to take advantage of that possibility.

The noise gates help considerably in cleaning up tracks, which is why I felt it was worth having one for each channel. However, they have more uses than just simple reduction of noise, as we will see under the noise gate section.

There is a headphone amp permanently connected to the cue bus for headphone monitoring. A loudspeaker monitor amp can connect to the output of either the main mixer bus or the cue bus, depending upon the setting of the monitor select switch.

Finally, the power supply that feeds this conglomerate of modules is not mounted inside the mixer, but rather in a separate, remote box. This type of approach minimizes hum pickup problems, since the supply can be located away from sensitive circuits such as reverb springs, guitar pickups, and mic preamp inputs that are prone to hum pickup.

Now that we have a functional overview, let's examine some of the electronic components we will be using to implement this mixer.

ABOUT THE PARTS

The star of our mixer-to-be is the *op amp,* one of those twentieth-century miracles you keep hearing about. It's a rather impressive device that consists of a whole batch of transistors and resistors crammed through chemical and photographic techniques on to a tiny crystalline wafer. This wafer is sealed in an epoxy case and various significant points in the op amp's circuit are brought out to little pins. The package containing the op amp (or sometimes several op amps) is referred to as an *IC,* or *integrated circuit.* An op amp is very much like a super-quality, miniature version of a musical instrument amp. However, the typical op amp is designed to handle low-level signals, so they are more properly classed as preamplifiers.

No op amp contains all ideal characteristics at the same time (i.e. low noise, great frequency response, low cost, and ease of use); as a result, you sometimes have to pick and choose for appropriate applications. The 741 is a very popular op amp, for example; it comes in an 8-pin package (see Figure 9–2) and is quite compact. It is also virtually indestructible and very inexpensive, but it is one of the noisiest amps around, and this makes it unsuitable for most of our uses.

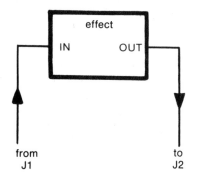

Single Effect.

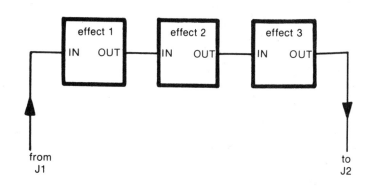

Multiple Effects.

139

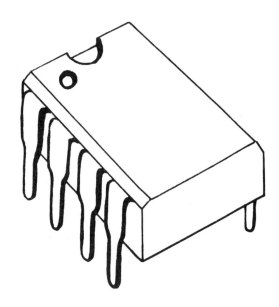

Figure 9-2. *8-Pin Integrated Circuit.*

However, there is a somewhat more expensive op amp, the 1556 (sometimes called a 1456), that has a much better noise figure and is still relatively foolproof and inexpensive. We use it for the main mixer and cue circuit boards, which handle high-level signals that mask the residual noise of the op amp.

One of my favorite ICs is the 4739. This is a dual op amp, which means that one IC contains two, complete, functional op amps. Despite the fact that these are low-noise, premium-type op amps, the cost is still reasonable. I have used 4739s in the preamp, EQ, and reverb sections, where low noise is of the essence.

The noise gate uses some other ICs. A 741 acts as a signal comparator; in this instance, we never hear the actual output, so noise is unimportant. The 555 timer IC is not an op amp at all, but is designed for industrial timing applications. It can be modified to suit our purposes, though; in the noise gate, it acts as a signal detector that opens or closes an audio 'gate' as required.

One point worth mentioning is that many op amps, like the 741, 1556, 4739, 4131 and several others are internally compensated; that means they are unconditionally stable, and do not generally require a bunch of external filtering circuitry since this circuitry is included in the IC. Since op amps are capable of

tremendous amounts of gain, sometimes they need to be *tamed.* Those that are internally compensated are tamed at the factory, and will not behave unpredictably if used in a conventional, relatively low-gain configuration. The drawback is that high-frequency response can suffer, but this is no problem in our situation, where we are dealing with audio frequencies which do not go much over 20kHz.

In situations where large amounts of high-frequency (say, above 10kHz) gain are required, engineers will pick uncompensated op amps and add external circuitry in order to tame the amp to the limits they desire. This external circuitry usually takes the form of a simple capacitor, although sometimes you may need to add a couple of capacitors and possibly a resistor or two. Popular uncompensated op amps include the 748, 725, 318, and many others. These may be substituted for the op amps in the mixer circuits if they are all you have around, but you will have to add compensation parts not included in the schematic. For this reason, I would recommend sticking to the exact op amp types recommended in the circuits unless you really know what you are doing and have data sheets on your parts around for reference.

Compensated op amps typically have two inputs, two power supply line connections, and an output. If, in the main mixer, for example, you wish to use an IC that has lower noise, you could use a 4739 in place of the 1556 by wiring up the appropriate points the way you did the 1556 (see Figure 9-3). However, I doubt that you would notice much difference in the overall noise level.

POTENTIOMETERS

Potentiometers (pots) have different characteristic tapers. Taper is the rate of change of resistance as you turn the pot from one end to the other. A *linear-taper* pot has equal amounts of resistance throughout its range—thus, if you have a pot whose maximum resistance value is 100k ohms, turning it up halfway would put the resistance between the wiper and either end at 50k. A *log-taper* pot is arranged so that a much greater amount of resistance is traversed by the pot as you turn it progressively further clockwise. This type of taper is usually used in consoles, as it

140

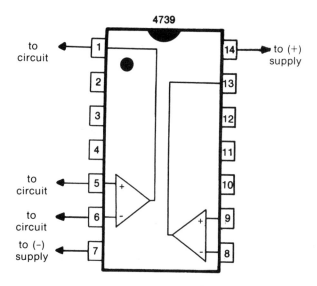

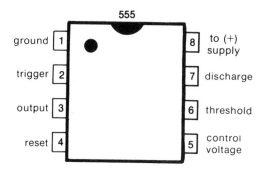

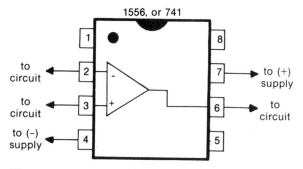

You can use one of the op amps in a 4739 for a 1556 op amp by making the following pin substitutions:

1556		4739
pin 2	equals	pin 6
pin 3	equals	pin 5
pin 4	equals	pin 7
pin 6	equals	pin 1
pin 7	equals	pin 14

Figure 9-3.

approximates the logarithmic response characteristic of the human ear, which requires progressively larger doses of sound to perceive a linear volume change. An *anti-log-taper* pot is rarer, and acts like the reverse of a log-taper pot.

Now, this may sound a bit confusing, but the only knowledge we really need to extract is that log-taper pots are desirable for volume controls and some other types of controls, since they follow the response of the ear. However, I have found that log-taper pots (or audio-taper pots, as they are sometimes called) are harder to find on the open market, and many times I have used linear pots to control volume functions. It is also feasible to approximate a log-taper pot by adding a small resistance between the hot and wiper terminals of a pot (see Figure 9–4); but to tell you the truth, and maybe I'm just lazy, I don't find taper to be all that significant a concern. If

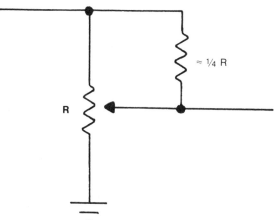

Figure 9-4.

you can find audio-taper pots, fine; but if you can't, it does not mean failure for your project. In the parts list for the various projects, we will specify which type of taper is preferable.

One other important characteristic of a pot is expense—and good pots are very expensive, starting at about $2.50 each for a super-hot pot. Quantity orders bring down the price, but who can afford to have 1000 pots lying around? On the other hand, using inexpensive pots can cause problems with scratchiness, short life, and all the other qualities associated with inexpensive devices. What I recommend is constructing your mixer so that all pots are readily serviceable and replaceable. This way,

141

you can use whatever pots you have around or can find at reasonable prices, and as you go along, you can upgrade and replace the older pots. If you replace each pot as it wears out with a nice, long-life, expensive pot, eventually you will have a fine mixer with nothing but quality controls.

In order to simplify wiring, the terminals of a typical pot are designated as terminals 1, 2, and 3 on the schematics. These correspond to the pot terminals indicated in Figure 9-5.

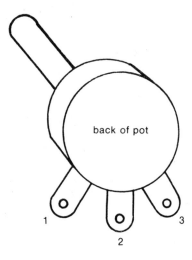

Figure 9-5. *Pot Terminal Designation.*

SWITCHES

I recommend using the smallest toggle switches you can find consistent with a good feel and sturdy operation. Be prepared for a shock—these babies go for about $2 each; so again, we have a basic, vital component that's not exactly cheap. Unlike pots, however, there are few inexpensive alternatives to the standard toggle switch, so you won't be able to start out cheap and then upgrade. But do make them easily replaceable, because from time to time a switch will break or the contacts will get old and worn, giving intermittent operation.

SOCKETS

Frankly, I think anyone who doesn't use sockets for ICs is asking for trouble. Sure, it may offend your sense of economics to pay 26¢ for a socket and only 25¢ for the IC it holds; but to not pay it would be false economy. First, using a socket prevents any possi-

bility of heat damage while soldering; second, should the IC ever fail—and they do from time to time—it is a hassle and a half to replace it if it is not socketed. With sockets, if you suspect that an IC is bad, you can replace it with a substitute known to be good and verify whether a problem exists in no time at all. Without a socket, you have no such option.

CIRCUIT BOARDS

There are several circuit board kits available on the market. These allow you to take printed artwork and turn it into circuit boards through various techniques. Some people really enjoy making circuit boards, watching the chemicals etch away at the copper, drilling the little holes—personally, I don't much like making circuit boards; and I'd just as soon not go into the process here in detail (if you want to know more, read *Electronic Projects For Musicians*). But there are alternatives to the standard circuit board: you can use Vector board that is pre-punched with little holes on .1″ grids, stick your parts through, and make any required connections with wire instead of copper circuit-board traces. Also, Bill Godbout Electronics (Box 2355, Oakland Airport, CA 94614) is offering circuit boards for the various projects, as they did for the projects in *EPFM*. Godbout's has boards that are made by large firms who deal in volume and have the equipment required to make really good boards.

If you want to fabricate circuit boards yourself, there is much literature available on the subject at electronic supply houses and in hobbyist magazines.

PACKAGING

Again, there is an extensive treatment on packaging in *EPFM,* so we won't duplicate it here; but there are a few considerations that are unique to packaging a mixing console.

First, it is crucial that you give yourself enough room in which to work. Use a chassis that comfortably holds all those pots, jacks, and circuit boards; lay out your pots so that they may be easily turned without turning the pot next to it. After you have figured out the size you need, increase it by 50%! The extra space comes in handy when doing maintenance (where you have to reach into corners and the like), and fosters an uncramped layout. I have worked on some super-high-density boards in my time, and on these it is very hard to keep track of which control actually goes with each channel.

Second, spend some time thinking about human engineering. Make sure that the controls you use the most are the most accessible, and that the board as a unit is easy to operate.

I fit my mixing console, exactly like the one described in this text less a few minor improvements, in a chassis 17" x 13" x 2" (with power supply and reverb springs mounted externally). This is about as small as I could go, and it was quite taxing to fit everything in that small space. So give yourself a break and opt for something a little bigger. Assembling the console on a small board takes a lot of planning on paper—drawing trial layouts with the various pots, switches, and circuit boards penciled in place. I also built up a lifesize front panel and indicated all the pot positions, then put knobs on top of this pseudo-panel and checked how comfortable the board would be to operate. There were several modifications made at this point in order to improve the logic of the signal flow. I would recommend placing the rows of pots for the various mixing busses (main, cue, reverb) horizontally along the bottom of the front panel, with the main mixer knobs at the bottom. Then extend the input modules vertically upwards above the faders (see Figure 9–6), and finally, mount the output selector and controls, like reverb cue and the like, off to the right-hand side. I stuck all the jacks along the rear panel of the console, but placed the break jacks on the front for easy access.

POWER SUPPLY WIRING/DECOUPLING

Distributing ground and power supply lines to the various modules should not be done in a random manner. Bring the power supply lines into the console from an external power supply, and have these lines terminate in several 3-lug terminal strips (see Figure 9–7) —one lug for (+), one lug for (–), and one for ground, which should bolt solidly to the chassis. Then, run the lines out to the various

modules in accordance with Figure 9–8. Although it may be a bit picky to run a wire out for each supply terminal to each and every module, I did it that way and I feel it does make a difference. In any event, all grounding should follow this type of single-wire system; with power-supply lines this is a bit less critical because there is *decoupling* built into most of the modules that helps clean up the supply lines.

Decoupling of the power supply simply means inserting a bit of resistance between the supply line and the point to be fed on the board; and then adding a capacitor to ground (see Figure 9–9). This combination helps remove any signals that have hitched a free ride into your module via the power supply lines. In the various modules a diode adds the necessary resistance, and also adds protection against accidental polarity reverses of the supply leads, which can be fatal to an IC. The capacitor can be valued anywhere from $2.7\mu F$ up to $100\mu F$ without affecting the performance of the mixer in any way. The holes on the circuit board artwork are set up so that fairly large capacitors (say, $100\mu F$) can be accommodated on the board, if that's what you have on hand. By the way, note that electrolytic and tantalum capacitors have a (+) end and a (–) end, just like a battery; and like a battery, they must be hooked up correctly for proper operation. The diode has an identifying band around it; this must also correlate with the component layout and schematic or the circuit will not work (see Figure 9–10).

GROUNDING OF JACKS

On each of the jacks in the schematics, you will see a little ground symbol ( ) which means that the shield of the jack should go to ground. If you have secured the jack into a metal chassis so that it makes good contact with the metal, it is not necessary to run a wire from this point to chassis ground, but it doesn't hurt in case a jack loosens up.

SHIELDING

Wires pick up spurious responses (like CB radios) because they can act like antennas under some circumstances. Shielding is another one of those subjects that could take an entire chapter, but here are the basics.

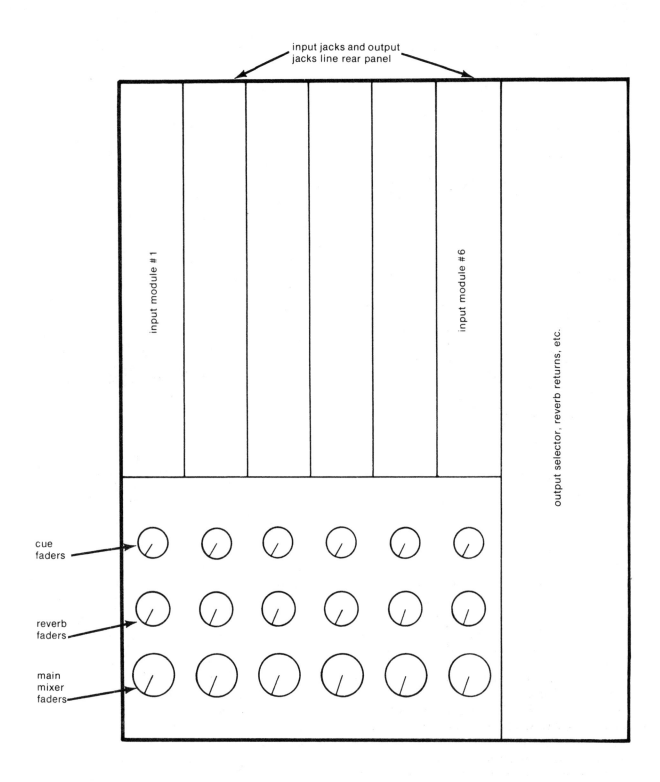

Figure 9-6.

144

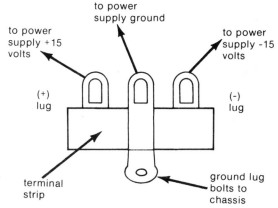

to power
supply ground

to power
supply +15
volts

to power
supply -15
volts

(+)
lug

(-)
lug

terminal
strip

ground lug
bolts to
chassis

Figure 9-7.

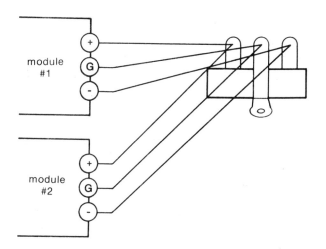

module
#1

+

G

–

module
#2

+

G

–

Figure 9-8.

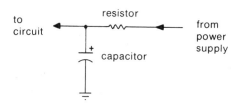

to
circuit

resistor

capacitor

from
power
supply

(a) *Decoupled positive supply line to module.*

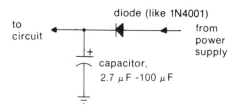

to
circuit

diode (like 1N4001)

capacitor,
2.7 μF -100 μF

from
power
supply

(b) *Our implementation.*

Figure 9-9.

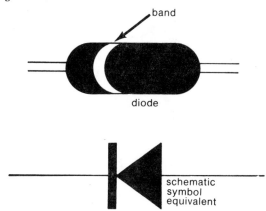

band

diode

schematic
symbol
equivalent

Figure 9-10.

First, build your mixer inside of a *metal* case. This is important! That way, the metal cases of the various pots and switches will contact the metal case of the mixer and be grounded to the supply through the ground lug of the terminal strip we discussed earlier. This will shield the pots and switches from hum.

Second, use shielded cable on low-level lines. Shielded cable preparation is discussed in detail in *EPFM*. The basic idea is to peel away the outer shield of the wire to expose an insulated inner conductor. The inner conductor carries the low-level signal we want to protect; the shield is wired to ground, at one end only. By being grounded, it diverts hum and garbage away from the inner conductor and off to ground. Shielded wire should be used with the inputs to the mic preamps, the wires going

to the gain control of the preamp, and the wires going from the reverb section to the springs. Actually, the wire going to the input of the spring doesn't have to be shielded; but the one coming from the output of the springs to the reverb module *must* be shielded.

The other modules work at high signal levels that swamp the residual hum that wreaks havoc with lower signal level devices, like guitar pickups. As long as you keep the wires reasonably short and dressed against the chassis, hum pickup should not present any major problems.

TESTING AS YOU GO ALONG

Sometimes people build their projects so securely that if something is miswired, it can take a tremendous amount of effort just to get at the wire and change it. When I made my mixer, I installed the basic mixer section first and tested to make sure it worked by touching the input points on the board and listening for hum (if you have a signal generator, that makes for a more accurate test); I then followed the same procedure for the cue mixer board. Next, I built one input module, connected it to the mixer, and tested it thoroughly. After testing and getting out a few minor bugs and mis-wired connections, I duplicated that input for all the other inputs.

I highly recommend acquiring a voltmeter if you don't already have one, if for no other reason than to test the power supply voltages before connecting the supply to the mixer. A mistake in the power supply could be the most expensive mistake in the whole board if you end up frying all your ICs (and probably some of the capacitors, too).

LEARNING FROM OTHERS' MISTAKES

After writing *EPFM*, I had the opportunity to see some units that didn't work. Although some folks figured out truly novel and exciting ways to prevent things from working, there were a few common problems that kept cropping up. Avoid these and you are at least partially on the way to success:

1) *Improper soldering.* Use a 25 to 40 watt pencil-type soldering iron with a fine point. Soldering stations with thermostatically controlled tips are best; these irons deliver more heat when required by hard-to-heat connections like jacks and ground lugs. Many builders use too much heat when heating up circuit board connections; it doesn't take much, after all, to warm up a little component lead and a thin strip of copper. These excessively hot joints pose a hazard both to the board and to heat-sensitive components. On the other hand, connections like the ground lugs of jacks thermally conduct to the metal chassis, which sucks away heat like a heat sink. This type of connection requires far more heat than a circuit board connection. The object is to apply enough heat so that solder melts and flows freely over the connection; if it takes 2

seconds for a circuit board connection, fine; if it takes 20 seconds to heat up a ground lug, that's fine too.

The type of solder you use is crucial. *Do not use any type of solder other than rosin-core solder,* preferably the kind recommended for electronic work. Silver solder, brass solder, acid-core solder, all of these are *no good.* Also, soldering paste is *not* required —or wanted—when using rosin-core solder. It will only gum up the operation of the board and give troublesome leakage paths. I'd recommend getting the thinnest gauge solder available, as it is much easier to use on small connections than thick solder.

2) *Improper grounding.* Each module board has a point labelled "G" that needs to be grounded. This must connect to the power supply ground line.

3) *Lack of patience.* This is probably the biggest project destroyer of them all. Hurrying through a project is asking for disaster. Not only is the work sloppy; but even if a device works right the first time, as the months go by you will pay as poor solder connections start to come undone. Also, unless properly tightened down, jack and switch mounting nuts will eventually work loose. As a result, you lose shielding and will probably pick up hum and other garbage.

4) *Improper use of shielded cable.* Unless the end of a piece of shielded cable is properly prepared, the shield can short to the hot wire (inner conductor). Additionally, too much heat applied to the cable connections can cause internal shorts. These may not be visible from the outside, but are detectable with an ohmmeter.

FINDING PARTS

These projects have supporting parts kits available with components, board, and pots from Bill Godbout Electronics. This arrangement worked out well with *EPFM,* especially for those who live a distance from well-stocked electronics distributors. Write for information on current kits and prices to Box 2355, Oakland Airport, CA 94614; once kits are introduced, they are updated as the technology changes.

If you live in a metropolitan area with a good industrial electronic parts distributor, then you are in luck. Most of the ICs are common; one possible exception is the 4739, which some people have reported as difficult to find. You can write to Raytheon Semiconductor Division, 350 Ellis Street, Mountain View, CA 94042, for the address of their local stocking distributor. Also, mail-order outlets similar to Godbout's sell individual parts; for the addresses and current prices of parts, check the ads in the backs of the various electronics magazines (*Popular Electronics, Radio-Electronics, 73,* etc.).

Unfortunately, many local electronic stores are not good places to get parts because they just can't stock all the components necessary to satisfy a wide variety of needs and still maintain low operating costs. On one hand you have TV supply houses, which can supply 100 flyback transformers but no exotic semiconductors; on the other you have chains like Radio Shack, which try to stock small quantities of as many different parts as possible. As a result, I order most of my parts through mail-order houses. Again, the best place to get addresses for catalogs and the like is in the backs of electronics magazines.

One point that often confuses beginners when they specify parts is IC nomenclature. For example, we referred to the 741 op amp, but no distributor would call it that. The numbers would have a letter prefix to indicate the manufacturer. For example, an LM741 would mean a 741 manufactured by National Semiconductor; an RC741 would be manufactured by Raytheon; a uA741 would indicate a Fairchild part; in other words, all manufacturers have their little codes, and sometimes the people behind a counter do not know that an LM741 is the same as what hobbyists commonly call a 741.

SUMMING UP
THE CONSTRUCTION SECTION

I said I would keep it short, but the problem is that there are many aspects of electronics that are obvious to some people and obscure to others, so to touch all bases would be very difficult in the few pages we have. I've attempted to cover the most important points, and to explain some of the problems that can torpedo a project. All of the circuits in my mixer have been tested using a variety of off-the-shelf parts, and it has been in service for almost a year as of this writing; but I also expect it to work for several more. Problems have been blissfully small; in fact, I haven't had to replace one IC yet, or spray one pot with contact cleaner. Also, functionally, the design has served me well: I have seldom been frustrated because this mixer couldn't handle a situation I presented to it. Of course, one design cannot suit everybody's needs; if your bag is recording a drum set with a dozen mics, then the mic inputs we have to play with don't look like they'll be enough. However, it is possible to add modifications that turn this mixer into a more complex device, and we will consider these modifications as we go along. But please: Don't just design something big for the sake of playing with lots of knobs. The simpler a mixer is, the simpler it is to use and maintain.

BASIC MIXER CIRCUIT

This unit is very versatile just by itself, even without the other mixer circuits described later. IC1, a 1556 low-noise op amp, is set up as a *summing* circuit. Pin 2 on this op amp is called the *summing junction;* it is a point that is at ground potential, although there is no physical connection to ground. We can mix a number of inputs into this summing junction with negligible crosstalk and interaction. Notice how a resistor comes back from this point for each input; the inputs are identified as points 1 through 8 on the circuit board.

Input 7 requires a little explanation. It may be ignored in the case of a 6-input mixer; or, you can install a 10k ohm resistor into location R7 on the circuit board and bring this pad out to another input, wired up like inputs 1 through 6. If you would like to add even more inputs, instead of adding R7, install a wire jumper so that pad 7 connects directly to the summing junction. You can then add more inputs if desired, as shown in Figure 9-11. These are wired up just like the six inputs already shown. However, you should know

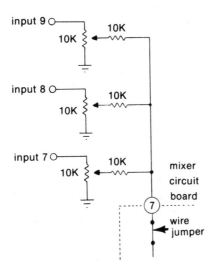

Figure 9-11.

that more inputs degrade the noise figure; although, in theory, you can add up to about 20 inputs, I'd recommend sticking to 12 or less for best results.

Input 8 accepts the reverb-return signal from the reverb system board and mixes it on to the main mixer bus. We'll talk about this some more when we discuss the reverb system.

The output point of the circuit board goes to a master output control that regulates the overall output of the mixer. SW7 switches

this combined output into one of the four inputs on your tape recorder, or into one of two dubbing outputs. R10 is not really necessary, but I happen to use that output with a particular piece of equipment and the loss of level is desirable. The output of this mixer also goes to the cue mixer board, so that you can monitor the output of the main mixer through the cue system.

The various inputs connect up to faders R11–R16. Terminal 1 of each of these acts as the input point for the channel; the outputs of the input modules connect to these input points, as pointed out earlier in the block diagram of the mixer system. Each input has a mute switch that can shunt the input to ground (we explained how to use mute switches in the mixing section).

The input points may be left unconnected until the input modules are ready to mate with your system. However, you can also connect these input points to some jacks and use the basic mixer module as is—it has many applications by itself. For example, if your instruments or microphones can feed a 10k ohm input impedance (which is the input impedance of the basic mixing board inputs), then you can mix them together and use the output-selector switch to send the mixed sound into

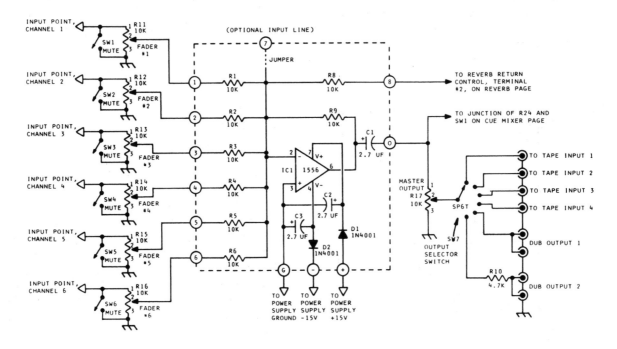

Main Mixer Schematic

one of the tape channels. Some instruments, like straight electric guitar, are loaded down when forced to drive a 10k ohm load (but a simple power booster, preamp, or similar effect box can overcome most loading problems); for these types of instruments, you will probably want to use ¼″ phone jacks at the inputs.

After you have recorded into three tracks of your recorder, you can use this basic mixer to mix those three tracks down into a fourth. Simply set the output selector to the track you want to record into, and mix the three tape outputs together through the mixer. In this case, you will probably want to have RCA phono jacks connected to the inputs, as most consumer-type tape recorders have that kind of termination. You can also use a switch to select between RCA phono and ¼″ phone jacks, as shown later in the mic preamp/input selector schematic. After filling up all four tracks of your recorder with recorded material, you can then use this mixer to mix down into another deck using a dub output; or you can patch a dub output to a monitor amp if you just want to listen without recording the mix into a second machine.

If you have just acquired a 4-track and need a simple mixer to get going, this basic mixer board fills all the basic requirements except that it lacks the ability to amplify low-level signals; but again, a booster or preamp, as mentioned previously, can take care of that. One low-cost solution would be to build just

one of the mic preamps shown later, and patch it into your mixer circuit when required. Using switchable phono and phone jacks at the inputs also adds flexibility. A final advantage is that this mixer doesn't draw much current; as such it can be battery powered by hooking up the power supply connections as shown in Figure 9–12. Although you won't have as much output potential with ±9V instead of the ±15V recommended, it is doubtful the reduced output swing will make much, if any, difference in your final sound.

Completion of this unit has you well on your way to a mixing board. If you don't want to stop at this point, let's check out how to add a cue system to the basic mixer.

PARTS LIST, BASIC MIXER CARD

R1–R9*	10kΩ ¼ watt carbon resistor (brown-black-orange)
R10	4.7kΩ ¼ watt carbon resistor (yellow-violet-red)
R11–R17	10kΩ potentiometers, log taper preferred
C1–C3	2.7μF tantalum capacitor, 20 VDC
D1, D2	1N4001 or equivalent diode
IC1	1556 op amp with matching 8-pin socket
SW1–SW6	SPST or SPDT toggle switches
SW7	Single pole 6-throw rotary switch
***R7**	Optional—see text

ALSO REQUIRED: (1) circuit board, (8) RCA phono jacks, knobs, solder, etc.

CUE MIXER CIRCUIT

The cue circuit is another mixer, very similar to the main mixer module; in fact, it even uses the same circuit board. The major difference between the two is that the cue system never shows up on tape, so we don't have to be quite as fussy about the sound.

The various cue faders connect to the input points of the various channels through isolation resistors, R18–R23. The purpose of these resistors is to isolate the cue bus faders from the main mixer faders, so that diddling

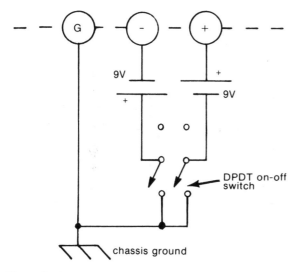

Figure 9-12.

with the cue faders doesn't alter the settings on the main mixer. However, these resistances, in conjunction with the faders, attenuate the input signals by a factor of 10 on their way to the mixer. Normally this would be a problem; but by using a 100k ohm feedback resistor at the op amp (R9), the op amp gives a gain of 10, which compensates for the signal loss at the inputs and brings everything back up to a proper level again. The price we pay for this gain is a slight increase in noise; but, as mentioned earlier, since this signal is only for cueing, we don't have to worry about this small increase.

With the cue mixer circuit board we use inputs 1 through 6 to monitor the equivalent main mixer channels. Input 7 listens to the output of the basic mixer (*output cue*). Input 8 accepts a reverb-return control for the cue system so that you may add reverb to your cue signals. The output of the cue mixer goes to a headphone amp, or headphone amps, depending upon how many you need to drive. Any low-power amp will work; *EPFM* has plans for a simple headphone amp based on the LM380 IC that costs about $7 to build. The cue mixer output can drive several headphone amps in case several musicians need headphone cueing.

A monitor amp can connect to either the output of the cue mixer or the output of the main mixer, depending on SW1's setting.

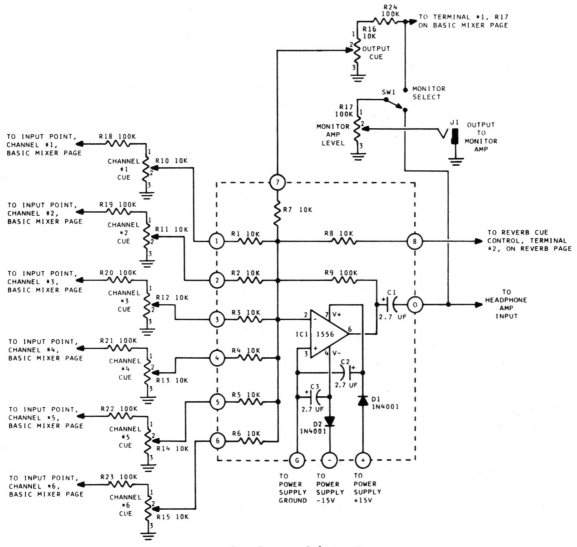

Cue System Schematic.

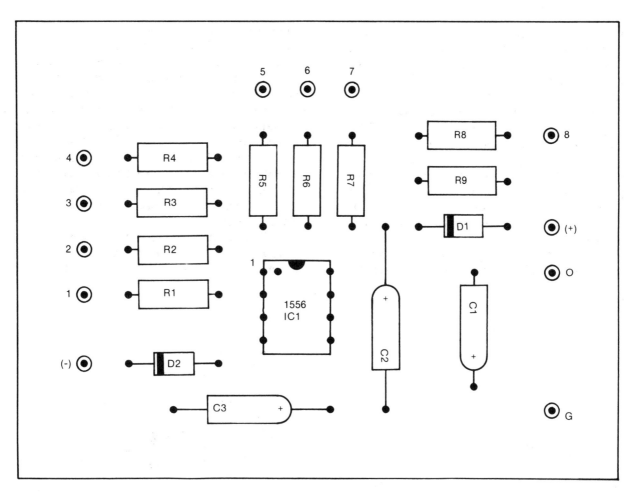

Main Mixer, Cue Mixer Component Layout

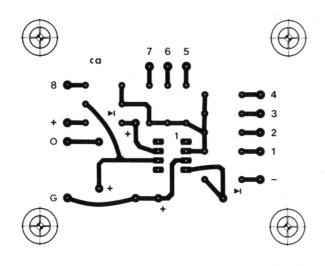

Main Mixer, Cue Mixer
Circuit Board Layout.

PARTS LIST, CUE SYSTEM

R1–R8	$10k\Omega$ ¼ watt carbon resistor (brown-black-orange)
R10, R16	$10k\Omega$ potentiometer, log taper preferred
R9, R18–R24	$100k\Omega$ ¼ watt carbon resistor (brown-black-yellow)
R17	$100k\Omega$ potentiometer, log taper preferred
C1–C3	$2.7\mu F$ tantalum capacitor, 20 VDC
D1, D2	1N4001 diode or equivalent
IC1	1556 op amp with matching 8-pin socket
SW1	SPDT toggle switch

ALSO REQUIRED: (1) ¼″ phone jack, (1) circuit board, knobs, solder, etc.

REVERB SYSTEM CIRCUIT

Here we have a variation on the cue mixer, with some differences (like an extra stage to amplify the signal coming out of the reverb springs).

The reverb mixer is built around IC1A. Again, we use isolating resistors (R16–R21) to prevent interaction; but this time, we have a switch that selects where the input of each channel of the reverb system connects. In one position, a reverb input connects to the input point, and picks up the signal that will have reverb added before it passes through the fader. In this 'pre' position, the amount of signal sent to the reverb mixer remains constant regardless of the fader setting on the main mixer. The 'post' switch position connects to the middle terminal of the fader, so that the amount of signal to which reverb will be added varies

with the setting of the fader. In other words, fader full up would give maximum reverb; fader full down would give no reverb at all.

Since the isolating resistors decrease the level going to the mixer, again we need to add some gain. But this time, we also need enough gain to drive the reverb springs; so, the mixer is set up to give lots of gain. This builds the level sufficiently so that the reverb springs are properly driven. Capacitor C1 rolls off some high frequencies; since the springs don't respond much over 5kHz anyway, there is no point in sending it extremely high frequency signals. This capacitor also removes most noise generated in the reverb mixer.

Because of the inductive nature of a reverb spring's input transducers, the impedance of the load changes with frequency. For this reason, the springs can sound bass heavy unless some kind of bass cut circuit is added

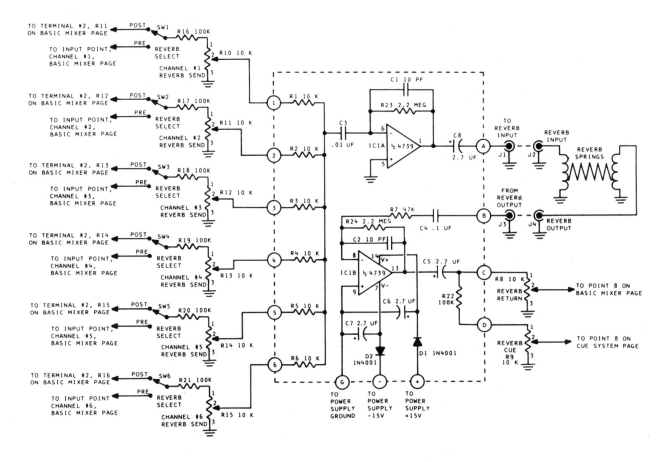

Reverb System Schematic.

to the system. In our reverb driver/mixer, C3 helps reduce response at lower frequencies to even out the overall frequency response of the reverb system.

Before we go any further, let's discuss reverb springs for a bit. They are generally fragile, fairly expensive, and give an outrageously low output. On the other hand, they are all we have to work with unless you have the bucks to lay out for a nice studio-type system using large plates or acoustical reverb. You can use the type of springs found in guitar amps, or you can order a new set of springs from PAIA Electronics, Inc. (1020 W. Wilshire Blvd., Oklahoma City, OK 73116) for approximately $10. The sound of reverb springs would never fool anyone into thinking that they are in a concert hall, but the simulation is pretty good. No doubt there are better ways to implement a reverb system using springs—perhaps some kind of parallel combination of a number of different springs would work best. However, the circuit we're using yields what I feel to be the best compromise between cost, complexity, and noise.

As mentioned before, the output of a reverb unit is extremely weak, giving signals in the millivolt range. To suitably amplify this

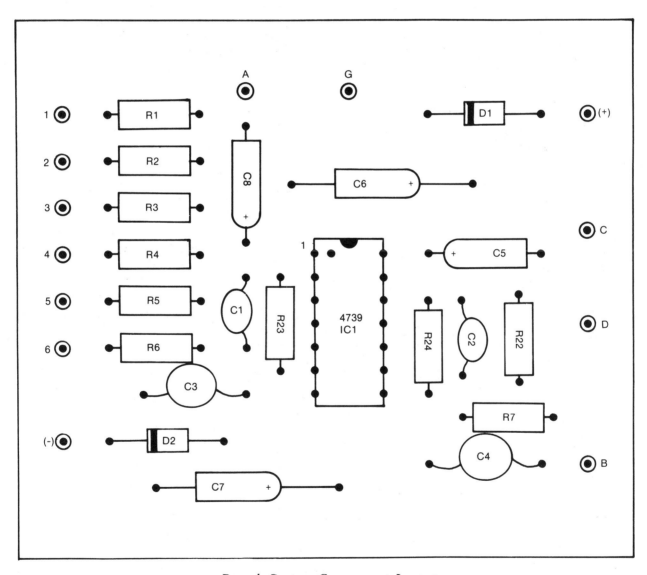

Reverb System Component Layout.

153

signal requires enormous amounts of gain, which causes correspondingly enormous amounts of noise. One way to help the signal-to-noise ratio is to drive the springs as hard as possible, so that there is maximum signal transfer to the springs' output; that's the reason for the extra gain in the mixer stage built around IC1A. Another way to help the S/N ratio is to avoid using excessive amounts of reverb on mixdown. There is a tendency for novice engineers and producers to use lots of reverb, but this just isn't necessary. It's not a good idea to add too much reverb to your music, just as you wouldn't add an excessive amount of spice to your food.

IC1B is the *recovery amp* for the springs, so called because it recovers this minute reverb signal and amplifies it. This stage has a gain of about 50, which I found to be the minimum you can get away with for moderate amounts of reverb. If this does not produce enough reverb effect for you, you can change R8 on the main mixer board to 4.7k ohms, which will make available about twice the amount of overall reverb. C2 rolls off high frequencies

and inhibits a tendency towards self-oscillation —exactly the kind of taming we touched on in the section on op amps.

Point A on the reverb mixer board terminates in an RCA type phono jack, J1, that connects to the input phone jack on the reverb springs through a length of shielded hi-fi cable. Similarly, run a cord from the reverb spring output jack to J3. Use as short a length as possible consistent with getting the springs away from hum-producing sources.

Points C and D of the reverb output stage connect up to the reverb-return controls, one of which works its way back to the main mixer bus and one of which goes to the cue mixer bus. As in the previous mixer circuits, there is on-board, power-supply decoupling.

When using the reverb system, try to keep the reverb-send controls as high as possible and the reverb-return as low as possible to maximize signal to noise. Also, use shielded cable between J3 and point B of the reverb mixer board to minimize hum pickup by the high-gain stage built around IC1B.

Reverb Mixer
Circuit Board Layout.

PARTS LIST, REVERB SYSTEM

R1–R6	10kΩ ¼ watt carbon resistor (brown-black-orange)
R8–R15	10kΩ potentiometer, linea taper preferred
R7	47kΩ ¼ watt carbon resistor (yellow-violet-orange)
R16–R22	100kΩ ¼ watt carbon resistor (brown-black-yellow)
R23, R24	2.2 MΩ ¼ watt carbon resistor (red-red-green)
C1, C2	10pF ceramic capacitor
C3	.01μF capacitor, mylar preferred
C4	.1μF capacitor
C5–C8	2.7μF tantalum capacitor, 20 VDC
D1, D2	1N4001 diode or equivalent
IC1	4739 dual, low-noise op amp with matching 14-pin socket
SW1–SW6	SPDT toggle switch

ALSO REQUIRED: (1) circuit board, (4) RCA phono jacks, (1) set reverb springs, knobs, solder, etc.

PREAMP AND INPUT SELECTOR

This is the first stage of our input module. SW1 selects either an output from the tape recorder, or an instrument/mic input. When using a low-impedance mic, you must use an external matching transformer for best results.

SW2 is a bypass switch for the preamp. In the *out* position, the signal flows directly from the input-selector switch to the next stage of the input module. Switched to *in,* the signal passes through the preamp before going on to the next stage.

IC1A is a buffer that places a negligible load on high-impedance instruments, thanks to an input impedance in the vicinity of 1 Megohm (the input impedance is a function of the parallel resistance of R4 and the input impedance of the op amp itself). C1 gives low-frequency response down to about 30Hz. If you use mylar or another stable type of capacitor, .01μF is a good value. If you use a

disc ceramic capacitor—whose value can vary considerably from its stated value—then use a .02μF unit to insure proper low-frequency response. The output of the buffer then goes to a rolloff switch, SW3. In the *flat* position, there is a smooth response down to 20Hz. In the *80Hz* position, the signal is attenuated by 6dB at approximately 80Hz. This position is good for removing excessive bass, microphone pops, room rumble, air-conditioning noise, 60Hz hum, and the like.

IC1B is a simple inverting amplifier with variable gain of 1 to 10. R2 prevents the gain from dropping below unity. The output of this stage couples back into the input-module signal path through C4, a 2.7μF capacitor.

On the circuit board, you will notice a lower-case 'g' pad located between points D and E. This pad connects to ground. Since you should use shielded cable with the wires going to R3, you may attach the shield directly to this point.

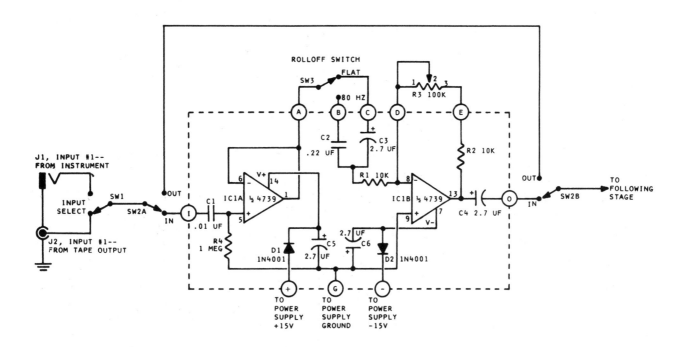

Preamp Stage And Input Selector Schematic.

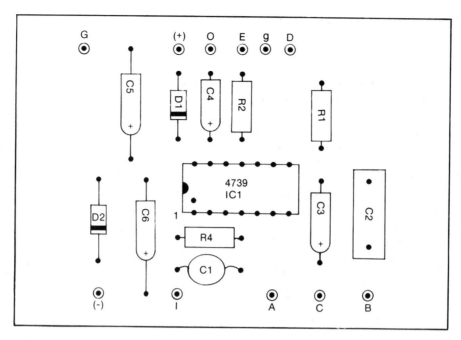

Preamp Component Layout.

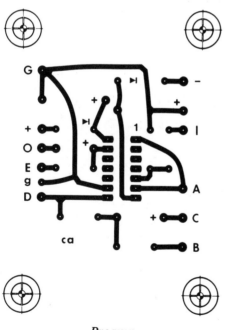

*Preamp
Circuit Board Layout.*

PARTS LIST, PREAMP STAGE AND INPUT SELECTOR

R1, R2	10kΩ ¼ watt carbon resistor (brown-black-orange)
R3	100kΩ potentiometer, log or linear taper
R4	1MΩ ¼ watt carbon resistor (brown-black-green)
C1	.01μF mylar capacitor
C2	.22μF mylar capacitor
C3–C6	2.7μF tantalum capacitor, 20 VDC
D1, D2	1N4001 diode or equivalent
IC1	4739 dual, low-noise op amp with matching 14-pin socket
SW1, SW3	SPDT toggle switch
SW2	DPDT toggle switch

ALSO REQUIRED: (1) circuit board, (1) ¼″ phone jack, (1) RCA phono jack, knob, solder, etc.

BREAK JACKS/TONE CONTROL CIRCUIT

The break jacks are closed-circuit types. Normally the signal flows from the preceding mic preamp stage to SW1. However, you can introduce other effects into the signal flow at this point by plugging into these break jacks.

For example, let's say you want to add a phase shifter. Plug a cord from J1 to the input of the shifter, and from J2 to the output of the shifter. The signal will now be diverted through the shifter. The logic of putting the break points where they are is discussed earlier in the chapter. If you have an effect that requires a low-level (or guitar-level) input, plug your signal source into the effect directly and plug the output of the effect into the mic preamp and forget about using the break jacks. Figure 9-13 shows how to use the break jacks to cascade mic preamps together to achieve greater gain than the gain of 10 offered by a single preamp. Note that once you insert plugs into J1 and J2, you break the signal path for that channel and no signal goes through to the tone control or any other subsequent stages.

SW1 is a simple in/out switch that functions like the one described for the preamp.

The tone-control circuit itself is a variation of the one I wrote for *EPFM* (project #11). The only changes involve lowering the input impedance from 1 Meg to 10k by changing R4, which also necessitates changing C3 to a larger value, in this case $2.7\mu F$. The output capacitor has also been enlarged so that the tone control can drive a 10k load satisfactorily. Other than that, the circuitry is identical.

The tone control in *EPFM* is a stereo unit; that is, there are two complete, separate

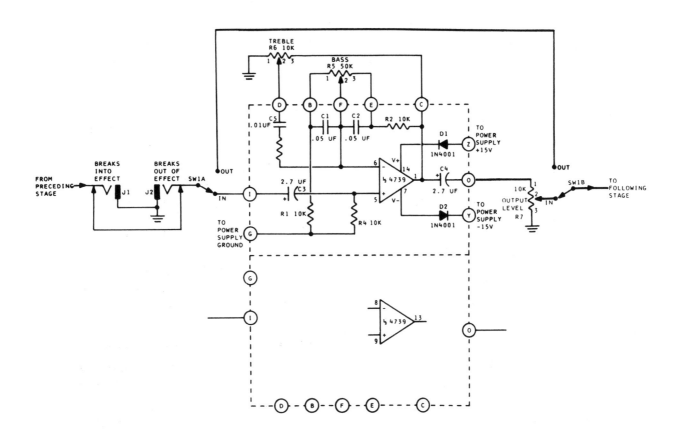

Tone Control Schematic.

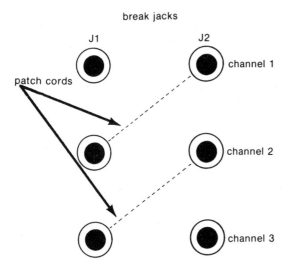

Greatly amplified mic signal appears at output of channel 3. Preamp must be switched in for all channels.

Figure 9-13.

controls on the same circuit board. Although we only show one channel on the schematic, the parts are exactly the same for the second channel, except that the power supply protection diodes are not required for the second half. Since each board has two channels, you only need a total of three boards to implement tone controls for all six input channels.

This particular tone-control circuit gives a gain of 2, which can be handy when you punch in EQ for something like a solo, and you want the equalized sound to stand out compared to the non-equalized sound. Should you not want extra gain, but would rather have a consistent volume level as you switch the tone control in and out, you may vary R7 to obtain the desired balance. In some cases, you may even want *less* level in the equalized position because the tonal changes may make the instrument stand out too much.

C1, C2, and C5 are capacitors that determine the tuning of the filter. Therefore, it's a

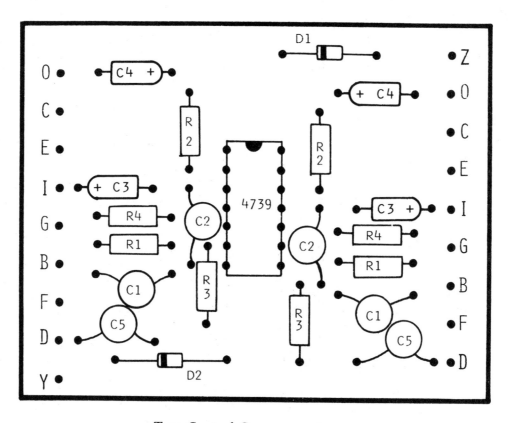

Tone Control Component Layout.

good idea to use mylar capacitors if possible in order to maintain stability and repeatability from unit to unit. If you must use disc or other less stable capacitor types, at least make sure, to give as much consistency as possible, that they are all the same model and made by the same manufacturer.

Although studios tend to use very expensive and complex equalizers, this simple and inexpensive equalizer (tone control) gives a good account of itself and will handle many of the situations, like hiss and low-end control, where you need EQ the most.

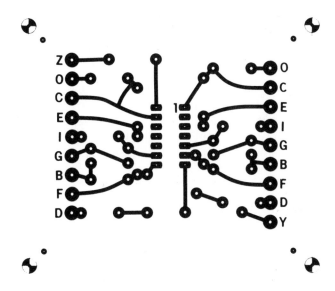

Tone Control Circuit Board Layout.

PARTS LIST, TONE CONTROL

R1, R2, R4	10kΩ ¼ watt carbon resistor (brown-black-orange)
R3	1kΩ ¼ watt carbon resistor (brown-black-red)
R5	50kΩ linear taper potentiometer
R6, R7	10kΩ linear taper potentiometer
C1, C2	.05µF capacitor, mylar preferred
C3, C4	2.7µF tantalum capacitor, 20 VDC
C5	.01µF capacitor, mylar preferred

D1, D2	1N4001 diode or equivalent
IC1	4739 dual, low-noise op amp with matching 14-pin socket
SW1	DPDT toggle switch
J1, J2	¼″ mono closed circuit phone jack

ALSO REQUIRED: (1) circuit board, knobs, solder, etc.

(Double these parts for two channels.)

NOISE GATE

A signal hitting the input of the noise gate splits into two paths: one path feeds IC1, a 741, and the other path goes through a photoresistor and couples into the output through C5.

IC1 is a *comparator;* simply stated, if an input signal level exceeds the level set by the comparator's threshold control, that signal produces an output voltage at the output of the 741 (pin 6). If the signal is below the threshold level, then there is no output from the 741. Since most signals are not static but instead move back and forth across the threshold, the output of the 741 resembles a square wave or series of pulses.

The 741's output then feeds a 555 timer set up as a missing pulse detector. As long as the input of the 555 sees a series of pulses at its input—which happens when an input signal is above the threshold—then its output, pin 3, is *high* (approaches positive supply voltage) and supplies current to two LEDs: D4, which indicates that the gate is open, and the LED located inside the CLM6000 opto-isolator. The CLM6000 consists of an LED and photoresistor mounted close to each other in a miniature light-tight package (see Figure 9–14). When current flows through the LED, light from the LEDs strikes the photoresistor; the photoresistor then acquires a very low resistance, (it's high when no light shines on it) and passes the input signal through to the output with little attenuation.

However, if the series of pulses stops (which happens when the input signal drops below the threshold of the comparator), then, after a few milliseconds, the output of the 555 goes *low* (approaches ground level). This

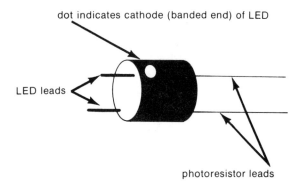

dot indicates cathode (banded end) of LED

LED leads

photoresistor leads

Figure 9-14.

allows current to flow through D3, indicating that the gate is closed. Simultaneously, current stops flowing through D4 and the CLM6000's LED. Since the LED inside the CLM6000 no longer shines on the photoresistor, the photoresistor returns to a high-resistance state. This interrupts the signal flow, and effectively prevents any audio signal from reaching the next stage.

The *reduction control* parallels the photoresistor. When turned up all the way it presents a short across the photoresistor, nullifying the effect of the noise gate. When the noise gate is in use, if the photoresistor is in its high-resistance state, then the reduction control determines how much the signal is attenuated on its way to the output.

This noise gate must see a 10k load at its output, which is just fine when working with our mixer because the input point of each channel is approximately 10k. If used in conjunction with other equipment, however, add a 10k to 15k resistor from point 0 to ground to insure proper gating action. This load resistance, along with the photoresistor, forms a voltage divider which attenuates the signal in the 'gate closed' mode. The maximum amount of noise reduction obtainable is about 10:1 (20dB).

SW1 is the time-constant control. Remember how we said that when the string of pulses stops, then in a few milliseconds the 555 goes low? The time-constant control determines just how many milliseconds it takes for that action to occur. In the 'fast' position it takes approximately 5 milliseconds; in the

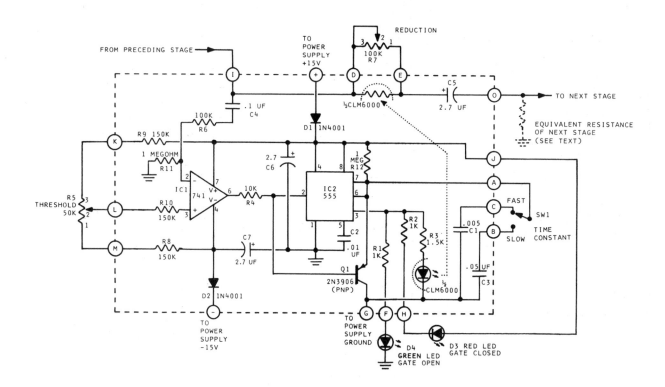

Noise Gate Schematic.

'slow' position, approximately 50 milliseconds. Use the 5ms position when you need a very fast noise-reduction effect (such as with percussive instruments), and use the 50ms position with signals like vocals, where you don't want the noise gate opening and closing on every little syllable.

To operate the noise gate, turn down any signal going to the gate and set the threshold just below the point where the 'gate open' LED comes on so that the 'gate closed' LED illuminates. Then, apply the signal and the 'gate open' LED should fire. When the signal goes away, the 'gate closed' LED should come back on. If it doesn't, move the threshold control slightly lower. Adjust the reduction control for the desired amount of noise reduction when the signal is off.

One of my favorite uses of noise gating is with vocals. Many times vocals do not run all the way through a song; as a result, there is an annoying tape hiss when the voice is not present. The noise gate effectively cuts out this hiss.

Another use for the noise gate is on fade-ins. By setting the noise gate as described two paragraphs back, when a signal hits the noise gate input, the 'gate open' LED lights up. Thus, if you want to fade in a drum part, you can leave the channel fader all the way off and watch the noise gate LED until the 'gate open' illuminates; this means that the drums are in the signal path. Slowly turn up the channel fader to create your fade-in.

Noise gates are a little tricky to set up and adjust; they are even trickier to use to maximum advantage. Lots of practice is the best way to understand how these things work. Also, re-read the section on noise gates under "Noise Reduction Techniques" for further understanding of how the noise gate works. The better you understand its workings, the better you can apply it.

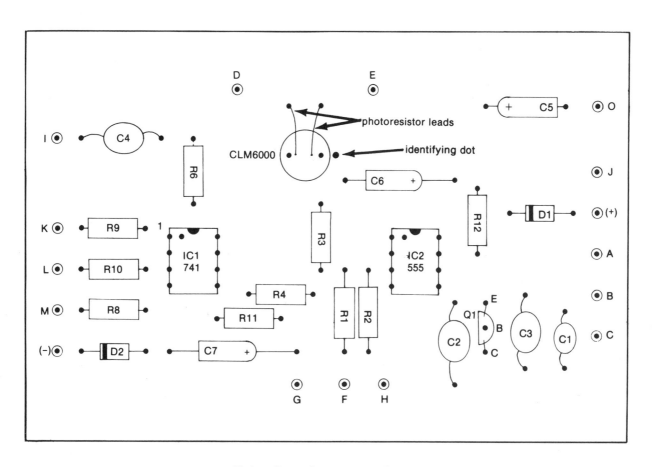

Noise Gate Component Layout.

161

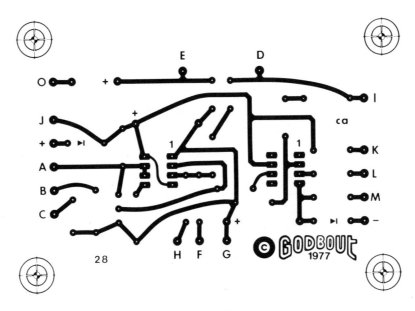

Noise Gate Circuit Board Layout

PARTS LIST, NOISE GATE

R1, R2	1kΩ ¼ watt carbon resistor (brown-black-red)
R3	1.5kΩ ¼ watt carbon resistor (brown-green-red)
R4	10kΩ ¼ watt carbon resistor (brown-black-orange)
R5	50kΩ potentiometer, linear taper preferred
R6	100kΩ ¼ watt carbon resistor (brown-black-yellow)
R7	100kΩ potentiometer, linear or audio taper
R8–R10	150kΩ ¼ watt carbon resistor (brown-green-yellow)
R11, R12	1MΩ ¼ watt carbon resistor (brown-black-green)
C1	.005μF mylar capacitor
C2	.01μF disc capacitor
C3	.05μF mylar capacitor
C4	.1μF ceramic disc capacitor
C5–C7	2.7μF tantalum capacitor, 20 VDC
D1, D2	1N4001 diode or equivalent
D3	Red LED
D4	Green LED
IC1	741 op amp with matching 8-pin socket
IC2	555 timer with matching 8-pin socket
Q1	2N3906 PNP transistor
CLM6000	Clairex opto-isolator
SW1	SPDT toggle switch

ALSO REQUIRED: (1) circuit board, knobs, solder, etc.

POWER SUPPLY

Every module discussed so far has three terminals going to the power supply, perhaps the most important module in your entire mixer. The power supply is the food that your mixer eats in order to stay alive, and should it fail, your session goes down the tubes. As a result, we will need to spend some time discussing this crucial final link in your system.

We will cover two basic ways of implementing the power supply. Neither is 'better' than the other; they just use different parts. This way you have a little bit of latitude in terms of choice of transformer and regulators.

The various mixer modules require two voltages, +15V referenced to ground and −15V referenced to ground. A console consisting of a main mixer, cue mixer, reverb mixer, six channels (each with mic preamp, tone control, and noise gate) and a headphone amp draws about 250mA from the positive supply and somewhat less from the negative supply. However, in keeping with the overall philosophy of conservative (worst-case) design, the supplies described can comfortably provide about twice this current. This has several advantages: normal operation does not overwork the supply, which reduces heat dissipation and heat sinking problems; also, you have some spare capacity available should you want to add additional effect modules. For example, I am currently powering a flanger from the power supply in addition to the mixer, and the supply doesn't mind one bit.

Power supply (A) is a simple 15V supply; by hooking it up as shown in Figure 9-15, we can obtain the +15V and -15V referenced to ground (this is called a bipolar supply, because it has two polarities).

The transformer specified is a 15 VAC type (if center tapped, just ignore the center tap). In an emergency, or if you can't locate a 15 volt transformer, you can tie a 12.6V and 6.3V transformer in series (Figure 9-16) to obtain an '18V' transformer. However, after hooking up these transformers in this fashion, be sure to measure the output voltage. If it reads somewhere around 18 VAC, fine. If you get a reading that's closer to 6 VAC, then reverse the two leads of the 6.3V transformer. Transformers have phase, and depending upon how they are connected, can either add or subtract—we want them to add.

This AC voltage then converts to raw DC through diodes D1–D4; the large capacitor then filters this raw DC into filtered DC. The

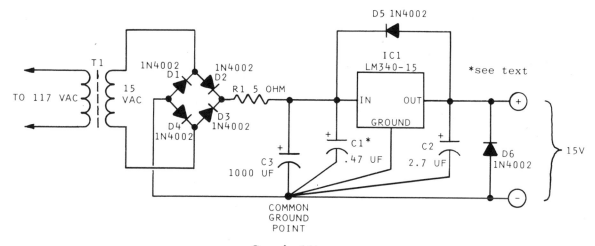

Supply (A).

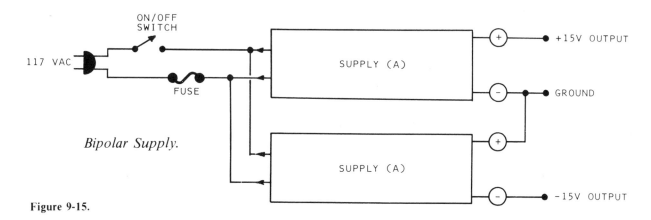

Bipolar Supply.

Figure 9-15.

163

filtered DC goes to the input of a three-terminal regulator, the LM340-15. This IC regulates our input voltage into a precise and stable 15 volts, regardless of load conditions.

Let's examine the three-terminal regulator for a bit. In pre-IC days, designing power supplies was a hassle; but the new IC regulators take care of all our problems, since they are virtually impossible to destroy and are very easy to use. They have built-in thermal overload protection; this means that should a regulator overheat, it does not turn into molten metal, but simply shuts itself off and waits for things to cool down a bit, at which point it turns on again. Also, if you short the output to ground, it won't curl up and die, but, again, just shuts off or limits the current until the short goes away. There are two ways, however, that these regulators can be fried: one failure mode occurs if the regulator becomes reverse-biased, which can happen if the filter-capacitor (+) end accidentally shorts to ground. Diode D5 protects the regulator by shunting destructive currents around it rather than through it. Also, should a negative (below-ground) voltage appear at the output, the regulator can latch up and self-destruct. Diode D6 shunts any negative voltages to ground. Although these situations seldom happen, accidents are possible or test probes can slip, and it only costs two diodes per supply to give us the protection we need.

These regulators come in two different types of packages. One type is called a TO-3 package and resembles a metal power transistor (see Figure 9-17); the other type is a plastic power package (TO-220 type). Either one is acceptable for our supply, although I'm prejudiced in favor of the TO-3 types for no specific reason.

When constructing the supply, you must allow for the fact that these regulators get hot and require *heat sinking*. A heat sink is simply a large chunk of aluminum attached to the regulator which helps draw away heat and dissipate it into the air. We don't need anything too elaborate, but the more heat sinking we add the cooler the regulators will run and the happier they will be. There are commercial heat sinks available for both types of packages, but a piece of aluminum will do the job almost as well.

Although the LM340 is designed so that the case is at ground potential, and may therefore use the grounded chassis as a heat sink, I do not recommend this approach because you will run into problems when building the negative supply, where the case of the regulator is *not* at ground potential. I generally build my power supplies on a piece of Vector board, and mount the heat sink under the transistor, sandwiched between the regulator and the Vector board. I also make sure that the heat sink cannot come into contact with the chassis. Figure 9-18 indicates some possible ways to heat sink the regulators. For extra heat transfer, coat the underside of the regulator with silicone grease—it conducts heat but not electricity, and therefore increases the heat exchange between the regulator and the heat sink.

The −15V supply is the same electrically as the +15V supply, and the same precautions apply. Mount both supplies in a nice large case, with lots of air circulation. Be nice to your power supply and it will be nice to you; you don't want the regulators to shut themselves off some hot summer day simply because you skimped on the thermal requirements.

Another subject involving safety concerns getting the AC lines into your power supply. Keep your AC connections away from the case and the power supply boards; make sure there is *no chance* they can short out to any other connections or to the case. Use a multi-lug terminal strip for securely attaching your wires. Make sure that no pieces of stranded wires can short out to the other terminals. Remember, we are dealing with

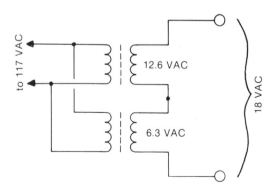

Figure 9-16.

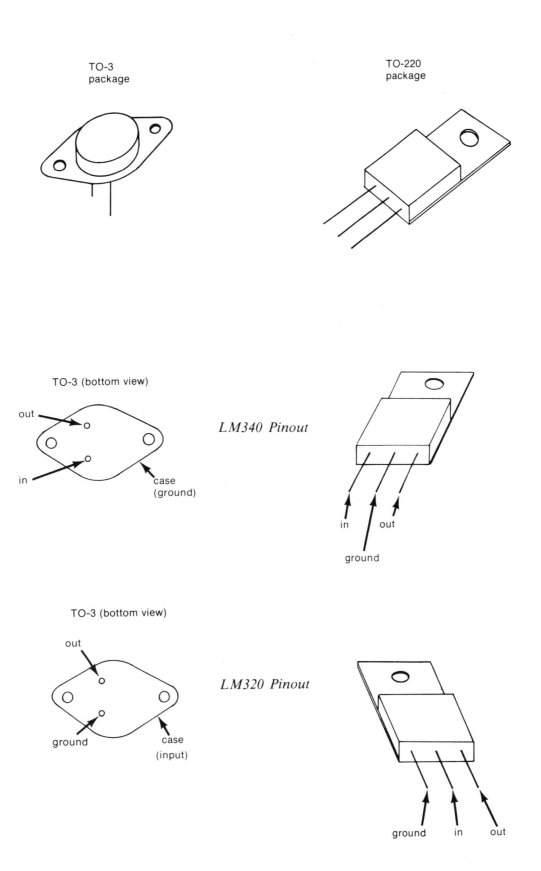

TO-3
package

TO-220
package

TO-3 (bottom view)

out

in

case
(ground)

LM340 Pinout

in   out

ground

TO-3 (bottom view)

out

ground

case
(input)

LM320 Pinout

ground   in   out

Figure 9-17.

165

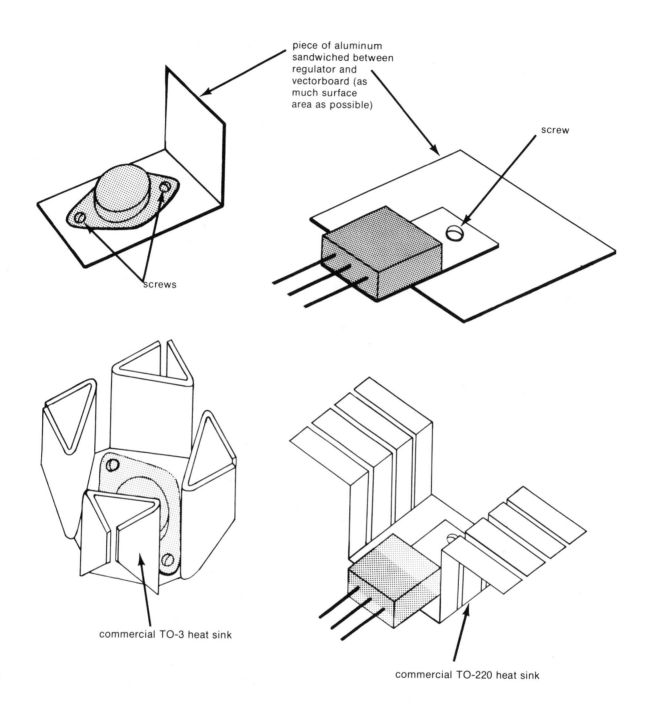

piece of aluminum
sandwiched between
regulator and
vectorboard (as
much surface
area as possible)

screw

screws

commercial TO-3 heat sink

commercial TO-220 heat sink

Figure 9-18.

166

potentially lethal voltages: you aren't going to have a great session if you get a jolt that knocks you across the room. Use a nice, heavy-duty switch that can handle several amps of current. Of course, the supply draws nowhere near that much; but be conservative for safety's sake.

Since the power supply is hopefully going to plug into a fused barrier strip as described earlier, we do not really need to fuse the primary. But again, just in case something catastrophic happens and someone spills water down into the supply, it's best to be prepared. A ½-amp fuse should protect you against blatant problems, such as a transformer primary shorting out.

Please be careful. After all, you are the most important piece of equipment in your studio. Take your time and make solid, well-soldered connections; work as though your life depended on it.

After you finish building your supply, make sure that the output voltages read (+) and (−) 15V. With no load, the voltage going to the input of each regulator should be somewhere between 20V and 25V; you might want to check this, too. Remember that when checking the voltages on the positive supply, the (−) lead of your voltmeter connects to

ground. When checking through the negative supply, the (+) lead of your voltmeter connects to ground.

Does everything check out OK? Fine. But don't hook the supply up to your mixer just yet. Let it sit there for a little bit and make sure it remains well behaved—just to make sure.

Power supply (B) (Figure 9–19) is a somewhat more elegant design, in that it only requires one transformer, four diodes instead of eight for rectification, and it uses both a positive regulator (the LM340-15) and a negative regulator (the LM320-15). Like the LM340, the LM320 requires heat sinking. It is specifically designed to handle negative voltages, and the protection diodes are oriented accordingly.

The capacitors indicated with asterisks may or may not be necessary. Data sheets for the regulators say that these capacitors are required if the leads from the filter capacitor to the regulators are long, as is often the case in systems where the transformer/filter combination feeds several regulators in remote locations. Maybe you won't find these necessary, but to tell you the truth, I always put them in—it gives one less chance for Murphy's Law to apply.

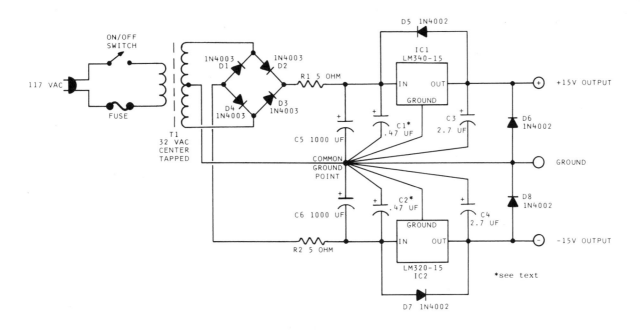

Figure 9-19.   *Supply (B).*

PARTS LIST, SUPPLY (A)

R1	5Ω 10 watt power resistor
C1	.47 to 4.7µF tantalum capacitor, 35 VDC
C2	2.7µF tantalum capacitor, 20 VDC
C3	1000µF Electrolytic capacitor, 35 VDC
IC1	LM340-15 three-terminal regulator, +15V @ 1A
D1–D5	1N4002 or equivalent power diode
T1	15 VAC to 18 VAC transformer (note: R1 may need to be increased with 18-volt transformers to bring voltage at input of regulator down to 25 VDC under no-load conditions)

ALSO REQUIRED: (1) fuse, (1) SPST on/off switch, wire, solder, heat sink, hardware, line cord, case, etc.

PARTS LIST, SUPPLY (B)

R1, R2	5Ω 10 watt power resistor
C1, C2	.47 to 4.7µF tantalum capacitor, 35 VDC
C3, C4	2.7µF tantalum capacitor, 20 VDC
C5, C6	1000µF electrolytic capacitor, 35 VDC
IC1	LM340-15 3-terminal regulator +15V @ 1A
IC2	LM320-15 3-terminal regulator, –15V @ 1A
D1–D4	1N4003 or equivalent power diode
D5–D8	1N4002 or equivalent power diode
T1	30 to 36 VAC center-tapped transformer (note: R1 and R2 may need to be increased with 36-volt transformer to bring voltage at inputs of regulators down to 25 VDC under no-load conditions)

ALSO REQUIRED: (1) fuse, (1) SPST on/off switch, wire, solder, heat sinks, hardware, line cord, case, etc.

USING YOUR MIXER

Well! The odyssey is complete. Hook the supply up to your mixer, experience a moment of trepidation, and plug in.

If you see any smoke, or hear sizzling sounds or small explosions, immediately un-plug and get ready to find whatever mistake is causing the problem. Chances are, though, that if you have been careful and followed all this advice, the only sound you hear will be the faint heart throb of 60Hz AC running through the transformers.

I have my mixer set up so that the tape recorder outputs from the 4-channel machine feed the first four inputs. I pretty much leave these inputs with the selector switch set to listen to the tape outputs; if I need to use the inputs for mics or instruments, then I set the input selector switch accordingly. I run the outputs from my second machine (a cassette deck) into inputs 5 and 6, and have the instrument inputs for 5 and 6 ready for patching to the outputs of various instruments.

The jacks that connect to the output selector run into the 4-channel machine inputs; one of the dub outputs goes to the second machine. Probably the best way to get a feel for the operation of the mixer is with some examples.

Plug an instrument, like a guitar, or a tone source, into input 6, and do the following:

1) Set the input selector to *instrument*.

2) Set the preamp in/out switch to OUT, turn gain to minimum, and set rolloff switch to FLAT.

3) Set EQ in/out switch to OUT.

4) Set threshold control on noise gate so that the 'gate open' LED lights; set re-duction control full clockwise.

5) Set mute switch on OUT.

6) Set cue bus fader, reverb fader, and main mixer fader fully counterclock-wise (off).

7) Plug headphones into output of head-phone amp. Now, we are ready to run some experiments.

Turn the cue control for channel 6 all the way up, and turn up the level of the headphone amp. Play your guitar or whatever; you should hear something. Is it a little weak in level? Flip the preamp in/out switch to IN, and slowly advance the preamp gain; that should increase the gain of the guitar. Set the rolloff to 80Hz; although the difference won't be too noticeable, the guitar should lose some bottom. This difference will be more apparent with bass, keyboards, and other instruments that go below 80Hz. We have now verified that the input selector, preamp, headphone amp, and cue bus are in working order (at least for channel 6). Set the EQ in/out switch to IN, and play with the bass/treble controls until you get a feel for their operation.

Next, practice a little with the noise gate. Turn the preamp up full so that the gate has a nice, strong signal to work with (it likes nice, strong signals). Stop playing for a moment, and turn the threshold control counterclockwise until the 'gate closed' LED comes on. Play your guitar; it should come through just as loud as before, but the 'gate open' LED should illuminate when you hit a note or chord. Next, turn down the reduction control; you should note that any residual noise and hiss dies out when you aren't playing. If it's a little hard to tell the difference, temporarily turn up the treble on the EQ to emphasize any noise; the difference between gated and non-gated sound should then be pretty plain. Note that you may need to reset the threshold control so that it is still above the noise level. Do not expect to become a noise-gate-control-setting expert in five minutes. Remember, for now, we are just getting a feel. You can develop your technique later.

Let's check out how the reverb is doing. Turn up the reverb-return control for the cue channel; you should hear some hiss coming from the reverb recovery amp. Set the reverb switch to 'pre' and turn up the reverb bus control for channel 6. You should hear a reverberated instrument.

Now let's see if this signal is making it to your recorder. Set the output switch associated with track 1 of your 4-channel recorder to source, and set the output selector on your mixer to channel 1. Turn up the main mixer fader for channel 6, then turn up the master volume control, and play. You should see the VU meter of your tape deck (channel 1) swinging back and forth. If it isn't, then check your output selector switch to make sure it is feeding the correct channel of your tape machine; check the cords; check whatever could be interrupting your signal path.

Now, turn down the cue control for channel 6, then turn up the output cue control; you are now monitoring from the output of the main mixer bus (what's going to the recorder) rather than from the cue bus. If you want to hear reverb, you will have to turn down the reverb cue control and turn up the master reverb-return control. Turn the output cue back down, but leave the master output and the main mixer fader for channel 6 up, so that the tape recorder VU meters still give an indication of a signal.

Next, set the input selector for channel 1 of your mixer so that it is picking up the output from channel 1 of your tape deck. Make sure channel 1 is set up the same way that we set up channel 6 at the beginning: preamp OUT, EQ OUT, mute OUT, etc. With the output cue and channel cue controls turned down, you should hear nothing. Making sure that the tape recorder output switch is still set to source, turn up the cue control for channel 1. Aha! You hear your instrument again, but this time, you are monitoring the signal *after* it has been sent to the tape recorder, gone through the tape recorder electronics, and been spit out the output of that particular channel. So there are three separate ways we can monitor our signal feeding channel 6: monitor channel 6 via the cue bus; monitor the signal going into the recorder via the output cue; or monitor the signal coming out of the recorder by monitoring, in this case, channel 1, via the cue bus. Had you sent your guitar into channel 2, everything would be more or less the same except that you would turn up the cue control for channel 2 if you wanted to monitor the output of your tape machine's channel 2.

Here is another example of the various ways to monitor a couple of signals. Say you have guitar and bass plugged into inputs 5 and 6, respectively. By monitoring input 5 only, via the cue bus, you can hear the guitar. By monitoring input 6 only, via the cue bus, you can hear the bass. By turning up the main mixer controls for channels 5 and 6, you can send both signals to whichever tape channel is selected by the output selector; and you can monitor this combined signal by turning up the output cue (but make sure the cue bus faders are down if you are monitoring in this mode). Finally, if you are sending your guitar/bass signal to channel 3 of your recorder, you can monitor the recorder output by turning up the cue bus fader for channel 3. With the tape recorder's output switch set to TAPE, you can also monitor the signal while the machine is recording (with a slight delay, of course) directly from the playback head. However, don't try to monitor with various combinations of monitor controls turned up; listen to either the tape output, the cue bus, or the output cue, but not two or three of these at once. Redundant monitoring may cause reduced levels or excessively high levels, due to cancellation or reinforcement of different signals that have different phase relationships with respect to each other.

There is so much you can do with a mixer like this; I could write another 100 pages on applications, but you will discover them anyway as you go along. Let's run through a couple more situations. Suppose you have tracks 1 through 3 recorded with guitar, bass, and drums, and you want to add a lead guitar part. To listen to tracks 1, 2, and 3, set the respective recorder output switches to tape, put all channels in SYNC, and adjust the cue bus faders for channels 1 through 3 to a comfortable listening level. Don't forget that the tape must be running in order for you to hear anything while the output switches are in the TAPE position. Next, plug your lead guitar into input 6; turn up the main mixer fader for channel 6 (the master level), and then set the output selector to send the lead guitar into track 4 (the remaining open track on the recorder). Now, you have three options for monitoring the lead guitar: the cue bus fader for channel 6, the output cue, or, with the tape output switch for channel 4 set to source, from the cue bus fader for channel 4. I would generally choose the cue bus fader for channel 4, simply because that monitors the signal the furthest down the signal chain; so if there is something amiss, I'll hear it right away. For example, if you are monitoring the cue bus for channel 6 and someone turns the output selector to the wrong channel, you will still

hear the guitar in your headphones. But if you listen to the tape recorder output, then any problem that shows up between your mixer and the tape recorder will show up in your phones.

Note that you *don't* want the main mixer faders for tracks 1, 2, and 3 up at all, or they will mix, along with your lead guitar part, into track 4. Remember, anything mixed onto the main mixer bus goes into the recorder; any sound mixed onto the cue bus goes into your phones.

With this mixer, you can readily add tape echo to a particular track. Suppose you are putting a vocal, via input 6, into track 4 of your recorder—a similar situation to the one we just described. And let's say you want to add some tape echo to the voice. To do this, turn up the main mixer fader for channel 4, and set the tape recorder output switch for channel 4 to tape. See what is happening? We are putting the mic into channel 4 of the tape recorder via the main mixer and output selector. But no sooner does that vocal get recorded at the record head, when we immediately pick up some of that signal from the playback head—delayed by a fraction of a second—and put it back into the main mixer. The delayed signal gets sent back into track 4, and the cycle repeats itself, creating an echo effect. But we run into a slight problem: If you monitor the output of track 4 from the cue bus, you will only hear a delayed sound; try singing along with a delayed sound sometime, it's not easy. In a case like this, your best bet is to set the echo for a suitable effect, then forget about monitoring it, and just monitor the cue fader for channel 6. This will make it much easier to sing along with the track. If you must hear the echo (for example, if you want to make sure it's not feeding back on itself), monitor via the output cue.

If this explanation of how to get echo is confusing, don't worry. One day you will hit upon it accidentally—whether you want it or not—and then you will find out for sure how this process works.

A musical instrument, sitting by itself, does not make a sound; it needs a person to bring out any beautiful music. But it takes a long time to learn fully about an instrument; I doubt that any musician can ever hope to extract everything possible from an instrument during a single lifetime. A mixer is a lot like a musical instrument, in the sense that you cannot just sit down and expect to be a master of the controls within a couple of minutes. You have to study the signal flow, why signals go where they go, why sometimes you do not get a sound even though you are *absolutely sure* everything is set correctly; only after that kind of study, coupled with hours of practice, an inquisitive mind, and a desire to learn, will you feel familiar with you instrument. These descriptions of how to use your mixer may sound unfamiliar—perhaps even a little frightening—and I would be the first to admit that running a mixer is no easier than learning how to fly. But people do learn to fly, and they do learn how to run mixers; and so can you.

There will be times when you will get discouraged. Despite years of experience, there are still times when I just cannot get a signal, only to find that I left a mute switch on by mistake or am monitoring from the wrong channel. You are embarking on an adventure that requires dedication, but the rewards are very gratifying.

Appendix A

WHERE CAN I LEARN MORE

This is always a difficult question to answer, because there is no one repository of recording knowledge. You need to pick up pieces of knowledge from a book here, from a magazine article there, from talking to engineers, from data supplied by manufacturers—in short, learning is a do-it-yourself proposition.

If you are interested solely in the technical/physics/mathematics aspect of sound, there are many excellent books on acoustics and electrical phenomena available. College libraries often have access to *Journal of the Audio Engineering Society, Sound and Vibration,* and other specialized publications; music departments frequently subscribe to current electronic music magazines (more on this later).

Books are for reference, for verifying technical facts, and for learning basics and theory. Magazines, on the other hand, carry the immediate news, the newest technical designs, the latest mixing and equalization ideas—in other words, current events. Although there are only a scattering of magazines written exclusively with the studio in mind, there are several general-coverage magazines that carry articles of interest from time to time.

Following are some books and magazines you may find helpful in your quest for knowledge:

BOOKS

Audio Cyclopedia, by Howard W. Tremaine (Howard W. Sams & Co., Inc., Indianapolis, IN 46268). Over 1700 pages of question-and-answer-type material on almost anything involving audio. While dated in some ways, this in nonetheless the recognized reference book for audio. The answer to anything you want to ask is probably in here, but finding it can be quite an operation. It's good to have around and fun to browse through, if you can afford it.

Handbook of Multichannel Recording, by F. Alton Everest (TAB Books, Blue Ridge Summit, PA 17214). A popular book, clearly written, that deals mostly with the professional multitrack studio.

Microphones: Design and Application, by Lou Burroughs (Sagamore Publishing Company, 980 Old Country Road, Plainview, NY 11803). The authoritative book on microphones.

Sound Recording, by John Eargle (Van Nostrand Reinhold Company, 450 West 33rd Street, New York, NY 10001). Fairly technical treatment; gives general overview of the complete recording process.

MAGAZINES

db, The Sound Engineering Magazine (1120 Old Country Road, Plainview, NY 11803). A magazine for sound engineers; concerns itself with new developments, electronics, new techniques, and the like.

Modern Recording Magazine (15 Columbus Circle, New York, NY 10023). This is a bi-monthly that deals with both musical and technical aspects of recording, mostly in a non-technical manner.

Recording Engineer/Producer (Box 2287, Hollywood, CA 90028). Leans a little more towards the production side than *db,* but also has many technical articles. Does a good job of combining both musical and technical aspects of a subject.

172

Songwriter Magazine (Box 3510, Hollywood, CA 90028). Although less technical than the other magazines mentioned, it's listed because many home recording enthusiasts are into writing songs.

Studio Sound (Link House, Dingwall Avenue, Croydon, England CR9 2TA). Similar to *db*, but covers the English scene.

The Audio Amateur (Peterborough, NH 03458). Although not devoted exclusively to recording, this magazine *is* devoted to audio and as such has some excellent tape articles.

NEWSSTAND MAGAZINES

Many magazines available to the general public carry occasional articles on recording; most of these can be found in a good library. *Hi-Fi Stereo Review* has an excellent column on tape recording, by Craig Stark. *Popular Electronics* has a hi-fi and tape column by Ralph Hodges, and also carries interesting projects from time to time (mixer, VU meter, etc.). *Radio-Electronics* has at least one or two audio articles per issue; it also carries comparison test type articles on tape that are very interesting. Other magazines include *Audio* and *High Fidelity*.

ELECTRONIC MUSIC MAGAZINES

Although none of these concentrate on recording, they are highly involved with audio and electronics and that makes them worth noting, especially for tape people who are into tinkering. These magazines are *Electronotes* (213 Dryden Road, Ithaca, NY 14850), *Polyphony* (published by PAIA Electronics, Inc., 1020 W. Wilshire Blvd., Oklahoma City, OK 73116), and *Synapse* (2829 Hyans Street, Los Angeles, CA 90026). Incidentally, I contribute regularly to these magazines as well as to some of the others mentioned earlier.

LOCAL MUSICIAN PAPERS

There are several local papers that cover specific music scenes, like *Musician's Classified* in New York, *Music City News* in Nashville, *Michigan Musician* in Detroit, and *Bay Area Musician* for the San Francisco Bay Area. These are good sources of information about local studios and local availability of equipment.

OBTAINING INFORMATION FROM MANUFACTURERS

If you need to know more about a particular product you may request information directly from the manufacturer. Listed below (in alphabetical order) are addresses of many manufacturers of audio-oriented equipment, but, naturally, any listing of this type cannot include all manufacturers of interest. Should you encounter any products, services, or publications not covered in this appendix that are of interest to home recording enthusiasts, drop me a line c/o *Guitar Player Books* (Box 615, Saratoga, CA 95070), and we'll see if we can work more information into subsequent editions.

When requesting information, limit yourself to equipment that really interests you. It costs money and people's time to send out information; take that into account.

Advent Corporation
195 Albany Street
Cambridge, MA 02139
—Speakers, cassette recorders

Akai America, Ltd.
2139 E. Del Amo Blvd.
Compton, CA 90220
—Stereo and 4-track consumer-type recorders

Bill Godbout Electronics
Box 2355
Oakland Airport, CA 94614
—Do it yourself parts kits for many of the
projects in the projects chapter

Crown International
1718 W. Mishawaka Rd.
Elkhart, IN 46514
—High-quality, 4-track recorders, amplifiers

dbx Inc.
296 Newton Street
Waltham, MA 02154
—Professional and consumer noise-reduction
equipment; compressors

Dokorder, Inc.
Box 8 (service department only)
Lawndale, CA 90260
—Stereo and 4-track consumer and semipro
recorders

Gately Electronics
57 Hillcrest Avenue
Haverstown, PA 19083
—Kits for mixers and other gear

Heath Company
Benton Harbor, MI 49022
—Kits for mixer, cassette recorder, amplifiers

JVC America, Inc.
58-75 Queens Midtown Expressway
Maspeth, NY 11378
—Consumer recorders and field cassette decks

Maxell Corporation of America
130 West Commercial Avenue
Moonachie, NJ 07074
—Cassette and open reel tape

Memorex Corporation
Consumer Products Division
41834 Higgins Way
Fremont, CA 94538
—Cassette and open reel tape

Nakamichi Research USA Inc.
220 Westbury Avenue
Carle Place, NY 11514
—Cassette and mixing equipment

Old Colony Sound Lab
Box 243
Peterborough, NH 03458
—Kits for equalizers, small amps, and parts

Opamp Labs, Inc.
172 S. Alta Vista Blvd.
Los Angeles, CA 90036
—Plug-in modules for custom mixing boards

Otari Corporation
981 Industrial Road
San Carlos, CA 94070
—Professional and semipro recorders

PAIA Electronics, Inc.
1020 W. Wilshire Blvd.
Oklahoma City, OK 73116
—Electronic kits, mostly synthesizer and
  effects oriented

Pioneer Electronics Corporation
75 Oxford Drive
Moonachie, NJ 07074
—Stereo and 4-track recording equipment;
  4-track field deck

ReVox
155 Michael Drive
Syosset, NY 11791
—Semipro stereo recorders

SESCOM
Box 590
Gardena, CA 90247
—Plug-in modules and parts for custom
  mixing boards

Shure Brothers, Inc.
222 Hartley Avenue
Evanston, IL 60204
—Microphones, mixers

Sony/Superscope
20525 Nordhoff St.
Chatsworth, CA 91311
—Stereo and 4-track consumer and
  semipro equipment

SWTPC
219 W. Rhapsody
San Antonio, TX 78216
—Kits for equalizer, amplifiers, simple mixer

TDK Electronics Corp.
755 Eastgate Boulevard
Garden City, NY 11530
—Cassette and open reel tape

TEAC Corporation of America
Box 750
Montebello, CA 90640
—Stereo and 4-track consumer/semipro

recording equipment, mixers,
mics, accessories

Uher of America Inc.
621 S. Hindry Avenue
Inglewood, CA 90301
—Specializes in portable recording gear

Yamaha
Box 6600
Buena Park, CA 90622
—Mixing boards

Appendix B

RELATING THE DB TO VOLTAGE AND POWER RATIOS

As promised earlier, here is the formula for relating the dB to ratios of voltage and power. It is stashed way in the back of the book so it wouldn't scare people off. If you want to know more, check out a good library.

For AC voltage ratios: $dB = 20 \left(\log \dfrac{V1}{V2} \right)$ $V = volts$

For power ratios: $dB = 10 \left(\log \dfrac{P1}{P2} \right)$ $P = watts$

(Power ratios are independent of source and load impedance values, but voltage ratios only hold when the source and load impedances are equal.)

Example 1: By measuring the peak-to-peak voltage at the output of an amplifier, you determine that, at minimum gain, the output is 0.25V peak-to-peak, and at maximum gain, the output is 5V peak-to-peak. To determine the ratio in dB between minimum and maximum gain,

$$dB = 20 \left(\log \frac{5.00V}{0.25V} \right) = 20 \, (\log 20) = 20 \, (1.30) = 26dB$$

Example 2: A microphone needs 60dB of gain in order to hit 0 VU on the tape recorder meter. Will a preamp with a gain of 1000 suffice?

$$dB = 20 \, (\log 1000) = 20 \, (3) = 60dB$$

Appendix C

SENDING YOUR DEMO TO A RECORD COMPANY

At some point, you may want to see if what you think is good music agrees with what a record company thinks is good music, and send a demo in for a company's consideration. If you really want to do the job right, give it some thought and effort. Here are some rules about sending in material:

Don't use up your chances prematurely. If you send in a not-so-hot tape, and then submit another a year later, don't expect the people who are listening to start off prejudiced in your favor. These people have memories. At the very least, show them you have a real, recognizable talent at loose on those tapes. If it's a band, make sure that it is at least as competent as the general music going around today or you won't stand a chance.

Don't waste the company's time. Quite a few people submit tapes to record companies, and it takes some time to sift through these. However, the companies *do* listen, because 1% of the stuff is good and warrants further investigation; it's worth wading through the other 99% if that 1% happens to be a Beatles or Sinatra or Elvis. Give them the best that you have got.

Keep it short. They don't want to hear concept albums, they are looking for hits—things lots and lots of people will buy. Unless you are a virtuoso, and a spell-binding one at that, do not submit more than about ten to fifteen minutes worth of material; three good, snappy songs will probably get you the most favorable response. There are exceptions, but in general, the name of the game for record companies is *hits*.

Send reel-to-reel, 7½ ips tapes. Some people submit 15 ips tapes, on the theory that the record company will be forced to listen to it on better equipment. This is logical, but I don't know if it makes sense. If someone has to use up studio time to listen to your tape, that may kill some of the incentive. A well-recorded cassette is usually all right, except that most people really don't have top flight machines, and neither do all lower-echelon company listeners. I think that submitting tapes in mono is the most foolproof approach, although I could be a little reactionary. A lot of people have had success submitting stereo tapes.

Include some information about yourself. Remember, you are sending a package. The tape's box should not be battered and illegible; give them something to read or look over while listening. A little background, perhaps, or the equivalent of liner notes. Don't get carried away, but give them a little idea of who you are, so they will know where you are coming from.

Send the tape to the A & R department of a record company. If you know a name or have a contact in that department, then send it to that person; but a tape sent to A & R Department will be listened to at some point.

Include a return mailer. Most companies will return tapes to you, but they have to cover that expense, which simply translates into higher record prices. Probably it's best to send your tape in a box; inside that box is another box for the return of your tape, and it's stamped, addressed, and ready to go. If they like your tape, fine; if they don't, at least they will be impressed by the fact that you are a considerate person.

Protect your songs before sending them in. No, companies as a rule won't rip off your songs, but people as a rule don't rob banks. Yet banks are robbed, and so are songs. I don't want to dispense any legal advice here about copyrighting and forming your own publishing company, but I will say that both of these endeavors are easier than you think, and it does not require a high-power attorney to accomplish these simple steps. There are books available on music law; frequently magazines and periodicals carry articles of interest to the musician about copyrighting and publishing. To get fully into the law of the whole thing would take some pages. Check out your local library and get the facts.

Don't do anything jive. Don't send contributions, threats, bribes, or promises of greatness. It will work against you.

Thank the company for its time. They don't have to listen to your tape, you know. They could just shove it into a trash basket and forget about it. But companies don't work that way, so let them know you are appreciative of the time they are investing in you.

Appendix D

ALTERNATE WAYS TO DO IT YOURSELF

If building something from scratch seems like too formidable a task, there are still ways to create a custom installation for less money than you would pay for a fully-assembled console. There are companies that manufacture complete subassemblies (mixing modules, power amps, mic preamps, equalizers, etc.) that you can combine into a console that suits your own particular needs. Here are some of the companies specifically catering to this type of market; write to them directly for details, as product lines and prices are subject to change. Note that these companies are professionally oriented and are not equipped to handle novices, so don't expect any 46-page manuals on how to solder, or much sympathy in case you get in over your head.

OLD COLONY KITS (Box 243, Peterborough, NH 03458). This company is affiliated with *The Audio Amateur* magazine, and carries kits and parts relating to previously published articles. Products include mixers, preamps, crossovers, medium-power amplifiers, VU meter kits, and the like.

OPAMP LABS INC. (1033 North Sycamore Avenue, Los Angeles, CA 90038). Opamp Labs offers modules applicable to professional and semi-professional recording studios. You should have a fair amount of electronic knowledge in order use these modules in a studio, but their well-laid-out and informative catalog is helpful and gives a pretty good idea of what to expect. Modules include low-noise op amps, mic preamps, test-tone oscillators, power amps for monitoring, transformers transformers, and the like.

SESCOM (Box 590, Gardena, CA 90247). SESCOM stocks a very complete line of (relatively) inexpensive building blocks for professional sound installations. Products include equalizers, mic preamps, RIAA and tape amps, splitters, snakes, power amps, compressors, test-tone oscillators, and a complete line of transformers. Like Opamp Labs, they also publish some excellent and helpful applications notes.

These are by no means the only companies catering to sound. Heathkit (Benton Harbor, MI 49022) offers a simple mixer; Southwest Technical Products Corporation (219 W. Rhapsody, San Antonio, TX 78216) has some good monitor amp kits; various magazines like *Popular Electronics* and *The Audio Amateur* have published mixer articles with supporting kits of parts; and new products are constantly being introduced to the scene. As usual, the best place to find out what's new is in the ads carried by magazines catering to the trade.

Appendix E

ABOUT THE SOUNDSHEET

The soundsheet is divided into three parts, each of which demonstrates different effects and aspects of the recording process. All basic tracks were recorded on a TEAC A-3340S. First, drums went on to track 1. In order to create a hiss level objectionable enough to demonstrate the noise gate, I purposely recorded the drums at a very low level and accented the hiss by turning up the treble EQ control. To make sure I would have enough drum track to work with, I recorded about five minutes of drums with a "1-2-3-4" count at the beginning so that I would know when to start.

After blocking out the song, I put on a bass track throughout the piece. Except for adding a touch of compression, this track was relatively straightforward.

I didn't want to have to do any premixing on the 3340, which meant restricting myself to a total of four tracks. One of the remaining two tracks held the rhythm guitar; the other track alternated between narration and lead guitar parts. This required a lot of punching in, where I would narrate the particular effect, stop the machine, then punch in an appropriate guitar part. Additional lead parts were punched in over the rhythm guitar when required. After completing all the tracks for this first part of the soundsheet, I mixed them down onto a Pioneer 8282 cassette deck (my second machine) using a TDK SA-60 cassette, and started in on the second part of the soundsheet.

The second part was recorded in more or less the same way, with rhythm guitar recorded all the way through and voice/effects added on to other tracks. As in the case of the first part, after all tracks were recorded they were mixed down onto the master cassette.

Since the soundsheet people required a reel-to-reel version to work with, I dubbed the first part, recorded on the master cassette, back into a fresh reel of tape loaded on to the 3340. I had mixed into the cassette deck at a high level to minimize noise, so there was a bit of decreased high-frequency response on playback, but since the SA tape takes chrome bias and EQ, changing the EQ position from chrome to regular gave a boost of the high frequencies on playback. I could then cut the treble back just a tiny bit on the way to the 3340, decreasing the noise while still retaining good frequency response. After verifying that the dub for the first part was all right, I then dubbed part two onto the 3340.

Part three was a special case. Since I wanted to demonstrate that you can layer tracks with a 4-channel machine, I chose one of my completed tapes to play in the background. This had already been mixed down on cassette, so I dubbed it on the 3340 master tape and included voice narration along with it. I made a few mistakes in the voice track, but that simply meant rewinding the cassette and starting over. Eventually, the third section was properly dubbed onto the master tape and I was almost finished. Before sending the tape out, though, I labelled the tape reel itself as to format (mono $\frac{1}{4}$ track, tails out) and speed (15 ips) so there would be no doubts as to what was on the tape.

Incidentally, I have prepared a cassette of my music that is being independently distributed through PAIA Electronics. The material was recorded over a period of about nine months, using the same equipment mentioned above. If you are interested in hearing just what is possible in a home recording environment, check it out. There are some pieces with as many as 11 tracks layered together, lots of vocal doubling, effects, and the like. Once you get a little practice, you can produce tapes that are equivalent in quality to many professional records (especially if you use noise reduction). As home recording becomes more commonplace, I expect to see more and more albums and tapes released to the public that have been recorded in peoples' homes rather than commercial studios.

180

INDEX

Continued on next page

181